Twayne's English Authors Series

Sylvia E. Bowman, *Editor*

INDIANA UNIVERSITY

William Beckford

TEAS   204

William Beckford
Portrait by John Hoppner

WILLIAM BECKFORD

By ROBERT J. GEMMETT
State University of New York, Brockport

TWAYNE PUBLISHERS

A DIVISION OF G. K. HALL & CO., BOSTON

Library of Congress Cataloging in Publication Data

Gemmett, Robert J
    William Beckford.

    (Twayne's English authors series ; TEAS 204)
    Bibliography: p. 175-83.
    Includes index.
    1. Beckford, William, 1760-1844 — Criticism and
interpretation.
PR4092.G4   828'.6'09   76-43256
ISBN 0-8057-6674-X

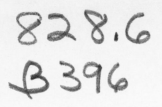
For
KENDRA
and
KERRY

Contents

About the Author

Preface

Chronology

1. Orientalism and the Age   17
2. The Emergence of an Orientalist   29
3. The Apprenticeship for *Vathek: The Long Story*   40
4. The Light of Reason: *Extraordinary Painters*   53
5. The "dubious visionary light": *Dreams, Waking Thoughts and Incidents*   64
6. The Central Tale: *Vathek*   79
7. Voices from Eblis: *The Episodes of Vathek*   103
8. The Light of Maturity   121
9. The Haunting Image   137

Appendix   149

Notes and References   159

Selected Bibliography   175

Index   185

About the Author

Robert J. Gemmett, the leading American authority on William Beckford, holds a B.A. degree from Siena College, an M.A. from the University of Massachusetts, and a Ph.D. from Syracuse University. He is the editor of an important edition of Beckford's *Dreams, Waking Thoughts and Incidents* which was favorably reviewed in America and Europe. He has also published editions of *Biographical Memoirs of Extraordinary Painters, Vathek,* and *The Episodes of Vathek.* The London *Times Literary Supplement* described Dr. Gemmett's volume in the series *Sale Catalogues of Libraries of Eminent Persons* as a "major contribution to Beckford studies." His publications include reviews and articles in *Philological Quarterly, English Miscellany, Gazette des Beaux-Arts,* and *Papers of the Bibliographical Society of America.*

Dr. Gemmett has taught at Clarkson College and the State University College at Brockport, N.Y. where he is currently Professor of English and Chairman of the English Department.

Preface

"Hardly any English writers until past the middle of the [eighteenth] century knew or apparently cared to know the East well, either through travel or through books; hence the pale and colourless quality of their Oriental fiction. Beckford was the first to introduce much picturesque detail." So wrote Martha Pike Conant in 1908 in her pioneer study *The Oriental Tale in England in the Eighteenth Century* — and I have used this statement as a point of departure for this study. Following the appearance of the English translation of Antoine Galland's *Arabian Nights* early in the century, the Oriental tale began its process of naturalization on English soil. It is against the background of this gradual assimilation of Oriental fiction into English culture that I examine Beckford's Oriental works, using the term "Oriental" here in a special, qualified sense to mean that which is more realistically Oriental than, for example, the sterile imitations of John Hawkesworth and Samuel Johnson. All of the Eastern tales produced by Englishmen in the eighteenth and nineteenth centuries were, strictly speaking, "pseudo-Oriental." One of my aims is to show how Beckford, through his own scholarship, advanced beyond the experiments of his predecessors in Oriental fiction, thereby heralding the more authentic Orientalism of the scholars and the poets who followed him.

I do not ask the reader, however, to judge Beckford's tales of the East solely on the basis of their relationship to the time in which they were written. I think it is essential to discover any permanent value they may have beyond their association with a specific historical period. For this reason, I also focus on the theme of alienation in Beckford's life and work — the rebellion of the self against the tyranny of outside forces. The extraordinary dedication with which he pursued his Eastern studies was, in fact, intimately bound with his desire to disengage himself from the society that restricted him.

The young Beckford was involved in a complicated struggle to find self-expression at any cost; and, constantly inhibited by the social circle in which he normally moved, he too often found himself a frustrated artist suffering from an acute desire to be free. It is precisely this struggle of the self against the restraining pressures of the external world that becomes the narrative seed for his Oriental tales — indeed, for his early works in general — and that enables them, I believe, to transcend the limitations of his time and to appeal to the modern reader.

So it is with a historical, mythical, and biographical purpose in mind that I study *The Long Story, Vathek,* and *The Episodes of Vathek* in the chapters following. I also discuss in this volume two additional early books, *Biographical Memoirs of Extraordinary Painters* and *Dreams, Waking Thoughts and Incidents,* which, though they do not number among his Oriental works, deserve to be examined in relationship to them. Both *Extraordinary Painters* and *Dreams* highlight the pictorial, satiric, and psychological character of the writing style that found its best expression in *Vathek.* Taken together, these five books mark a particular phase of Beckford's life; for they reflect the young man, spoiled, undisciplined, and eager to display his artistic sensibilities — an artist so absorbed with his own image that he easily became one of the sublime solipsists of his era.

I have also dealt briefly with the travel books he produced in his seventies, *Italy; with Sketches of Spain and Portugal* and *Recollections of an Excursion to the Monasteries of Alcobaça and Batalha,* and with his two unknown burlesques, *Modern Novel Writing* and *Azemia.* These four works were produced after his interest in writing Oriental tales had waned and are interesting in what they reveal about the mature Beckford once his youthful ardor had somewhat cooled and his spirit had tempered with age.

In preparing *William Beckford,* I have benefited greatly from those who have studied Beckford before me. I acknowledge my debt to all of them here and especially to Boyd Alexander, Guy Chapman, and J. W. Oliver for their invaluable books. I must give special acknowledgment to Dr. André Parreaux's study *William Beckford, Auteur de Vathek: Etude de la Création Littéraire;* for, as my notes reveal, it was particularly helpful to me. I can only hope that someday this important work of scholarship will be translated into English and achieve a wider audience here in America. For background material on the development of the Oriental tale in England, Dr. M. P. Conant's survey was indispensable.

Preface

I wish especially to express my gratitude to Mrs. James T. Babb of New Haven, Connecticut, who graciously allowed me to quote in this book from some unpublished material in her husband's Beckford collection. I owe a special debt to the late James T. Babb for many acts of kindness and for his unfailing assistance in my ongoing Beckford research.

I am grateful to the Research Foundation of the State University of New York for the financial assistance awarded to me during the course of writing this book; to A. G. Nizet of Paris for permission to quote and translate extensively from Dr. Parreaux's book; to Philip L. Gerber for encouraging me to write this book for the Twayne English Series in the first place and then for making working conditions conducive to writing it; and to the following individuals for their aid: Herbert W. Leibert, William Fleming, Sidney Thomas, Patricia Strimple, and Elaine Taylor. I owe much to the encouragement and the example of a former undergraduate professor of English, the Reverend Matthew Conlin, who had an incalculable influence on the fact that I am an author and a college professor today.

I wish also to express my appreciation to the Beinecke Rare Book and Manuscript Library of Yale University, where a major Beckford collection is now housed; to Oxford University Press for permission to quote material from J. W. Oliver's *Life of William Beckford;* to Constable and Co. for permission to reproduce quotations from Guy Chapman's edition of *The Vision;* to the Duke of Hamilton for permission to quote from Beckford's notes in Samuel Rogers' presentation copy of *Italy;* to Sylvia Bowman for her close reading of the text and for her many helpful suggestions; to the libraries of the State University College of New York at Brockport, the British Museum, Oxford University, and the Library of Congress.

ROBERT J. GEMMETT

State University of New York,
Brockport, 1975

Chronology

1760   William Beckford born September 29 in a town house on the corner of Greek Street and Soho Square, London, to William Beckford, Lord Mayor of London, and Maria Hamilton Beckford.

1770   Father dies in June.

1772   Decision is made to educate William at home; with the aid of Lords Chatham and Lyttelton, Mrs. Beckford resists successfully the efforts of guardians to force her through legal means to send Beckford away to school.

1772 -   Undergoes stiff educational program in the Classics directed
1776   by Reverend John Lettice and overseen by Lord Chatham; meets Alexander Cozens who helps to encourage his more exotic tastes.

1777   Leaves Fonthill with Lettice for Geneva to complete his education; comes in contact with artists and writers, such as Jean Huber, Paul Henri Mallet, and Voltaire, who exercise a profound influence on his life; begins composing *The Long Story* by year end.

1779   On a tour of England meets and becomes instantly infatuated with William Courtenay, a boy of eleven.

1780   In April, publishes *Biographical Memoirs of Extraordinary Painters;* in June, begins Grand Tour of Europe.

1782   Composes first draft of *Vathek* in one sitting sometime in January; begins extensive correspondence with Samuel Henley concerning the development and translation of *Vathek;* embarks on a second European tour.

1783   Has five hundred quarto copies of his travel notes, *Dreams, Waking Thoughts and Incidents,* printed and ready for publication in March; family orders its withdrawal on the grounds that some of the material in it is objectionable;

marries Lady Margaret Gordon in May following family pressure to do so; completes at least one tale of *The Episodes of Vathek* before the end of the year.

1784 Elected as a member of Parliament for Wells but a few months of the dull business of the House oppresses him, and he seeks a peerage with the title of Lord Beckford of Fonthill; hopes of obtaining the peerage are blasted by a public scandal accusing him of a homosexual affair with William Courtenay.

1785 Finishes a second companion-piece to *Vathek;* in April, wife gives birth to their first child, Maria Margaret; flees England with wife and child under the continued pressure of the scandal.

1786 Brings a third *Episode* close to completion by the opening of the year; wife dies suddenly in May after giving birth to their second child, Susan Euphemia; without his knowledge, Samuel Henley publishes the English translation of *Vathek* on June 7.

1786 - Remains in virtual exile from England traveling for the next
1796 ten years throughout Switzerland, France, Italy, Spain, and Portugal; publishes the French edition of *Vathek* in Lausanne and a more refined French version in Paris later in 1787; unauthorized editions appear in Wien, Mannheim, and Leipzig the following year.

1796 Returns to England; devotes time to building and landscape gardening on his new Fonthill Abbey estate; publishes *Modern Novel Writing,* a satire on the extravagances of contemporary novelists.

1797 Publishes a second burlesque of contemporary novelists under the title of *Azemia.*

1798 Mother dies in July; leaves for Portugal in the fall; he resides there for almost a year.

1799 - *The Story of Al Raoui,* a translation attributed to Beckford,
1806 published in 1799; expends creative energies supervising the construction of Fonthill Abbey and the laying out of the grounds; accumulates books, paintings, and rare art objects for the Abbey.

1807 Orders his father's mansion demolished; moves into the Abbey.

1809 Allows Henley's translation to be published again, using the original sheets of the first edition.

1815   Hints at the possible publication of a confederated edition of *Vathek* and *The Episodes* in the preface of a revised French edition of *Vathek.*

1816   Issues a revised edition of Henley's translation; unauthorized edition of *Vathek* appears in America for the first time.

1819   *Repertorium Bibliographicum,* an account of the great libraries of England, on which he collaborated with William Clarke, appears for the first time.

1822   Weighed down by financial debts, he sells Fonthill and moves to Lansdown Crescent, Bath, where he sets out to create a second "Fonthill."

1823   Publishes some trifling poems in the *Literary Gazette* under the title, *Epitaphs.*

1828   Begins writing *Liber Veritatis,* a work of no significance, dealing with the pedigrees of some of the titled families in England.

1833   Bargains with Richard Bentley for the publication of *The Episodes* but fails to extract from him "a sum as round as the great globe itself"; as a result, the tales not printed during his lifetime.

1834   Publishes in July, *Italy; with Sketches of Spain and Portugal,* a revised form of the suppressed *Dreams, Waking Thoughts and Incidents,* with additional material on Spain and Portugal.

1835   In May, publishes another travel book, *Recollections of an Excursion to the Monasteries of Alcobaça and Batalha.*

1844   On May 2, following a bout with influenza, Beckford dies in an unadorned truckle bed, after several years of relative quiet among his books, his prints, his gardens.

CHAPTER 1

Orientalism and the Age

W HILE residing in France in 1781, William Beckford wrote to a friend that he had decided after an extended stay in Paris to remain there "a month or six weeks longer" because "this is the land of oriental literature."[1] Written to a native of the East, this statement might have provoked laughter; but Beckford echoed in making it the feelings of most educated Englishmen who knew something about the growth of Oriental fiction in the Western world. Stirrings of a movement had begun in France between the years 1704 and 1717 when Antoine Galland had published his translation of the manuscripts containing the curious Arabian stories he had found in Aleppo.[2] *Les Mille et une Nuits, Contes Arabes,* as the completed French work was called, but better known today as the *Arabian Nights,* was received with instant enthusiasm in France; and it rose in popularity so suddenly that it excited a plethora of imitations. Original translations, pseudo-translations, philosophical tales, and parodies of all kinds burst forth almost immediately and kept the new interest alive. Petis de la Croix's authentic translation *Les Mille et un Jours, Contes Persans* appeared as early as 1710–12 and then Thomas Gueullette created his famed pseudo-translations — *Contes Tartares* (1715), *Contes Chinois* (1723), and *Contes Moguls* (1732) — in order to meet an intense popular demand. Before the eighteenth century came to an end, the French reading public saw unfold from the press almost seven hundred works that could be loosely classified as "Oriental."[3]

I Aladdin Comes to England

Before the appearance of Beckford's *Vathek* in 1786, the rise of the Oriental tale in England coincided almost chronologically with the movement in France; indeed, the English interest developed, to

17

a great extent, in response to it. Nonetheless, the English were alive
to the East long before 1700 because of the tales of Marco Polo's
adventures, the fables of Bidpai in Thomas North's *The Morall
Philosophie of Doni* (1570), the philosophical romance of Edward
Pococke's Latin translation *Hai Ebn Yockdhan* (1671), and even the
satiric pseudo-letters of G. P. Marana's *Turkish Spy* (1687) which
had nurtured English interest in the East. But the English translation of Galland's *Les Mille et une Nuits*, which came out sometime
between 1704 and 1712,[4] marked a profound change, as Martha Pike
Conant has already indicated, in the identity of Oriental fiction in
England: "The sudden advent of the *Arabian Nights* full of the life,
the colour, and the glamour of the East — even in the Gallicized version of Antoine Galland — naturally opened a new chapter in the
history of oriental fiction in England."[5] Numerous translations from
French sources flooded England thereafter. As for the *Arabian
Nights*, its celebrity in England was such that it proceeded to a
fourth edition only nine years after the appearance of the first
English edition, and a fourteenth edition emerged from the press in
1778.

This does not mean that no distinctions are to be made between
the two movements as they evolved in France and England. At the
outset, the French seemed to have fewer inhibitions than the
English regarding the assimilation of the Oriental tale into their
culture. Commercial expansion under Colbert had brought the
Orient closer to the home country; and the highly descriptive travel
accounts, especially those by François Bernier, Jean-Baptiste Tavernier, and Jean Chardin, had documented the customs, dress, and
topography of these far distant countries and had sufficiently whetted the appetite of the French for more of the same material.
Furthermore, in an age dominated by Nicolas Boileau's Classicism,
there was something new and unconventional about these tales that
was powerful enough to awaken an incipient Romantic spirit and to
encourage the French public to recognize that it was coming into
contact with refreshingly different literary material. But perhaps
more important to the nature of the movement in France was the
simultaneous appearance of Charles Perrault's fairy tales with all
their insular appeal to the French. The mixture of the fairy element
with Oriental imitations of the *Arabian Nights* helped to produce
works more richly imaginative than was customary and became "one
of the most striking characteristics" of the French movement.[6]

On the other hand the Anglo-Oriental movement, at least

throughout a large part of the eighteenth century, failed to capture the deep imaginative tone of the French movement. Following the first appearance of the *Arabian Nights* in England, the tendency of English writers in their own imitations was to approximate only the externals of the Oriental tale — the machinery and setting without the spirit and the philosophy of the Orient.[7] For the more picturesque versions of the Eastern tale, the English continued to rely heavily on the French supply. For example, next in importance to Galland's collection in England was the work of Petis de la Croix, another Frenchman, whose gathering of tales was turned into English early in the century under the separate titles of the *Turkish Tales* (1708) and *The Thousand and One Days, Persian Tales* (1714–15). As for the popular imitative tales, or pseudo-translations, such as Gueullette's *Chinese Tales* (1725), *Mogul Tales* (1736), and *Tartarian Tales* (1759), or J. P. Bignon's *Abdalla, Son of Hanif* (1729), which succeeded in capturing some of the warmth and spirit of the Orient, they, too, came to England from France, as did the less popular works of G. de Brémond, J. Regnauld de Segrais, the Comte de Caylus, and F. Huguet de Graffigny.[8] As for the reason for this English dependence upon the French, part of the explanation lies in the fact that English writers were reluctant to take the Oriental tale seriously; it was, they felt, an alien and aberrant literature in a society devoted to Classical ideals. Bishop Atterbury's celebrated remark that Arabian tales "gave a judicious eye pain" represented a fairly commonplace view at a time when the literate gentleman was reared to respect the Classical tradition. Although the Oriental tale was eventually naturalized in England, in the beginning "the environment proved stronger than the new organism."[9]

Some English writers did attempt, however, to create their own Oriental tales, though no one as successfully as Beckford in the eighteenth century. The application of the term "Oriental" to these productions, it should be borne in mind, is admittedly misleading and must be accepted with the greatest reserve throughout this study. These tales by Englishmen were Oriental only in the vague imitative sense; and the imitation, compared to the work of the French, was generally of an inferior quality. Furthermore, these tales were not always *primarily* imitative; they were simply English works presented in the guise of the Oriental tale. Perhaps it might be more accurate to view the progress of the Oriental tale in England during the first three quarters of the eighteenth century as occupying the first phase of its development — a pseudo-Oriental phase — leading to the more authentic Orientalism of the early 1800's and to the years following until it reached maturity in the Oriental scholarship of Alexander Kinglake and Richard Burton in the mid-nineteenth century.

II *The Oriental Tale as Utilitarian Enterprise*

The direction of the Oriental tale's development in England was largely along moralistic lines. Not surprisingly, the didactic writers of the century made it serve their ends. So strong was this moralizing tendency in the literary tradition and so difficult was it to resist that even Beckford, in spite of his innovations, adhered to it in his own works. Essayists like Joseph Addison and Richard Steele attempted to mold the Oriental material from France into a shape that would be more palatable to the Neo-Classical man of taste; and, as a result, their references in the *Tatler*, the *Spectator*, and the *Guardian* to the tales of Galland and Petis de la Croix, though frequent indeed, were almost always made for the restricted purpose of illustrating a moral lesson. What justified the more extensive use of such "extravagant" stories, these authors felt, was their ability to reinforce the didactic spirit of the essays in which they appeared. Thus, "The Fable of the Two Owls" from the *Turkish Tales* provided Addison with an excellent means of insinuating his moral in *Spectator*, No. 512. "There is nothing so difficult," he theorized, "as the art of making advice agreeable." But, "upon the reading of a fable, we are made to believe we advise ourselves."[10]

Elsewhere, Addison concluded an essay devoted to the "subject of hope" with Alnaschar, an "Arabian fable . . . translated into French by Monsieur Galland" as an appropriate coda to his theme.[11] In *Guardian*, No. 162, Steele employed "Santon Barsisa" from the *Turkish Tales* to illustrate his particular moral reflection. Oriental fables, in other words, afforded these men an oblique method of inculcating Augustan virtues without the necessity of being offensively direct. Even Addison's original stories, like *The Vision of Mirzah* (1711) and *The Story of Hilpa, Harpath, and Shalum* (1712), followed the same intentional pattern. The result was that, in spite of the exotic flavor of these tales, they were generally pale in their Oriental coloring and thin in their character portrayal. In Addison's hands, the Oriental tale was reduced to method, chastened to eliminate the imaginative elements, and corrected to satisfy the literary codes of the day.

Under the control of later periodical essayists, like Dr. Samuel

Johnson and John Hawkesworth, the Anglo-Oriental tale continued its didactic trend but with a deeper, more serious quality than before. Since both writers found it a suitable vehicle for philosophical reflection, neither made any attempt to particularize the Orient. Johnson believed it was the business of the artist to examine "general properties" and "large appearances" — to avoid, in other words, the particular and the idiosyncratic; hence, he used only the slightest degree of Oriental coloring and constructed only the barest background for such essays as "Ortogrul of Basra" in *Idler*, No. 99, and "Obidah and the Hermit" in *Rambler*, No. 65. The characters he fashioned served his critical purpose, too: they were abstractions designed to speak to men of all ages and races.

Hawkesworth, though less restrained in his employment of imaginative elements, was likewise satisfied with feeble Oriental embellishments to dress his philosophical tale. His concern, as he expressed it in *Adventurer*, No. 4, was that literary performances of this kind never violate the law of probability; presumably, too much of what he conceived to be Oriental would do just that. In good Neo-Classical form, he insisted that the action of the story proceed with regularity, the characters "act upon rational principles," and events take place "as may naturally be expected from the interposition of superior intelligence and power."[12] On this foundation, he composed the "History of Nouraddin and Amana" (1753) and "Carazan" (1754), tales that one would characterize as Oriental with embarrassing hesitancy. Hawkesworth held that Eastern stories provided a useful means of sermonizing about the value of meditation, the vanity of human ambition, the necessity of religious faith, and other such solemn subjects.

Johnson's employment of the Oriental guise for his philosophical narratives came to fruition in *Rasselas* (1759), the best-known work of this kind before *Vathek*. Obviously not written for anyone familiar with the Orient, Johnson's didactic romance turned out to be a longer version of one of his favorite themes: the absurdity of exhausting one's life in search of perfect happiness. Rasselas, the Prince of Abyssinia, leaves the Happy Valley to survey the conditions of the world; and he gradually learns that "human life is everywhere a state in which much is to be endured, and little to be enjoyed." He also discovers that man must simply fill the vacancies of time with constant physical and mental activity and then endure with the hope of a better life to come. This remedy was Johnson's universal one for boredom and a main concern of *Rasselas*. As for

Oriental features, the tale did little to assimilate any: the Oriental setting was faint, local color was absent, and the language did not approximate Oriental style. With Johnson's *Rasselas*, as Ernest Baker has observed, it was "a question of putting native wine into bottles of foreign make," but "it was the quality of the vintage not of the imitation bottles that mattered."[13]

What appears today to be an obsessive concern of Neo-Classical writers like Johnson and Hawkesworth for rationalistic art also accounts for the adaptation of Oriental material to satiric ends in the eighteenth century. Initially, this literature took the form of Oriental pseudo-letters, a species of literary composition introduced to Europe by G. P. Marana's *Turkish Spy* (1687–93) and developed in France by Charles Dufresny's *Amusemens sérieux et comiques* (1699). The external structure of these works consisted of a series of letters composed ostensibly by an Oriental who was visiting a city in Europe for the first time. His running commentary about European manners and institutions as a naive, uncorrupted observer created the satiric situation. In the face of the ideal, in other words, the shortcomings of the actual could be made terrifyingly apparent. This satiric format provided the startling justaposition of opposites that the English satirists liked so well — one that Jonathan Swift employed effectively in parts of *Gulliver's Travels*.

In the Oriental-satiric vein, Thomas Brown borrowed liberally from Dufresny to produce *Amusements Serious and Comical Calculated for the Meridian of London* (1700), while Lord Lyttelton, inspired by Montesquieu, wrote *Letters from a Persian in England to his friend at Ispahan* (1735). Oliver Goldsmith finally brought this genre to full maturity in his effective handling of the disguised Oriental in his collection entitled *The Citizen of the World* (1762). But the point to be underscored again is that a work of this kind was neither created nor read for its relevance to the authentic East; for, to serve the same purpose, the critical observer could well have been an American.

Thus Oriental fiction from Addison to Goldsmith was consistently made to conform to the Augustan codes of art. To put it more accurately, the surface aspects of the Oriental material imported largely from France were used to adorn the Augustan tale. Rationalistic Classicism, with its heavy emphasis on morality, philosophy, and satire, prevented the genre from developing as freely in England as it had in France. Yet, paradoxically, the more imaginative Oriental tales brought into the country from Paris continued to be read avidly side by side with the sterilized "Oriental stories" of the English. Interest in Persian and Arabian tales did not cool in London simply because English writers were reluctant to recapture the spirit of Oriental romance in their own literary compositions. There was still something refreshingly wild and irregular about imaginative Oriental literature that quickened the heart of an age that was otherwise dominated by the ideals of reason, order, and good sense. The English mind was not used to it, to be sure, but the alien nature of this kind of fiction was curiously alluring for precisely the reason that it was a breath of fresh air in the Classical environment of colorless art.

Furthermore, extravagant Eastern tales were sufficiently tabooed to intensify interest in them — to make them, in other words, even more enticing to English readers than they perhaps deserved to be. It is significant of this interest that Alexander Pope, the leading spokesman of the Neo-Classical period, enjoyed the *Arabian Tales*, recommended them to his friend Bishop Atterbury, and thought of writing a Persian fable himself. "It would have been a very wild thing if I had executed it," he surmised, "but [it] might not have been unentertaining."[14]

III   *The Oriental Threat to Augustan Taste*

Few Classicists seemed to have considered the Oriental tale in its imaginative forms, whether authentic or imitative, as a serious threat to accepted standards of taste until the middle of the eighteenth century. But, when it became clear in the 1750's that the vogue of these tales was only one manifestation of a widespread mania for many kinds of Oriental art, some supporters of Classical esthetics were for the first time openly alarmed.[15] They began looking upon the craze for the Eastern style in porcelain, furniture, and architecture as well as in fiction as a direct challenge to the establishment. After all, here was art that all too frequently neglected order and abstract design in favor of asymmetrical and naturalistic schemes. To many orthodox Classicists, it had become apparent that Orientalism in England was a disintegrating force which had to be opposed.

Between the years 1753 and 1756, a systematic attack against the Oriental vogue found its most prominent outlet in Robert Dodsley's publication *The World*. Three notable writers — Sir James Marriot, the poet laureat William Whitehead, and the critic Joseph Warton — sought in the pages of this periodical to prevent Oriental art from attaining additional artistic acceptance. "A few years ago every thing was Gothic," wrote Whitehead, "but, according to the present prevailing whim, every thing is Chinese."[16] All three men believed that taste was founded on fixed and universal principles supposedly discoverable in nature; but the "new-fangled" taste — confined as it was to nothing but whim, caprice, and novelty — introduced anarchy, they felt, into the realm of art. Productions of this kind were barbarous, argued Marriot; they were ruinous "of that simplicity which distinguished the Greek and Roman arts as eternally superior to those of every other nation."[17] Going a step farther, Joseph Warton insisted that the violation of Classic simplicity was fraught with grave moral consequences. He even claimed that, if "simplicity" were "venerated as it ought to be[,] it would at once banish from the earth all artifice and treachery, double-dealing and deceit."[18] The implication was, of course, that the admiration of "whimsical and grotesque figures" and other such "splendid deformities" on Indian screens, wallpaper, or like objects violated the moral as well as the esthetic codes of the day. Twenty years later, William Pitt protested on similar grounds young Beckford's exposure to the *Arabian Nights*.

How did the Oriental tale fare during this rising protest? Since the force of most of the satire was directed against the abuse of Classic simplicity, the failure to supply moral instruction, and the undue stress on the principle of irregularity in art, only the authentic and the closely imitative forms of Oriental fiction were attacked at this time. In particular, only the authors who attempted "to write in the true Eastern style" were severely chastised by the critics. Oliver Goldsmith, for example, unleashed his protest against this group in Letter XXXIII of *The Citizen of the World* in which he provided his readers with an archetypal author of Oriental tales who describes the nature of his composition:

I have written many a sheet of eastern tale myself . . . and I defy the severest critic to say but that I have stuck close to the true manner. I have compared a lady's chin to the snow upon the mountains of Bomek; a soldier's sword, to the clouds that obscure the face of heaven. If riches are mentioned, I compare them to the flocks that graze the verdant Tefflis; if poverty, to the mists that veil the brow of mount Baku. I have used *thee* and *thou* upon all occasions, I have described falling stars, and splitting mountains, not forgetting the little Houries who make a very pretty figure in every description. But you shall hear how I generally begin. "Eben-ben-bolo, who was the son of Ban, was born on the foggy summits of Benderabassi. His beard was whiter than the feathers which veil the breast of the penguin; his eyes were like the eyes of doves, when wash'd by the dews of the morning; his hair, which hung like the willow weeping over the glassy stream, was so beautiful that it seem'd to reflect its own brightness; and his feet were as the feet of a wild deer which fleeth to the tops of the mountains." There, there, is the true Eastern taste for you; every advance made towards sense, is only a deviation from sound. Eastern tales should always be sonorous, lofty, musical and unmeaning.[19]

Goldsmith undoubtedly had the "French imports" in mind when he wrote this passage; but three leading French writers — Voltaire, Caylus, and Antoine Hamilton — had been ridiculing the excesses of the literary tradition in France for some time.[20] The pseudo-Oriental tales of the English naturally escaped this kind of criticism; for Addison, Johnson, and Hawkesworth, as we have seen, did little in this genre to offend the Classical tradition. On the contrary, their use of it manifested their reluctance to change; and the works that followed theirs in the 1760's like John Langhorne's *Solyman and Almena* (1762), James Ridley's *Tales of the Genii* (1764), and Mrs. Frances Sheridan's *History of Nourjahad* (1767), also demonstrated the same penchant for inculcating moral truths and, like their predecessors, for displaying English manners more accurately than the Oriental ones.

But some signs of change in England relative to the Oriental tale were appearing by the 1780's when Beckford entered the picture. The derision of writers like Goldsmith and the onslaught of the essayists in *The World* were, in the end, important manifestations of a growing realization that interest in the Eastern mode was beginning to run deep in the country. The steady inundation of the British market by reprints and new editions of Oriental tales imported from France was bound to alter taste in some significant way. In addition, the establishment of Indian chintz and Chinese laquer, porcelain, wallpaper, and other items as fashionable in the 1750's and 1760's had effectively stimulated appetites for more art in the Oriental style. The outcome was that what had begun at the opening of the century as a trifling curiosity had gradually turned into a serious interest; interest soon bred familiarity; and familiarity began to change the whole nature of the Oriental movement in England.

IV   *The Naturalization of the Oriental Tale*

England in Beckford's day was actually entering a new era of intimacy with the East. Contemporary knowledge of these distant lands since the beginning of the century had been vague and ill-defined, based almost entirely on French translations of the *Arabian Nights* and on a handful of travel books; but, after the 1750's, the East became more accessible to the English. Expansion of colonial interests in India through the settlements of the English East India Company contributed to the lessening of distance between the two worlds; and so did the growth of scientific archaeology in England, which encouraged expeditions to Greece, Asia, and Egypt. The Continental wars played an equal role by closing Western Europe to sightseers during the latter part of the century.[21] As a consequence, travel accounts of Eastern lands and manners entered England at a rapid rate; and they provided more accurate source material about the unknown East than ever before. Indeed, they enriched the Oriental movement in England and ultimately gave new life to an anemic literary genre.

The numerous firsthand accounts of the East were accompanied by activity in the field of Oriental scholarship. Although this academic movement can be said to have begun in a serious manner in the first half of the century when Simon Ockley published the first volume of *The Conquest of Syria, Persia, and Egypt* in 1708, followed by George Sale's translation of *The Koran* in 1734, it did not achieve momentum until John Richardson and Sir William Jones brought their work to light in the 1770's and 1780's.[22] Richardson's *A Dissertation on the Languages, Literature and Manners of Eastern Nations* and Jones' direct translations from Arabic literature received wide recognition and spurred the development of Oriental research dominated later by Johnathan Scott and William Ouseley and brought to fruition by Kinglake and Burton in the Victorian era.

The effect of this search for accuracy on the quality and production of Oriental fiction was considerable. Besides the travel books, the scholarly studies made available a fresh body of Oriental material that presented vivid descriptions and realistic detail from which a fiction writer could draw inspiration. The glamorous East suddenly came alive; and, portrayed in all its local color, it seized the imaginations of English readers whose tastes were already verging on the Romantic; and English writers, beginning with Beckford, began incorporating the same picturesque detail into their own tales of the East.

England's period of pseudo-Orientalism, therefore, was beginning a serious transformation during the days when Beckford was writing Oriental tales. A stronger, deeper Orientalism was starting to emerge in the final decades of the eighteenth century; but these were only transitional years — years that were leading to the full-blown Oriental antiquarianism of the 1800's. One must guard against placing the mainstream of accurate Orientalism too early in the century;[23] for, despite the effort to gather correct historical detail, either through travel or scholarship, knowledge of the Orient remained imperfect for many years; and the use of authentic material in literature before the Romantics was infrequent and, at best, only tentative. Eastern students of this period have argued that the early Oriental scholarship in England was uncertain by present measurements of judgment. Such scholarship seldom joined, for example, with other spheres of study in order to "present a field of knowledge sufficiently well-attested . . . to prevent imaginative writers . . . from building up a literature based upon a self-centered and inaccurate use of the researches of scholars."[24] In fact, realistic Orientalism was just beginning to take hold during the final stages of the eighteenth century; and, with the exception of the works of William Beckford, it did not reveal itself in imaginative literature to any noticeable extent until the Oriental verse tales of Lord Byron, Thomas Moore, and Robert Southey, and even then it was an Orient with "a lurking odor of old leather bindings."

To recognize the continued presence of vague and fanciful notions about the East and the uncertain state of scholarship during this period, however, is to appreciate more deeply Beckford's work in this area. As the age moved toward Oriental realism, Beckford was the first Englishman to produce imaginative works in the Oriental vein which reflected the new dramatic trends. Viewed against the background of pseudo-Orientalism, Beckford's *The Long Story; Vathek, The Tale of Prince Alasi and the Princess Firouzkah; The Tale of Prince Barkiarokh;* and *The Tale of the Princess Zulkaïs and the Prince Kalilah* show significant signs of departure from the past and rise above the experiments of their predecessors. The tone of Beckford's works, as will be shown, was more subjective, exotic, and emotional; and the content of his tales was more greatly enriched by the imaginative use of local Oriental detail than any previous English tales of the East. One tale, *Vathek,* came, of course, to occupy a more important place in the history of pseudo-Orientalism because, unlike Beckford's other Oriental works, it was published and available to the reading public of his generation. As a transitional prose tale of the Orient, it anticipated the Romantic Oriental verse tales of Byron, Moore, and Southey. With this work, as André Parreaux concluded in 1960, the Oriental tale in England ceased to be either a French importation or simply a utilitarian enterprise;[25] it then began to display its own autonomous colors. The alien resident, in other words, was well on its way to becoming thoroughly naturalized.

CHAPTER 2

The Emergence of an Orientalist

BECKFORD's early life was marked by constant discipline and repression from which he frequently sought relief in his Oriental studies. Born in 1760 when the fashion for things Eastern was finding expression throughout England, he could hardly have avoided some contact with the East; but his having such contact was certainly not meant to constitute any part of his formal education. His mother, Maria Beckford, a member of the old aristocracy, daughter of the sixth Earl of Abercorn, was of a family too solidly committed to the Classical style to tolerate the "Asian rage." Beckford's father, twice Lord Mayor of London, was a political figure of national prominence and one of the richest men in England. As the offspring of such a union of wealth and noble blood, Beckford spent his time with the Classics, as was the tradition of the eighteenth-century gentleman. His parents were convinced that he would excel his contemporaries; and they designed, from the day of his birth, a future for him that would be commensurate with his social position. They wanted him to become a statesman and a respectable figure in public life, but his artistic tendencies pushed him into different and, to their mind, undesirable directions.

I The Dream of Politics

The curious irony in the life of the young Beckford is that, although his parents longed for him to become a glamorous political figure, they actually forced him into leading a different and less acceptable kind of existence. The Lord Mayor and his wife seemed too obsessed with the notion that *they* could create a rich political career for *him;* and the consequent pressures they applied in their efforts to do so were too much for the sensitive William to bear. He began to despise politics and the responsibilities of the world, and he escaped them whenever possible by finding solace in nature and in art.

Young Beckford's political future must have been in mind when the Lord Mayor asked William Pitt, the secretary of state, to be his son's godfather. The christening took place on January 6, 1761, with Lord Effingham as proxy for the minister who was unable to attend. "I consider it the greatest honour," wrote Beckford's father, "to have such a sponsor to my child. . . . No endeavours of mine shall be wanting to instill into his tender mind principles of religion, honour, and love of country. It is true, these are old-fashioned principles; but they are such as you approve of, and practise."[1] While Alderman Beckford handled his son's political contacts, Mrs. Beckford fostered in the growing boy "the pride of birth and descent" and made certain that he was "inoculated with the vanity of wealth and power."[2] And, as might be expected from zealous parents, no expense was too great for William's education. A fully developed program to stimulate his talents was introduced at a very early age. The result was that, at the age of four, he spoke French with as much fluency as English; and he began his Latin studies at six. Mozart is said to have given him lessons in musical composition when Beckford was five and Mozart only nine! "He passed some time at Fonthill," Beckford wrote, "having been engaged, though quite a child, to give me — his junior by four or five years — lessons of composition."[3] Years later Beckford told a friend that an air he had improvised during one of the sessions with Mozart, *le non più andrai*, was used by the master in his opera, *The Marriage of Figaro*.

Pampered by both parents and relatives, Beckford was thoroughly spoiled as a young man and remained so throughout his life. "He flew into tantrums as soon as he was opposed," writes Boyd Alexander, "but collapsed in the face of difficulties; he would call loudly on his mother or tutor or agent to 'devise some plan' to extricate him from them; he cursed and blamed everyone except himself."[4] Robert Drysdale, Beckford's first resident tutor, described him in 1769 as a "boy of 8 years, exceedingly sprightly. . . . He has been accustomed to speak and read French since he was 3 or 4 years old, and had begun Latin about a year before I came here. He is of a very agreeable disposition, but begins already to think of being master of a great fortune. I am apprehensive that both his father and mother, contrary to their own desire and inclination may hurt him by indulgence." And a year later the tutor added with foreboding: "May God preserve him and render him such a man as may answer the fond wishes of his parents and the hopes he gives of extraordinary abilities at present to every one that knows him."[5]

The death of the Lord Mayor in 1770, when Beckford was only nine, did not alter the plans that had been devised for his future; in fact, the absence of the father may have accelerated them because he was then left exclusively in the hands of an autocratic mother. Perhaps to a greater extent than her husband, she was determined to direct her son's career and resisted angrily any deviation from the plotted course. As a woman of strong will, she usually got her way by the use of threats; indeed, her behavior caused Beckford to nickname her the Begum "on account of her strong tendency to a sort of oriental-like despotism."[6] Sometimes she played upon his emotions to make him submit to her wishes. "Awake, for Heaven's sake, awake," a friend once implored him, "and let a Mother's sorrows touch your heart. Oh, Beckford, she has wrote me such a letter, so full of passionate tenderness and anxiety about you that, was you to see it, every instant would appear to you an age till you could by your presence cheer her drooping spirits. . . . The whole tenor of her letter convinces me that *you* are the only physician who can give her relief."[7] She loved him with a violent affection and complained frequently to friends that she could not live without him. "A person told me the other day," a correspondent wrote to Beckford, "that Mrs. B. absolutely pined in your absence, that she existed only for you and said such things of her affection for you that would have melted a heart of Adamant."[8]

Her possessiveness was also evident in the intensity with which she devoted herself to her son's religious education, for she did everything in her power to impress upon his mind the evangelical principles that so possessed her own life.[9] On this basis, she had selected Mr. Robert Drysdale as Beckford's first tutor. "Very lately Mrs. Beckford told me," Drysdale explained to a friend, "that she could have found great numbers extremely well-qualified in what is called the knowledge of the world, but that she was afraid of committing her son into the hands of these fine gentlemen."[10] In the same letter he underlined Mrs. Beckford's dedication to her cause: "She prefers virtue and religion to every other accomplishment; may Almighty God succeed her pious devices and intentions in the religious education of her son." The strong sense of sin and guilt that pervaded Beckford's writings later was a consequence, perhaps, of these "pious devices."

Mrs. Beckford's desire to dominate her son and to preserve him from the world's vile influences made her also refuse to send him to a school or to a university. Two unpublished letters now on file in the Public Record Office of London reveal how she imperiously spurned the advice of several guardians who had been appointed by her husband's will to decide upon such matters.[11] They recommended the boy be sent away to a public school, but she insisted he continue his education at home "under her eye." Two of the guardians, one of whom was Sir John Gibbons of Middlesex, were so troubled by her tactics that they petitioned Charles Camden, the Whig Lord Chancellor, in 1772 to issue a legal order which would force her to send William away to school. But this act was desperate and to no avail; for, when Lord Chatham and Lord Lyttelton interceded for her, Camden dismissed the petition in the fall of 1772. The result was that throughout his formative years Beckford lived at Fonthill in the company of tutors, dowager aunts, and people removed from his generation. This mistake was one about which he was bitterly aware most of his life, and was also the one that created the stifling atmosphere that eventually bred rebellion. As his American artist friend, Benjamin West, once recalled: "Incense was offered to him and flowers strewed in his way wherever he went. He seemed to think his education had not been conducted judiciously, and that being brought up in private, he had not experienced those checks which are useful. That at public school he should have been exposed to make his way among others, taking the consequence of things as they might happen."[12]

II A Repressive Education

The major objective of Beckford's private education was to "look upon taste and sentiment as acquisitions of less importance, than the right use of reason."[13] To accomplish this end, Mrs. Beckford called upon Lord Chatham to oversee the whole educational program; but, unfortunately for William, he only served as an additional disciplinary force. When a guardian tutor, the Reverend John Lettice, formed a plan for advanced Classical instruction, Chatham, who decided that it was not sufficiently exacting, offered such stiff additions to the curriculum, that their severity caused the Reverend Lettice to express reservations about them. In one of Lettice's progress reports to Chatham, he revealed that, had it not been for the example of the statesman's family, he would not have considered it "practicable to adopt so severe a plan, at the age in which it was wished my charge should make the experiment." He then indicated, moreover, that the work initially proved to be torturous for the pupil:

It was likely that our first setting out in this thorny path should prove rather irksome to so warm an imagination; and so, indeed, it happened: but we had been at Burton [Pynsent, Chatham's residence], and were fired by example too much to retreat, though little charmed with the rugged prospect before us. It is true, that for some time we scarcely took a single step on mathematical ground without stumbling, and I fear we trod but tenderly when we were last at Burton; but since our return, I have had the satisfaction of concluding, that the good impressions Mr. Beckford received there have had a lasting effect, from the unusual attention with which he had lately applied himself that way; an attention, which has been by no means unsuccessful, and which promised much in his favour.[14]

Behind Chatham's decision to plan Beckford's educational program was his concern over his discovery that Beckford had suddenly developed an unusually strong interest in Oriental literature for a boy of his years. According to Lewis Melville, the boy's infatuation began with a copy of the *Arabian Nights* which he had found in his father's library. "He read and re-read these stories with avidity," Melville writes, "and the impression they made on him was so strong that Lord Chatham instructed Lettice that the book must be kept from him. The precaution came too late, for, though the injunction was obeyed and for some years the *Arabian Nights* was withheld from him, the Oriental tales had taken possession of the impressionable reader to such an extent that he could never forget them. They had fired his youthful mind and held his imagination captive; their influence over him never waned all the days of his life."[15]

Such enthusiasm for frivolous tales constituted in Chatham's mind a violation of the "right use of reason"; and, to correct this influence, he did more than Melville indicated — he actually ordered Lettice to confiscate *all* Oriental materials at Fonthill. The tutor responded in a letter of December, 1773, that the "splendid heap of oriental drawings, etc.," had been sacrificed at the "shrine of good taste." "Mr. Beckford," he added, "had firmness enough to burn them with his own hand. I hope that as his judgment grows maturer, it will give me an opportunity of acquainting your Lordship with other sacrifices to the same power."[16] Although Beckford had committed his Oriental treasures to the flames, he did so against his will; and such a repressive effort, so dramatically displayed, served only to create misunderstanding and fear in the mind of a thirteen-year-old boy. It failed to curb his fascination with the East; indeed, it may well have promoted it.

This incident was a traumatic experience that he never forgot, for he re-enacted the scene several years later in an early unpublished work, "L'Esplendente." In it, he described a Mohammedan father in a convulsive state of anger over the discovery that his son had acquired a perverted taste for "impiously drawing the human form." Upon ordering his son to abandon forever what he believed was a devilish art, "he furiously snatched up the leaves [drawings] which were scattered about, and tearing them asunder, committed them to the winds and the torrents. The youth sobbed, not daring to reply or to make any attempt to save the children of his fancy. But the loss affected him more than can be imagined; he turned angrily from his father, and hiding his face with his hands, gave way to violent indignation. What can my father mean, what crime have I committed?"[17]

The young artist's response to suppression was not unlike that of Beckford; both reacted with deep indignation at the outrage committed against them. Nor was this attempt the only one to stifle Beckford's creative imagination, to insulate him from the "deleterious effects" of Orientalism. In the years to follow, a sustained effort was made to convert him to be the civic-minded gentleman that the family wished him to be. Oriental literature was something they felt people of sound, cultivated taste should regard with alarm. Mrs. Beckford undoubtedly considered it an influence that would lead her son astray from pursuits more worthy of gentlemanly investigation and from the legacies of Greece and Rome.

Consequently, Beckford became more noticeably secretive in the enjoyment of the pleasures of the imagination which were viewed with so much suspicion by the grown-ups at Fonthill. He read his Oriental tales on the sly, and he shared his deepest thoughts with only a few intimates who happened to become part of his circle. Furthermore, he grew morbid and melancholy as he became more and more aware of the fact that his artistic tendencies isolated him from many of his contemporaries. These feelings swelled within him until he was resentful of his elders and scornful of all those who conformed to the dictates of an orthodox and artificial society. He was, as Chatham had feared, too much "compounded of the elements of air and fire" to be settled by any "proportion of terrestrial solidity."[18]

III   *Cultivating an Oriental Taste*

The fact is that other forces at work within the confines of Fonthill helped to nurture rather than to discourage Beckford's natural fondness for Oriental literature. The first influence was that of Alexander Cozens, who came to the Beckford household sometime before 1775 as a special tutor; for Cozens had an Eastern taste of which Mrs. Beckford and the other adults at Fonthill seemed unaware. Among the Beckford papers today is a small sketch of an Oriental subject on which is written: "Given to A. Cozens by Agamine, the Persian at Petersburg, 1730." Guy Chapman believed that it was Cozens "who first inclined Beckford towards his Persian and Arabic studies,"[19] for Cozens had traveled widely and had relished hearing tales of China and Persia during his own youth in Russia. As a prominent water-color artist, he was supposed to school Beckford in the standard methods of drawing; but, upon discovering the boy's devotion to the East, he stimulated this interest with extravagant visions from his own past. That Beckford was profoundly impressed is clear from the many letters he drafted to "The Persian," as he secretly nicknamed Cozens. "Could I have imagined," he wrote in one of them, "any person so penetrated with the same rays as you are with those that transfix me? Strange, very strange, that such a conformity should subsist."[20] Reading these letters, as Chapman observed, "ones sees that despite Lord Chatham's veto, the study of Arabia, Persia and India went on, and that by some means the forbidden books were secured to the ardent scholar."[21]

One other tutor, Sir William Chambers, could also have played a role in cultivating William's exotic taste. When this relationship began is difficult to determine; but Beckford told a friend that he "was a pupil of Sir W. Chambers when he was building Somerset," which could place the date as early as 1775. However, Beckford's signed and dated presentation copy of Chambers' *Dissertation on Oriental Gardening* reveals that they knew each other as early as "19th March 1773."[22] Like Cozens, Chambers was something of an Orientalist; for, while a young man, he had made one or two voyages to China while serving as the official in charge of the cargo and the commercial interests of the Swedish East India Company.[23] At Canton, Chambers had spent some time making sketches of the architecture and the costumes which supplied the primary material for his *Designs for Chinese Buildings* published in 1757. He was later given the opportunity to realize this interest in Chinese architecture at Kew Gardens, where he erected several buildings in this style, including the House of Confucius and the Great Pagoda. By the 1770's, moreover, he had achieved a reputation in England as the chief propagandist for Oriental gardening with the publication of his *Dissertation on Oriental Gardening*. Although his assigned task was to instruct Beckford in the principles of "classical" architecture, he must have shared his Oriental ideas with such an eager young student. If he did not ignite Beckford's interest in this new lore, he may well have fanned the flames.

So, to the dismay of Beckford's family, the hope of wrestling William from the sway of Orientalism was not to be realized. Nor could his warm imagination be chilled by any repressive means. For Beckford, Arabian tales not only provided a stimulating relief from the dryness of his Classical studies but also helped him to fill the long periods of isolation which characterized his childhood and to imaginatively escape the obligatory society fostered so persistently by the adults at Fonthill. Whenever troubled or discontented, he could find at least temporary freedom in the rarified atmosphere of the land of Aladdin. In his solitary hours, his visionary flights to Egypt or Persia could provide a vent for the emotions that were bottled within. It is not difficult to see that, in the beginning, Beckford sought in the East the solace of a simpler world — a world free from the cares and frustrations of his own.

IV   *Expressions of Selfhood*

Beckford was sent with Lettice to Switzerland to complete his education in 1777, which marked a turning-point in his life. It was an important year not only because he was emancipated from the claustrophobia of his home life for the first time, but because Geneva, where he stayed, was a brilliant intellectual center filled with people who had a deep respect for the arts. At home, he felt inhibited by the watchful eye of his mother; but in Geneva he was fortunate in meeting several illustrious men who, like Cozens and Chambers, encouraged the development of his creative talents. At this time, he became friendly with Jean Huber, the artist and musician; Charles de Bonnet, the naturalist; and Horace Benedict de Sassure, the author of *Voyages dans les Alpes*. Beckford also studied under Paul Henri Mallet, the author of *Northern Antiquities;* and he was even in the company of the sardonic Voltaire, "a very dark-complexioned, shrivelled, thin old man, stooping much from age."[24] All of these men welcomed the impressively curious boy from England into their circles; and, through his association with these notables, Beckford became more convinced than ever that the artist's life was respectable. The very presence of such accomplished writers, philosophers, and painters created an ambience that stimulated him to creative activity. As a result, he was rarely without a pen in hand during this year, for he was constructing prose descriptions of breath-taking Alpine scenery or writing confessional reveries for the eyes of friends back in England, particularly for his half-sister, Elizabeth Hervey and for Alexander Cozens.

Significantly, many of Beckford's confessional letters at this time contain expressions of growing rebelliousness. The dull civilities of polite society bored him, depressed his spirits, and sometimes stirred in him a sense of outrage:

Delivered up to a Sword, Bag and pretty Cloathes, I am obliged to go dangling about to assemblies of sweet dear, prim, tulipy, variegated Creatures, oppressed with powder and pomatum, and tired with the lisping nonsense I hear all around me. . . . At home I am infested with a species which, like mathematical points, have neither *parts* nor magnitude — Alas, fat Bulls of Basan encompass me around. — Tubs upon two legs, crammed with Stupidity, amble about me. Some of them mere trivets and Footstools, supple, pliant, and complaisant.[25]

What horrified Beckford was that he often saw himself as becoming one of these "prim Creatures" if he, as he feared he would, accepted the tedious business of parliamentary politics. His personality was too volatile, too subject to change, he would say, to fit into any regular groove. To Mrs. Hervey, his half-sister, he revealed the state of his mind as being quite different from what his elders had expected: "I think I heard you say, 'What, nothing but hobgoblins and old tapestry stories? The boy's head is turned, I believe.' Granted. The boy's head whirls about like a Catherine wheel."[26] To Cozens, he felt even freer in being explicit about his restlessness:

To receive Visits and to return them, to be mighty civil, well-bred, quiet, prettily Dressed and smart is to be what your old Ladies call in England a charming Gentleman and what those of the same stamps abroad know by the appellation of *un homme comme il faut*. Such an Animal how often am I doomed to be! To pay and to receive fulsome Compliments from the Learned, to talk with modesty and precision, to sport an opinion gracefully, to adore Buffon and d'Alembert, to delight in Mathematics, logick, Geometry and the rule of Right, the *mal morale* and, the *mal physique*, to despise poetry and venerable Antiquity, murder Taste, abhor imagination, detest all the charms of Eloquence unless capable of mathematical Demonstration, and more than all to be vigorously incredulous, is to gain the reputation of good sound sense. Such an Animal I am sometimes doomed to be! To glory in Horses, to know how to knock up and how to cure

them, to smell of the stable, swear, talk bawdy, eat roast beef, drink, speak
bad French, go to the Lyons, and come back again with manly disorders, are
qualifications not despicable in the Eyes of the English here. Such an
Animal I am determined not to be![27]

To be a gentleman was to "suffer the encroachments of Fashion and
crouch beneath the influence of solemn Idleness and approved Dis-
sipation."[28] Instead, Beckford preferred to be among the rugged
mountains of Geneva where he could enjoy wild vistas and digest the
contes Arabes without fear of disapproval. He wished, at seventeen,
to enjoy his dreams, his fantasies, and his singularity — "however
irksome and discordant to the Worldlings around."[29]

   It is important to recognize, however, that Beckford's hostility to
the restrictions of custom and authority during this period was
limited to the intimacy of letters to sympathetic friends; for his was a
very secret revolt. He was still an adolescent, not secure enough to
be openly rebellious. At times, he was wracked by feelings of guilt
for failing to obey the family commands; he was even ready to fulfill
his mother's wishes and yield to conventions he often said he
despised. At other times, he wanted to be free — free to wander in a
pure, idyllic, and indolent world of his own imagining. This situation
made the nature of his character seem contradictory: one side of his
mind yearned for greater freedom; the other nervously expressed a
need for stability and order.

   Beckford's internal struggle sometimes found expression in his
taste. One minute he would advocate indulging in melancholy and
sneering at Classical writers — they are so "different from us"; the
next, he would condemn the architecture of a city precisely because
" 'tis so unclassic a place."[30] Indeed, he regarded himself as a
traveler of two worlds. "My reason or my fancy is continually
employed," he declared, "when abandoned by the one I obey the
other. These two powers are my sun and moon. The first dispels
vapours and clears up the face of things, the other throws over all
nature a dim haze, and may be styled the Queen of delusions."[31]
Freedom and self-reliance he might achieve in time. Meanwhile, he
had to satisfy himself with bold expressions of selfhood in the
privacy of letters, rhapsodical essays, and finally in his Oriental tales.

   A work of fiction which incorporated Beckford's personal struggle
in the guise of an Oriental tale was not long in coming. By the winter
of 1777 - 78, he was deeply engaged in the process of composing one

such work, "the long Story," as he called it. At the time of writing, he had been absorbed in the lore of the East — legends, mysteries, religions, customs — and no bit of information, however small, escaped him. His Oriental studies had even begun to assume the character of scholarship. His knowledge of this kind of material was more than sufficient to fire his imagination. The result was a work which, though never completed, served as an apprenticeship for his more sophisticated Oriental tales that were to follow.

CHAPTER 3

The Apprenticeship for Vathek: The Long Story

BECKFORD composed at least part of *The Long Story* in the chateau of Baron Prangin at Nyon "in a Bedchamber 30 feet square, hung with old Hobgoblin Tapestry full of savages and monsters slaughtering one another."[1] He referred to the work for the first time in a letter dated November 24, 1777: "I have but a very scanty portion of my time to write my Centrical History."[2] By the end of December, the work had taken sufficient shape to permit its dedication to Cozens, the only man, Beckford felt, who would appreciate his effusions:

Geneva, De. 25th, 1777
What may very well be called a Dedication

You ought to be extremely cautious to whom you show the long Story, for certain I am the greatest number of readers would despise, ridicule or make neither head nor Tail of it. They would probably exclaim — what can these high flown descriptions of Grottos and Glittering Forms and Beings mean! and the Dwarfs too — a charming set of little Fellows who to use a Newmarket expression are literally got down in the *Devil's Ditch and nowhere.*

All that concerns the Sanctuary is too *solemn* and *sacred* to be prophaned. The subject is very grave and serious. When I reflect that you see and feel the Scenes and the actions I describe, their being concealed from eyes in general does not at all concern me. It is to you then that I deliver up my work, and it is in your Bosom that I deposit it. . . . Your approbation is to me the approbation of a Multitude. It is all I desire and all I seek for in venturing to commit to writing the inspirations of my Fancy, those pleasing Dreams in which perhaps consist the happiest moments of the Life of

WILLIAM BECKFORD.[3]

Except for three slight references to the work by Beckford in 1778, 1784, and 1785, not much more is known about its history;[4] nor is it certain that he ever finished his task.

40

When Guy Chapman uncovered a portion of the manuscript among the Hamilton papers in 1929, he described it as "a fair copy written in a folio exercise book," bearing the inscription: "Written about the end of 1777." "Whether the manuscript was ever completed," he added, "it is impossible to determine, but since the last few pages are transcribed on both sides of the paper, whereas the earlier ones are on the recto page only, it may be hazarded that the transcriber was trying to get the whole as it existed into one book."[5] Satisfied that he had gathered all of the material that there was to be found, Chapman published the small manuscript of eighty-seven pages in 1930 and provisionally named it at that time *The Vision*.

I "*My Centrical History*"

The story, as it appears in the Chapman edition, begins as an autobiographical narrative, a "Centrical History," as Beckford described it. It opens with a description of the moon's illumination of the rugged cliffs which surround the house where the author was residing in Switzerland. The speaker's voice is distinctively Beckford's:

I happened accidentally to open my Casement: the Moon shone bright in the clear Sky illuminating the Mountains. I stole away silently from the gay circle of Company and passing swiftly the Garden of Flowers, the Orange trees and the Grove betwixt the House and the Rocks set my feet to some steps cut in their solid sides. Luckily I had mounted the hundred steps which lead to the first Crag of the Mountain before a dark grey Cloud fleeting from the North veiled the Moon and obscured the light which conducted me. What could I do! the steps were too steep, too precarious, too irregular, to descend in darkness; besides, tho' darkness may prevail for a moment light will soon return; I must not despair. (3)

The moon is Beckford's usual symbol for imagination, irrationality, delusion; for "My Reason or my fancy . . . are my Sun and Moon." In this story, the moon becomes the magnetic force which lures the narrator away from the "gay circle of Company" into an *Ossian*-type landscape. "When the Moon emerged from her concealment shewing the leafy woods and the Rocks beneath," he writes, "my mind was travelling in another world of fancy" (3–4).

Initially, Beckford has a difficult time sustaining his moonlight visions. "Mean sorrows" keep stealing in to trouble his enjoyment — to toll him back to himself. At one point, he imagines the presence of "haggard wretches abandoned by the mercy of Heaven, a miserable few shrinking from mankind and burying themselves in this gloom to work mischief and pour destruction on those who ages past may have offended them." He even imagines he hears their voices "yell amongst the mountain peaks on high" (5-6); but his reverie is suddenly invaded by his own sense of guilt as he berates himself for his excess of imagination: "Art thou so sunk, William! art thou reduced to the level of such as these? Is thy conscience troubled, is thy reason fled, fearest thou the harmless gust of air that makes mock melody amongst the cliffs? Arise then from thy abject posture, cast away thy feverish fancies and resume the attitude of man" (6).

Reason does gain temporary ascendancy, but the moon is an irresistible force; it continues to loom overhead and to entice him into the world of dreams. The temptation to yield to its sovereignty becomes so great, in fact, that he has to tear his eyes "from these glories finding the attraction of the moon too powerful" (7). Then, in an obvious, self-conscious reference, the thought disturbs his mind that the "cares of this vile earth" will rob him in a few years of these secret enjoyments. The "projects of ambition," the "sordid schemes of interest," and "all the occupations of the World" must by their very nature consume the hours that he could give to the playland of the imagination. When he remembers the vocation that has been prepared for him, he vows that he will repulse its influence: "If I must waste those hours in cabinets and councils, if the evening must be sacrificed to debates and to watchful consultations, still they shall not rob me of the midnight moon" (9).

The tension of the narrative increases as his struggle with his conscience continues. "Whilst I lay indulging . . . amongst the wilds," he declares, "a thought intruded unwillingly upon me of the good people I had left at home. What will they think become of me? Their imagination will form wild beasts to eat me up, robbers to murder me, rocks to give way and roll me from their summits mangled at their feet" (10). But the anxiety is not severe enough to induce him to return home; instead, he decides to continue his nocturnal adoration in what becomes a symbolic search for independence. After he makes this decision, his conflict somewhat subsides; and the first phase of the narrative comes to an end. Beckford announces this closing by referring once again to the moon:

> — It was now the hour
> The holy hour, when to the cloudless height
> Of yon starred concave climbs the full orb'd Moon. (12)

Reason is then rendered impotent as he finally yields to the "soft delusion" and surrenders himself to a prolonged dream which lasts in the second section until the story comes to an abrupt end.

So far, the first part of *The Vision* reads very much like many of the sensitive letters Beckford had drafted in Switzerland for the pleasure of his friends at home. But, in the dream sequence, which occupies the more substantial portion of the book, the presence of Beckford as the tortured personality is much diminished; less of the self is apparent as he starts the process of fictionalizing the substance of the dream-vision. The author is no longer so intrusive, for his subjective, personal voice begins to merge with the more literary, imaginative voice of the objectifying artist. The esthetic distance that Beckford establishes between himself and his material is still not very great, but it does strengthen the literary quality of that part of the narrative which remains, and it does anticipate the more sophisticated handling of his material in *Vathek*.

II   *The Dream of Initiation*

Beckford begins the second part of *The Vision* by describing the experience of being translated into the dream:

A soft delusion like a descending dew stole on my senses and I sunk down on the grass, the scene still distinct before my eyes, my mind in a delirium. Sounds seemed to proceed from the cavern, long protracted sounds wafted over the dark bubbling river, swelling peals of distant harmony. Soon I thought the notes of some silver toned instrument accompanied by an angelic voice stole into the porches of my ear filling me full of rapture. Now a full accord, now a majestic pause; now wildly warbling notes dying away amidst the recesses of the caverns. Silence prevailed for a moment. Then the distant murmur in the woods, on the cliffs, on the vapours, on the waters, melody as faint as a departing mist floated in the Aether ascending higher and higher till but a vibration remained on my ear. An universal calm succeeded for many moments till it was broken by a faint whisper issuing from the Cave. My soul was all attention, every sense on their utmost stretch: the sound increased till I could distinguish something like the human voice modulating in two different tones, one deep and faltering, the other clear, smooth and delightful as the voice I had heard before. (12–13)

For the first time, the story now assumes an Oriental character as Beckford perceives two majestic figures standing silently at the entrance of a wide cavern: "The tallest wore the figure of a majestic sage, his hoary hair bound by a golden fillet inscribed with unknown characters, his beard waving over an ample robe of deep azure of the colour of the meridian sky and concealing his feet and arms with its folds. . . . The other . . . a woman who had an imperial mein, a sublime port and a spirit in her opal eyes, a fire which I dare not describe" (13). The sage is Moisasour, a Brahmin, and the woman with him is the beautiful Indian girl Nouronihar. They have been engaged in a search for a magical herb which has the power of expanding the mind, of opening it to the "source of all perfection," the *"ALL WISE,"* whose very name makes the "inmost soul glow with sensations of Love, of gratitude, of awe" (15).

Discovering the intruder-narrator, Moisasour recognizes instantly that the young man craves for the acquisition of "more than worldly knowledge." He proposes, therefore, that he undergo a purification trial in the course of being initiated into the secrets of "the Shastah, that Fountain of Knowledge" (19). The author-narrator consents and willingly enters the cavern under the supervision of two preternatural beings, Malich and Terminga. He is then committed to searing flames and to an eddying whirlpool; his body endures several shocks of cold, heat, and violent wind. All during this rigorous process, he penetrates deeper into the subterranean world — through crystalline caverns, grottoes, and endless passages. When he finally arrives at the "Halls of the Glorious," Moisasour places at his disposal the tables of adamant on which are engraved, in letters of brilliant light, "the Eternal Records of Truth!" (65).

The author is permitted to read these records in the "language of intuition," and he discovers that they constitute the six thousand years of knowledge gathered by sages on earth together with additional knowledge that has been deliberately kept obscure from ordinary mortals. When Moisasour subsequently directs the narrator's eyes to a different table, the "register of human actions," appearance succumbs to reality. The mask of deceit is torn away as the heroes of mankind — kings, conquerors, philosophers — are reduced to their true size and figure; for in this place, Beckford explains, "no characters are blazoned in perfidious colours, no crimes extenuated, no merit concealed: the best, the greatest of them, the few whose hearts e'er felt the love of truth retain not here one half of their historic stature" (66). And the Sage concludes: "This . . . is all thou art permitted to see. . . . But mark well . . . the true scope of thy initiation. 'Tis the knowledge and government of thyself. Let it sink deep into thy spirit. Let it remain there indelibly fixed that the register of human actions, which thou hast seen, was not copied from fame or flattery or from the judgement which one man passes on another; it is a rigid transcript of what every man's conscience writes in the register of his own heart. Be wise" (66–67).

The newly initiated member of the subterranean society is thereupon conveyed through a different set of caverns to view golden landscapes of groves, islands, and lakes that are even more astonishing to the eye than anything he had previously experienced. This excursion leads him ultimately to another meeting with the beautiful Nouronihar, who promises to recount the tale of her misfortune and to disclose to him "the secret of her birth." To avoid an approaching storm, they seek refuge in a sequestered cave, which turns out to be a sumptuous apartment carved in rock of yellow jasper and lit by a myriad of crystal lamps which engulf the room in a continuous glow of evening light:

The pavement was intirely covered with mats of the nicest workmanship, on which some skilful artist had imitated fruits and flowers with so much success that at first sight they could not be distinguished from bunches of real ones. . . . A pile of aromatic wood, neatly cleft, was placed by the side of a cheerful fire, fed with the same fuel and three large baskets heaped with cocoa nuts and all the variety of fruits the valleys produced stood on the other side. The fountain I heard in the dark trickled from a nook in the interior grot and was received in a cavity on the brink of which were placed a variety of clear crystal vases, some empty, others filled with cinnamon and wild roses in full bloom. (85)

As the storm rages in the valley outside, the two delicate beings enjoy the "perfect security" of their cell. Nouronihar pipes melancholic songs on her lute, and then sinks languidly into a carpet of flowers. Upon awakening from a gentle sleep, she runs into the interior grotto and returns "with two large volumes covered with mystic writings," which she lays before her partner. Seating herself beside him, she sets out to explain the strange contents (88); but, before a word is uttered, the story ends.

III *An Imaginary Eastern Voyage*

To characterize this tale, one would have to say it is essentially an initiation story devoted to what was to become a typical Beckfordian theme: the search for self-determination. "Mark well," commands Moisasour, "the true scope of thy initiation. 'Tis the knowledge and government of thyself" (66). But Chapman's *The Vision* represents only a fragment of a larger work, for additional portions of what was to constitute a longer history exist in the form of forty-four pages of rough draft that were printed by André Parreaux in 1960. These selections now make it possible to know more about the general design of Beckford's entire project: they establish, for example, that the continuation of *The Vision* was an imaginary voyage composed in the manner of the *Arabian Nights*.[6]

Parreaux was granted permission in 1955 to examine these fragments among the Beckford manuscript archives then in the hands of Boyd Alexander of England, and the forty-four pages of text break down as follows:

1. Around five and a half pages, of which the first three and a part of the fourth constitute a variant of the text published by Chapman, starting with "I was admiring the cheerful air of the cave" (85) to the end of the printed fragment (88). Only the first of these three pages carries a number (116); the others are not particularly interesting variants.

The continuation of this fragment (two and a half pages) presents us with Nouronihar reading passages drawn from the mysterious volumes; she converses with the author and agrees, on his demand, to tell him the story of her life.

2. Eighteen manuscript pages, numbered from 1 to 18, contain the beginning of this story.

3. Four pages numbered from 19 to 22 are only a resumption, an amplification, a development, and a clarification of a part of the preceding fragment (and notably of pp. 12–13) — always in Beckford's hand.

4. The rest of Nouronihar's narration is represented by diverse fragments, which form a total of sixteen pages:
   a) Four pages, not numbered, in Beckford's hand (and of which the first begins with the words "I looked around").
   b) Eight pages numbered 1 to 8 entitled "For the Keladet where N. remains six months."
   c) One page not numbered (beginning with the words "We saw a light at a distance").
   d) Two pages not numbered of which the first opens thus: "a whirlwind of sand clouds the air," and of which the second ends with an unfinished phrase: "Said had just performed the last rites over the body of."
   e) Finally a few lines without apparent connection with what precedes but which probably agrees with the same story ("The Deer which bounding across the vast Forest of Amrin . . . ").[7]

Referring to the whole construction of Beckford's tale as *The Long Story*, Parreaux has reconstituted the grand lines of the work into two principal parts:

1. The initiation story which Chapman published in full [*The Vision*], with the exception . . . of five manuscript pages which still should be reattached to this story. This first part, though it is now depicted as part of a longer manuscript, was truly the shorter of the two, and constituted, as it were, a long preamble to the so-called history.

2. The life of Nouronihar and her ancestors recounted by herself. In this second part, one is able to distinguish the following divisions:
   a) A history of Nouronihar's ancestors which was, at the same time, an historico-mythical account of the origins of India.
   b) The story of a sacrilege committed by Nouronihar, which formed at one and the same time the culmination point of *The Long Story* and the essential change of the action.
   c) The expiation and the adventures which happen to the heroine during the course of this expiation — This final part was without a doubt the most considerable in length.[8]

It is now possible, based upon the manuscript quotations which appear in Parreaux's book, to summarize the missing segments of the long romance of which *The Vision* was only intended to be the apparent preamble. We have seen how abruptly Beckford ended *The Vision:* the new material makes it clear that he was working on a more adequate conclusion to this opening portion of the narrative. For example, the contents of the two large volumes inscribed with mystic writings, which Nouronihar had carried from an interior grotto, are explained as representing the diary of a sage who had once lived in the same sumptuous cave. On the pages of these tomes, the sage had recorded the results of some extended research, particularly his impressions of life in the "central world." He, in addition, expressed his admiration for Moisasour; and he proclaimed in the form of hymns the great serenity of his own soul that had been achieved by living in this retreat. Nouronihar explains to the narrator that she found solace in reading these passages whenever the specters of her past life on earth haunted her imagination. Too curious to resist, the narrator presses Nouronihar to tell the history of her life. She demurs at first and then begins the "tissue of misfor-

tunes" as the end of the first part comes to a respectable close: "She
fetched a deep sigh and turning towards me began."[9]

With the prologue concluded, the principal body of the book was
to follow. As the section in which Nouronihar describes the origin of
her ancestors and her own personal history, including her tragic sin
and final atonement, it also constitutes the *voyage imaginaire* to the
East. She opens her story by tracing geographical, historical, and
mythical scenes of India, descriptions which she feels are necessary
because Europeans in general do not understand the Eastern
countries over which they claim so much dominion. Geographically,
the woods of Pegu, the deserts of Mien, the interior of Ashem, the
source of the Siamboc River, and numerous other locations remain
unexplored by Europeans. "The Realms of Puronka from whose
Mountains the Ganges derives its Origin, is my native land. A long
series of these valleys, between innumerable Hills surrounded by
Cliffs and precipices, forms my Fathers Empire which his Ancestors
have ruled ever since the Race of the Prophets was extinguished."[10]
Thereafter, she recounts certain myths and legends of spiritual
rulers, like Bruma, Pourrous, Krisna, which she claims are neither
known nor understood in the West; and she also suggests that she
herself is a descendant of a celestial spirit.[11]

Related in other fragments are the details of Nouronihar's sin
which were supposed to frame, of course, the climax of the history.
As this part of the story continues, she is seen alone with a prince
named Humaioon in the sacred temple of her ancestors where she
suddenly becomes overcome by passion. A struggle with her conscience follows, but she yields to her desires and indulges in sexual
intimacies with him. To make the sin more horrible, she reveals that
her consciousness of the sacrilege she has committed in this holy
place actually enhances her pleasure: "Tho' conscious of my
sacriledge, the crime served but to inhance the delights of those
guilty moments. . . . Whenever I thought, whenever my situation
suggested itself to me, its Horrors, instead of cooling, inflamed my
Love and I pressed Humaioon to my bosom with redoubled ardour."[12] Later, when she regrets her act, she pleads to the gods for
forgiveness; but it is too late. The final portion of her history is thus
devoted to her atonement, which consists of wandering in exile for
an unspecified period of time.[13] Finally, she is admitted to the
"central world," which brings the narrative full circle.

IV   *Foreshadowings of* Vathek

Such is the substance of the fragments which form the continuation of *The Vision*, the whole of which is more properly titled *The
Long Story*. The significance of this early work in the canon of
Beckford tales is, first of all, that it anticipates in many ways the
scenes, characters, and atmosphere of *Vathek*. Chapman, in his edition of *The Vision*, has already noted foreshadowings of *Vathek* in
the use of the name Nouronihar, "though the bearer is a very different figure from the unscrupulous little consort of Vathek"; in the
employment of dwarfs, "with the qualification that the author has
not yet acquired the ironical touch with which he portrays those in-
effably tedious little beings in his later fantasy"; and, finally, in the
sketches of the "paradisaical groves and pastures of this magic
land," which prefigure in *Vathek* "the Mountain of the Four Foun-
tains, the caves of Fakreddin, and the flowery meadows of Rocnabad" (xiv). In addition, we should also mention that the description of the Halls of the Glorious in *The Vision* could well serve as a
preliminary draft for the Halls of Eblis in *Vathek:*

In a few instants we gained the extremity of the valley where something that
resembled human portals raised over the mouths of as many yawning
caverns. On a nearer survey I perceived those portals to be no more than a
sort of niche or entablature on which was engraved a variety of characters
entirely unknown to me. . . . My motion, which had abated during a space
just sufficient to allow my observing in the most cursory manner the objects
which presented themselves around, again returned and hurried me
together with my guides into one of the vast caverns I have mentioned. It
was divided by at least three thousand massy columns into the most stately
halls decorated with colonades of slender pillars inconceivably striking. The
lesser order of pillars was formed of a clear white crystalisation, exquisitely
beautiful. They supported neither frieze nor cornice, nor any ornament in
the least degree consistent with the rules of architecture we observe on the
surface of the earth, but sustained on their airy capitals a variety of glisten-
ing garlands composed of spars and intermixed like the branches which form
our bowers. The pavement in some measure corresponded with the roof.
Figure to yourself a variety of marble, agates, jaspers and other stones some
of which you are utterly unacquainted with, all painted by the hand of
nature with an infinity of elegant veins, all gleaming with the polish of a
mirror and reflecting every object in the same manner. Mark how the pavement, like a lake of marble, extends amongst this spacious labyrinth of

columns as far as your eye can reach. . . . We darted along a gallery of prodigious length, the pavement, roof, and walls entirely formed of polished agate which reflected our forms like a looking glass. We passed too hastily for me to observe with any degree of certainty the objects in the gallery; but I could not help being struck with two ranges of colossal statues placed regularly in niches on each side illuminated by a line of bright lambent flames which played about the sceptres they held in their hands. These fires blazed on innumerable golden altars with a vivacity that dazzled my eyes. Just as I was about to enquire the meaning of the sculptures around me, we arrived at a vast arch closed by a portal of ebony, whose valves flying open of a sudden with a sound that rung amongst the altars, displayed an immensely spacious concave, unsupported by any visible cause and glowing with a refulgence that proceeded from an orb of the most brilliant hue suspended from the centre by chains that, almost imperceptible, wore the appearance of sunbeams. Under the orb I beheld a flight of many hundred steps covered with a rich carpet of purple which imitated the mossy herbage of the subterraneous valleys. On every step sat a lucid form increasing in glory and stature the nearer they approached Moisasour who was seated on the summit of the steps while Nouronihar reclined at his feet. (37-39)

In the character of Moisasour, we can also see the future Eblis: both are victims of pride; and both are leaders of underworld regions, though the one is the land of the redeemed, the other of the damned. Moisasour is a fallen angel who had atoned for his transgressions; and, because of his inordinate passion for knowledge, he once challenged, like Satan in John Milton's *Paradise Lost*, the omnipotence of the "MOST HIGH." When he and other rebel angels attempted to pry into mysteries that they were commanded only to revere, they were forced into exile and were to "wander for ages" in the body of an inferior creature. But, unlike Eblis, Moisasour was allowed to make reparations for his wrongdoing. Beckford left room for hope, therefore, in *The Vision;* but, when he wrote the catastrophe of *Vathek*, hope gave way to despair.

It used to be observed of *The Vision* that it contrasted markedly in atmosphere with *Vathek*. "Many readers," writes Fatma M. Mahmoud, "were struck by its atmosphere of luminous wisdom and natural goodness, much in contrast to the sense of evil that hangs over *Vathek*."[14] But the emergence of the successive additions to *The Vision* not only alters this conception but also establishes a greater similarity between the two works. In particular, the revelation of Nouronihar's sin, intensified by the guilty pleasure she derives from its commission in a sacred place, looks forward to the baleful tone of parts of *Vathek* as well as to segments of *The Episodes of Vathek*. The newly discovered material shows that Beckford's profound concern for forbidden pleasure in his later works — his exquisite sense of evil — found its first stage of growth in this precocious early composition. Experience had already rubbed some of the bloom off the boy-author's heart; but not "all of the bloom" has disappeared, as John G. Lockhart later perceived upon reading a copy of *Vathek*.[15]

Something further can be noted about *The Long Story* that indicates its strong kinship with *Vathek:* although it is by no means an Oriental tale in the sense that *Vathek* might be, the constant references to the East throughout the body of *The Vision* reflect at this early stage in his career a strong liking in the mind of the young writer for Eastern detail. Besides the appellations, Moisasour and Nouronihar, for example, Beckford mentions the "groves of the Bramins"; cites Gehbil, "a mountain in the interior of India," and Zennana, a Persian term signifying a harem; and makes reference to the Hindu deity, "Padmani" (Padmapani). The geographical setting for the dream fantasy, though subterranean, is faintly Eastern; for the location is given identity occasionally by means of a comparison like, "On the right of the level space grew several cocoa trees . . . and near them flourished a grove of palms, resembling the Talipot of Ceylon" (81).

There are also allusions to religious mysticism, when, through fasting or the using of potent herbs, the "inmost soul glows with sensations of Love, of gratitude, of awe, too fervent for the mortal frame" (15). Furthermore, the narrative looks forward to another major characteristic of *Vathek* by including notes to elucidate a few of the obscure Oriental references, such as the one to "Shastah": "The Shastah is a Book written on the leaves of Palmtrees of very remote antiquity. Contains all the Learning and mythology of the Bramins. Its contents scarce ever reached Europe. Mr. Bathurst, a Bookseller in London, possesses a few leaves of this inestimable treasure but none are sufficiently learned in the Sanscrit language to expound them" (19).

It is likewise apparent, finally, from the newly discovered fragments of Nouronihar's history with their wealth of Oriental names and allusions that Beckford was making use of the varied material that was offered him in academic studies of the East long before *Vathek*. Parreaux has identified J. Z. Howell's *Interesting Historical Events, Relative to the Provinces of Bengal, and the Em-*

pire of Indostan (1766–71) as one of the sources Beckford used in
The Long Story; and he has also suggested several other possible influences.[16] That Beckford drew upon this kind of material to supply
some of the details of an imaginary voyage is especially significant in
view of his preoccupation with concrete Oriental details in *Vathek*
and in *The Episodes of Vathek.* Even without a precise listing of
source books, Nouronihar's numerous geographical references and
her history of Indian legends and religions illustrate that her creator
at the early age of seventeen had arrived at a bookish knowledge of
Indian history and geography that few older Englishmen of his time
had achieved. Only a few years would have to pass before he would
bring this unusual knowledge to bear on a more sustained piece of
literary Orientalism.

CHAPTER 4

The Light of Reason:
Extraordinary Painters

IF *The Long Story* revealed the Romantic side of the young
Beckford, his *Biographical Memoirs of Extraordinary Painters*, a
second apprentice work composed about the same time, exposed a
different, more restrained and rational side of his personality. Written under Cozens' influence and encouraged by the Reverend Lettice, *Extraordinary Painters* gave evidence of Beckford's extensive
knowledge of painting which was to give his highly pictorial style of
writing its shape and character; but it also demonstrated the satiric
skill which was to find its way, somewhat uncomfortably, in the fantasy world of *Vathek*.

I *Origin and Composition*

The account of the origin of *Extraordinary Painters* comes to us
unfortunately second hand: from Beckford's contemporary biographer, Cyrus Redding, a man prone to inaccuracies, and from
Henry Venn Lansdown, a Bath artist and teacher of drawing. According to Redding in a journal article printed in the *New Monthly
Magazine* shortly after Beckford's death, *Extraordinary Painters* was
designed originally to be a perfectly "laughable book" and was inspired partly by the imaginative descriptions that Beckford's
housekeeper provided when she was showing visitors the collection
of fine paintings in the galleries of Fonthill Splendens, the mansion
owned by Beckford's father. With the confidence of an expert, she
was in the habit of expatiating on the lives of the artists and the
merits of their compositions when she knew nothing about either.
Beckford, who was supposedly amused by the amount of gross mis-
information and inaccurate detail she exhibited to gullible strangers,
hit upon the idea of writing a guide book that would incorporate a
similar degree of fantasy. In his own reported words,

My pen was quickly in hand composing the *Memoirs*. In the future the housekeeper had a printed guide in aid of her descriptions. She caught up my phrases and her descriptions became more picturesque, her language more graphic than ever! . . . Mine was the textbook, whoever exhibited the paintings. The book was soon on the tongues of all the domestics. Many were the quotations current upon the merits of Og of Basan, and Watersouchy of Amsterdam. Before a picture of Rubens or Murillo there was often a charming dissertation upon the pencil of the Herr Sucrewasser of Vienna, or that great Italian artist Blunderbussiana of Venice. I used to listen unobserved until I was ready to kill myself with laughing at the authorities quoted to the squires and farmers of Wiltshire, who took all for gospel. It was the most ridiculous thing in effect that you can conceive.[1]

A slightly different version is given in H. V. Lansdown's privately printed pamphlet entitled *Recollections of the late William Beckford, of Fonthill, Wilts; and Lansdown, Bath.* Consisting largely of reconstructed conversations with Beckford and descriptions of his Bath residence which were made during the course of a few visits there, it is presented in the form of five letters written in the fall of 1838 to his daughter Charlotte Lansdown. The letters remained in manuscript for fifty-five years before Charlotte decided to print them in 1893. The material relating to *Extraordinary Painters* is recorded in the last letter, dated November 10, 1838, in which Lansdown recalls Beckford's explanation of how his book came to be written:

The origin of Beckford's *Lives of Extraordinary Painters* was very odd. When he was fifteen years old the housekeeper came to him, and said she wished he would tell her something about the artists who painted his fine pictures, as visitors were always questioning her, and she did not know what to answer. "Oh very well; I'll write down some particulars about them." He instantly composed *Lives of Extraordinary Painters*. The housekeeper studied the manuscript attentively, and regaled her astonished visitors with the marvellous incidents it contained; however, finding many were sceptical, she came to her young master and told him people would not believe what she told them. "Not believe? Ah, that's because it is only in manuscript. Then we'll have it printed; they'll believe when they see it in print." He sent the manuscript to a London publisher, and inquired what the expense of printing it would be. The publisher read it with delight, and instantly offered the youthful author £50 for the manuscript. The housekeeper was now able to silence all cavilers by producing the book itself.[2]

These two accounts cannot, of course, be taken too seriously; both suffer from a certain degree of imaginative distortion. Other evidence exists, as will be shown, which demonstrates that Beckford did not compose this work at fifteen years of age and that he certainly did not complete it, as Lansdown suggests, in one sitting. It is possible, however, that the housekeeper's comic role was catalytic; and it is also likely that Beckford gave these explanations to Redding and Lansdown. But, at the same time, it must be remembered that Beckford loved colorful conversation and that he was not beyond distorting the truth. The book at any rate had a much more serious intent; for, whatever the initial creative impetus, *Extraordinary Painters* was an ingenious burlesque of artistic excesses propagated by various schools of painting, most notably the Dutch and the Flemish, and a masterful parody of certain biographies dedicated to capsulizing the life and work of individual artists.

Attempts to determine the composition date of *Extraordinary Painters* have been attended with similar problems.[3] Redding maintained that the entire work was finished before Beckford left England to complete his education in Switzerland in June, 1777, when he was only sixteen years old;[4] and testimony from two other sources furthermore seems to strengthen this statement. The first source is an anonymous article in the *European Magazine* in 1797, authored apparently by someone who knew Beckford well, which claimed that "The Lives of the Painters" was "written at sixteen years of age."[5] Second, an extant copy of *Extraordinary Painters*, once owned by Elizabeth Hervey, has her signature on the flyleaf, the date "1798," and the phrase "Written by Will. Beckford, Esq. when he was in his 18th year."[6] Since Beckford's "18th year" fell between September 29, 1777, and September 29, 1778, it would still be possible, as Boyd Alexander has pointed out,[7] that 1777 was the correct year of composition. The foregoing evidence, therefore, would seem to invalidate the conclusion set forth in the official Beckford bibliography that he composed the *whole* work between the autumn of 1779 and the spring of 1780.[8]

But two important letters by Beckford's tutor, the Reverend John Lettice, must not be overlooked in this discussion; they require close reading in any endeavor to date the composition of *Extraordinary Painters*, for they show clearly that Beckford wrote at least the last section of this book in the early months of 1780.[9] It is evident from the first letter, dated December 12, 1779, that this work was done at Lettice's special request. He apparently had indicated a willingness to guide the finished product through the press for Beckford, but he hesitated to do so because of its brevity. The letter discloses that the

manuscript which Lettice had in his possession in December and
which he was showing to his colleagues at Sidney Sussex College was
incomplete, containing only four of the final five stories. "To go to
a more agreeable subject," Lettice wrote to Beckford,

Mr. Hunter (who by the by is a very superior critic) and I have read together
Aldrovandus and Og of Basan [the first two lives] with great delight. I think
they please me better than ever, especially the latter, and my friend is not a
whit behind me in admiration of them. I shall today shew them to several
others of my friends. The Master was unfortunately gone out of College
before they came and will not return soon enough to read them, which mor-
tifies me much; as I am sure he would have done it with particular pleasure.
Hunter and I have this moment been reading the two last lives [Sucrewasser
and Blunderbussiana]. We agree that [Sucrewasser's][10] chosen name has
many charming strokes of humor in it and that Blunderbussiana is the *chef
d'oeuvre* of the whole.

Lettice wanted his student to write at least six stories. "I wish you
would write two more lives," he added; "and if they are as well done
as these I should have no objection to midwifing it to the world in
the spring, if you have no one, as I do believe they would be extremely well received. We will talk more about it when I get to
Fonthill. In the meantime I will take care to give them such corrections as they may want."

As it actually happened, Beckford followed his tutor's advice, in
part, by composing one additional biography after he had received
the December letter or, perhaps, after Lettice's predicted visit to
Fonthill. This may be inferred from Lettice's assurance in the letter
of March 23, 1780: "I have shewn Watersouchy [the fifth and final
biography] to nobody; because it might make the publication of the
lives less a secret than we wish it to be. I like it perfectly well, now I
see it written out fair, and do not think it any way unworthy to appear among the rest."[11] Since Lettice had shown the biography of
Watersouchy "to nobody," it is reasonable to conclude that it was
not part of the earlier manuscript passed around so freely in
December and that it was drafted during the winter months of 1780
as an acceptable conclusion to the book. In this case Redding's ap-
pointment of 1777 as the year in which Beckford produced the whole
of *Extraordinary Painters* is somewhat misleading. With the
evidence that has been surveyed, it would be more accurate to conclude that, although Beckford may have begun weaving his satire in
1777, he did not complete his task until the early part of 1780. Only

after the account of Jeremy Watersouchy was fashioned did Lettice
send it to the printer with his own engaging preface affixed. The little volume finally appeared on the London bookstalls shortly after
April 10, 1780;[12] it was bound in marbled paper wrappers and offered for two and six.

II *A Beckfordian Satire*

As for the work itself, *Extraordinary Painters*, like so many
Beckford creations, is for the most part a fantasy, a product of his
own virile imagination. But his fantasy is shot through with the
humor of a satirist — a work, we might say, which is both absurd and
meaningful. This intention is evident almost at first sight in the
proper names invented by Beckford for his assortment of characters.
In the case of three of his leading artists — Sucrewasser, Blunderbussiana, and Watersouchy — there is a direct correspondence
between the artist's name and the style or method of his work; and
Beckford's criticism is inevitably implied. Sucrewasser of Vienna is
devoted to painting in fresco on the walls of casinos, and his most
characteristic compositions are as bland as his name: "The subjects
were either the four Seasons or the three Graces. Now and then a few
blind Cupids, and sometimes a lean Fury, by way of variety. The
colouring was gay and tender, and the drawing correct. The faces
were pretty uniform and had all the most delightful smirk
imaginable; even his Furies looked as if they were half inclined to
throw their torches into the water, and the serpents around their
temples were as mild as eels."[13]

Blunderbussiana, on the other hand, who is appropriately the son
of a bandit chieftain, is preoccupied with the study of anatomy as a
necessary stage in the development of his art: "His father's band frequently bringing bodies to their caves, he amused himself with dis-
secting and imitating the several parts, till he attained such a perfection in muscular expression as is rarely seen in the works of the
greatest masters. . . . He never was without a leg or an arm, which he
went slicing along, and generally accompanied his operations with a
melodious whistling; for he was of a chearful disposition, and, if he
had had a different education, would have been an ornament to
society" (85–86). What Beckford is attacking here, of course, is the
commonly held view of Renaissance art criticism that anatomical
research was the key to the greatness of Italian art.

Finally, there is Watersouchy, whose name, as André Parreaux has
already pointed out, is a corruption of the Dutch word *waterzootje*,

or "boiled fish."[14] His forte, as we might suspect, is painting pieces of still life that range from glossy flowers to eatables. Beckford describes Watersouchy's first compositions as "an arm chair of the richest velvet, and a Turkey carpet." "The exquisite drawing of these pieces," he continues, "was not less observable than the softness of their tints and the absolute nature of their colouring. Every man wished to sit down in the one, and every dog to repose on the other" (95).

A burlesque nomenclature critically suggestive of the nature of the character described extends to the minor figures as well. After meeting the scholarly professor, Clod Lumpewitz, who preserves for all time the memory of Aldrovandus Magnus in a Latin epitaph, and Soorcrout, the ingenious artist who recommends "white of egg" as a replacement for "oils in general," the reader is entertained by the royal Prince Henry Suckingbottle, by his friend Felt Marshall Swappingback, and then by two illustrious patrons of the arts, Cardinal Grossocavallo and Count Zigzaggi, before he is introduced to the famous Italian painter, Insignificanti, whose specialty is painting lap-dogs on velvet cushions, and to the exquisite Baise-la-main, "an encourager of the fine arts," who combines "the greatest wealth with the most exemplary politeness." All of these names contribute to the general prankish spirit of the comedy; and, even if read for this level of humor alone, *Extraordinary Painters* could be considered successful.

But what lends special force to the comic spirit of this work is its strange blend of the real with the burlesque, the authentic with the farcical — a commingling of disparate elements that looks forward to *Vathek*. Thus, interwoven with the fictitious figures are real historical personages who speak, act, and occupy significant roles in the stories. There are imaginary painters, but there are very real artists, too, such as Hemmelinck (Hans Memlinc), Giulio Romano, Francis Mierhop, Gerard Dou, Maria Sibylla Merian, Albert Dürer, Cornelis van Poelemburg, and Joseph Porta; and all these persons are worked into the essential fabric of the stories. In addition to the painters, there are other celebrities who sometimes appear when we least expect them. Professor Lumpewitz, for example, is obviously a creation of Beckford's fancy; but John Ogilby, the translator of the Latin epitaph, really lived in the seventeenth century and was satirized by John Dryden and Alexander Pope for his voluminous translations of Homer and Virgil. The imaginary story of Drahomire, "who in the year 921 was swallowed up by an earthquake," is based on the actual story of Drahomira, the princess of Bohemia who murdered her mother-in-law in 921. Dolgoruki, furthermore, is in actuality the name of a Russian noble family; and George Podebrac is George Podebrady, who was king of Bohemia in 1458. Almost all the biographies, moreover, contain popular historical material, such as the reference to Cardinal Ippolito's abuse of the poet Ariosto, the attribution of the invention of oil painting to the Van Eycks, and the legends concerning St. Denis' martyrdom and St. Anthony's oratorical skill.

The result of this unusual mixture of the absurd and the authentic is that it often achieves the effect of double-edged satire in which romance and reality deride each other. It may not be surprising to discover, therefore, that the reading public in 1780 was considerably puzzled by *Extraordinary Painters*. The book, endowed as it was with such a melange of the burlesque and the authentic, resisted easy interpretation. Even critics were thrown into a miserable humor over the "sense" of it. Although it was generally felt that the anonymous author was "by no means a bad or uninformed writer," and that "in his performance the reader will meet with some good descriptions," the total effect of the comic elements were felt to be lost in the "vexatious obscurity" which seemed to permeate the whole work.[15] The reviewers in the *Gentleman's Magazine*, the *Critical Review*, and the *Monthly Review* admitted frankly that the central meaning of the work and the general intention of its author totally escaped them:

Those *connoscenti* who expect here a Bellori or a Vasari, a De Piles or a Walpole, will be disappointed. The six "extraordinary painters" here celebrated never existed but in the author's brain. . . . Some ridicule on particular characters may perhaps be intended, but the meaning (if any) is much too latent for us to discover.[16]

There may . . . , for aught we know, be much hidden wit and humour in it, but the line of our understanding is not, we must acknowledge, long enough to fathom the depth of it.[17]

Not content with studying this performance carefully, we have consulted both professors and virtuosos concerning it; but still remain in the dark with respect to the Author's real drift.[18]

For the reader of 1780, the only conceivable explanation was that the book satirized certain contemporary artists under feigned names,

but who those artists were could not be determined: "On the first
view of the performance, it naturally occurs, that the Author meant
to draw some modern or living characters: but if such was his intention, we confess that we are not of that class of readers who can iden-
tify any one of them in this mingled mass of true and fictitious
history."[19] Yet, in spite of the mystery that seemed to enshroud the
book, a second issue of the first edition appeared before the year
ended.

The publication of the second edition in 1824 by William Clarke
was better received, but not because any deeper understanding of its
content existed. The book was of interest because it was known by
then that its creator was the author of *Vathek,* and the popularity of
Beckford's major work was enough to make any other work of his an
object of curiosity. *Extraordinary Painters* displayed, it was felt, the
early efforts of the fervent imagination which spun the story of the
tormented caliph. One observant critic detected a "corresponding
perception and development of the effects of regret, remorse, and
unavailing repentance, on the intellectual faculty" in *Extraordinary
Painters;* and he also noticed that "the touches of playful satire
which frequently occur to relieve the sombre character of the narrative, in some parts of *Vathek,* are not less visible in these
Memoirs."[20] Even more specifically, he recognized that the description of the imaginary hall in Noah's ark in the tale of "Andrew
Guelph and Og of Basan" contained "much of the wild sublimity
and mysterious interest which characterize the account of the hall of
Eblis in *Vathek."* The passage to which this early reviewer alluded,
if taken out of context, could indeed find a place in Beckford's
Oriental masterpiece. The similarity in style, tone, and image is very
striking:

He [Og of Basan] represented a vast hall in the ark, supported by tall
slender columns of a strange unknown architecture. Above were domes,
which admitted a pale watery light, diffusing a sacred gloom over the whole
apartment. On the foreground he placed the venerable patriarch in extasy at
the sight of an angel, descending majestically on a rainbow, which cast its
vivid tints on the cornices of the hall, gleaming with gems. These bright
hues were powerfully contrasted with the shade that prevailed in the
background, where a line of portals, inscribed with mysterious characters,
seemed just emerging from the darkness. The form of the angel seemed to
hover in the air. It was lucid and transparent, its hair seemed like waving
sun-beams, and its countenance was worthy of a minister of the Deity. The
rays which darted from the angel struck upon several altars, vases and
golden ornaments dispersed in various parts of the apartment. (69)

Apparently, not until the appearance of the third and last edition of *Extraordinary Painters* in 1834 did readers show signs of coming to terms with Beckford's satire. When the edition appeared in early August under Richard Bentley's imprint, it was promptly reviewed in William Jerdan's *Literary Gazette*. "The follies of art are ridiculed in the happiest vein," the article commended; and this task required "what the author of Vathek eminently possesses — a thorough knowledge of his subject, a fine taste, and a judgment equally alive to beauties and to blemishes." From it, the review concluded, "the soundest lessons in art may be readily learnt."[21]

The comments were brief, but it was just the kind of commendatory notice that fed Beckford's vanity. He left his reaction to it among the still unpublished letters to his bookseller George Clarke:

If the Painters do not go off like a sky rocket, it will not be Jerdan's fault. His Gazette of last Saturday speaks a volume of praise in a very few lines. What precedes the extracts is a charming little vignette, and the plain energetic recommendation at the end forms a "Cul de Lampe" the publishers ought to be pleased with. Send me a Literary Gazette, and to the Duke of Hamilton another. I am certain he will be *pleased* with it. I do confess *I was*. Not having looked into the book (further than the plate of Sr D[enis] with head in hand) this long while, I felt much exhilarated by the extracts, and had a hearty laugh at Aldrovandus and the Burgomaster Van Gulph. . . .[22]

The man who really helped to establish a new understanding of the text, however, was John Gibson Lockhart, the biographer of Walter Scott. In the introduction to a review of *Italy; with Sketches of Spain and Portugal,* published a few months before the above review, Lockhart made several observations about *Extraordinary Painters*, ones which Bentley used as part of an advertising program to promote the sale of the volume.[23] Lockhart first sought to establish that it was meritorious in its own right as a work of art, beyond the fact that it was composed originally by one of the most controversial young eccentrics in England: "Mr. Beckford, it is said, appeared as an author at the early age of *eighteen*, but the *Biographical Memoirs of Extraordinary Painters* would have excited considerable attention, under whatever circumstances they might have been given to the world." Lockhart then undertook to clarify what had baffled his predecessors. These combined biographies, he explained, were "a series of sharp and brilliant satires on the Dutch and Flemish schools — the language polished and pointed — the sarcasm at once deep and delicate — a performance in which the bouyancy of juvenile spirits sets off the results of already extensive observation, and the judgements of a refined . . . taste."

Beckford saw this review and later brought it to Cyrus Redding's attention.[24] This man Lockhart, he felt, showed some understanding of his book; for *Extraordinary Painters* certainly exposed to ridicule the strained and artificial mannerism prevalent among many works of the Dutch and Flemish artists or, for that matter, any other artists who may have adopted a similar style.[25] To Beckford's mind, literal realism in painting was too disciplinary to be pleasing because it represented a commitment to fussy detail that stifled the imagination. "When I find [Rubens] lost in the flounces of the Virgin's drapery, or bewildered in the graces of St. Catherine's smile," he once wrote, "pardon me, if I withhold my adoration."[26] His feeling was akin to that of Keats when he looked upon Benjamin West's picture "Death on the Pale Horse": there was simply nothing to be intense upon, no emotional reality.

A final objective of Beckford's book, and one which even escaped the sharp eye of Lockhart, was to satirize certain biographical or critical studies of painters published in the eighteenth century. "It is true enough," Beckford confided to Redding, "that I designed to hit the criticisms and memoirs upon Dutch painters. How could I fail to do so with such an opportunity — their fooleries and trash so very obvious!"[27] One item in particular seems to have inspired these hits: Jean-Baptiste Descamps' *La Vie des Peintres Flamands, Allemands et Hollandois* (1753–64). Using Descamps' book as the principal source for *Extraordinary Painters*, Beckford endeavored to parody its style, or what Redding called, its "biographico-pictorial authorship."[28] Occasionally, he followed the text so closely that words and sentences were transcribed almost verbatim; sometimes for comic effect, he purposely exaggerated the tone or inflated the language dealing with trivia. The result was a whittling down, a diminishing of both the manner and the subject of Descamps' book, or indeed any similar work which could not withstand the following treatment:

At length he [Watersouchy] began: Ambitious of shewing his great versatility, and desirous of producing a contrast to the portrait just finished, he determined to put the lady in action. She was represented watering a capsacum, with an air of superior dignity mingled with ineffable sweetness. Every part of her dress was minutely attended to; her ruffle was admirable; but her hands and arms exceeded all idea. Gerard Dow had bestowed five days labour on this part of Madam Spiering's person, whose portrait was one of his best performances. Watersouchy, that he might surpass his master, spent a month in giving only to his patroness's fingers the last touch of perfection. Each had its ring, and so tinted, as almost at first sight to have deceived a discerning jeweller.

When he had finished this last masterpiece he found himself quite weak and exhausted. The profound study in which he had been absorbed, impaired his health, and his having neglected exercise for the two last years brought on a hectic and feverish complaint. The only circumstance that now cheared his spirits was the conversation of a circle of old ladies; the friends of Madame Gulph. These good people had ever some little incident to entertain him, some gossiping narration that soothed and unbended his mind. But all their endeavours to restore him could not prevent his growing weaker and weaker. At last he took to cordials by their recommendation, became fond of news and tulips, and for a time was a little mended; so much indeed, that he resumed his pallet, and painted little pieces for his kind comforters; such as a favourite dormouse for Madam Dozinburg, and a cheese in a China dish with mites in it for some other venerable lady, whose name has not descended to us. (106–07)

Beckford's various satiric methods in *Extraordinary Painters* seem, on the whole, to be properly Neo-Classical. But, despite the display of eighteenth-century wit, the book suffers at times from a slippage of tone, from an uneven quality of style which suggests that the author could not sustain his own point of view. If he begins by satirizing the art historians for their Romantic indulgence, he ends by indulging himself in his own biographical fantasy. The story of Og of Basan is a case in point. Og is a Romantic painter who engages in a monomaniacal quest for the ideal subject; and, in the manner of the artist in Percy B. Shelley's *Alastor*, he does so at the expense of love and ends by paying for his extravagance in a violent death.

Although the story deals ostensibly with the danger of such excess, the moralizing role of the satirist is not sustained. Instead, as the story unfolds, Beckford's flippant humor diminishes and is replaced by his own obvious attraction to Og's sense of abandonment and criminal guilt, and to the forlorn and Gothic settings in which the artist finds himself. When the author says of Og during his stay in Rome that "he would now walk by moonlight through the lonely galleries, and revolve in his mind the instability of human grandeur," the satiric voice has yielded to sympathetic identification and with it the book's Neo-Classical posture. Yet, in a curious way, the resultant stylistic unevenness seems less a literary fault and more a significant revelation of Beckford's own personality. As a young man, he was too mercurial to keep his natural passion under control for any length of time. The hard light of reason yielded inevitably to the soft deluding power of imagination.

CHAPTER 5

The "dubious visionary light": Dreams, Waking Thoughts and Incidents

BECKFORD returned to England from Switzerland in 1778 and during the next few years prior to the composition of an unusual travel book, *Dreams, Waking Thoughts and Incidents,* and his major work, *Vathek,* found himself pulled in different directions by various emotional problems. During a tour of England in 1779, for example, he met and developed almost instantly a "strange wayward passion" for William Courtenay, the eleven-year-old son of Lord Courtenay of Powderham Castle. "I grew sensible," Beckford wrote later, "there was pleasure in loving something besides oneself and felt there would be more luxury in dying for him than living for the rest of the universe."[1] The precise nature of this relationship may be subject to varying interpretations, but there can be little doubt about its disturbing emotional effect. Following the initial contact, Beckford experienced constant anxiety in his efforts to keep in touch with the "little C."; and he was also frequently agitated by the efforts of his family to dissolve what it felt was an unwholesome relationship. In addition, Beckford faced at this time a second emotional struggle that involved an affair with the unhappily married Louisa Pitt-Rivers, the wife of Beckford's cousin, Peter; for their relationship had flamed into passion by the end of his European tour in the spring of 1781. To these complex relationships were added for Beckford the troubling responsibilities connected with his wealth and his social position. His only relief was the escapism of self-induced visionary states in which he increasingly indulged during the months immediately preceding his departure for the Continent. "Visions play around me," he wrote of himself, "and at some solemn moments I am cast into prophetic Trances. Lost in Dreams and magic slumbers my Hours glide swiftly away. I have none to awaken me — none to sympathize with my feelings. Those I love are absent. Thus desolate and abandoned I seek refuge in aerial conversations and talk with spirits whose voices are murmuring in the Gales."[2]

A ten-month Grand Tour of Europe, which provided material for most of the letters in *Dreams, Waking Thoughts and Incidents*, became then for Beckford a period of deep self-analysis interfused with dark moments of despair. If the family council at Fonthill believed that this tour would somehow cure the vagaries of his personality, it had been seriously mistaken; for his travel simply added to his panoply of disorders. On June 19, 1780, he set out from Margate with the ubiquitous Lettice and embarked on the first portion of the journey, moving at a rapid pace through the Low Countries, where he grew "as scurrilous as Dr. Smollet" in his complaints about Dutch and Flemish taste. But, when he reached Venice in August, some new poison entered his system.

Sometime during his month-long stay, Beckford became involved with the decadence of Venetian high society, largely through the help of the adventuress, Madame de Rosenberg, and her *cavaliere servente*, Count Benincasa; and, before long, Beckford was drawn into a homosexual entanglement with a young member of the aristocratic Vendramin family which left him in a feverish and agitated state. Years later he attempted to explain the relationship in discreet terms as "a passion of the mind — resembling those generous attachments we venerate in ancient history, and holy writ — what David felt towards the brother of his heart, the son of Saul."[3] But the immediate impact on him was traumatic, and, for the rest of the tour, his mind was haunted by one object: "One image alone possesses me and pursues me in a terrible way. In vain do I throw myself into Society — this image forever starts up before me. In vain do I try to come up to the great expectations formed of me — my words are cut short and I am halted in mid-career. This unique object is all I hope for — and I am dead to everything else."[4]

By the time Beckford reached Naples in November, he had worked himself into such an overwrought state of mind that he could no longer contain his feelings. As a result, he unloaded all his emotional freight upon the shoulders of a new friend and confidante, Lady Hamilton, the first wife of Sir William Hamilton, the English ambassador to the Court of Naples. Beckford stayed with the Hamiltons for a month during which time Lady Hamilton acted as a positive and fortifying influence; and, disapproving completely of his Venetian affair, she made him aware of the dangers he might be led into if he continued it. With her aid, he made an effort to discipline himself, though reasonable behavior was a struggle for him to sustain. When he left Naples in the first week of December, Lady Hamilton attempted to continue her influence through a series of letters in which she urged him to remember the "harsh truths" she had forced him to face.

But he was on his way to Venice again, to Vendramin, and to the "pestilential air" that Lady Hamilton had urged him to avoid. "Resist nobly a sentiment that in your soul you cannot approve," she pleaded, "and which if indulged must end in your misery and in the destruction of a mother who dotes on you."[5] In Venice at the end of December, Beckford wrote assurances that he would not yield to the "insinuating whisper of a soft but criminal delight,"[6] and she answered with a letter imploring him to continue the resistance: "Every day you will find the struggle less — the important struggle! What is it for? No less than *honor, reputation* and all that an honest and noble Soul holds most dear, while Infamy, eternal infamy (my soul freezes while I write the word) attends the giving way to the soft alluring of a criminal passion."[7] Beckford apparently surmounted the temptation, because by January 10, 1781, he had abandoned his "Venetian state" and with it his "fatal connection."

If leaving Venice raised Beckford's spirits, the relief was shortlived. Once out of Italy, the proximity of England and the unwelcome responsibilities it held for him loomed large in his mind. By early February, he was in Paris where he deliberately lingered for two months trying to forget the "sullen realities" of business and politics; and his business included the Chancery proceedings against a bastard brother for which he would have to prepare before his twenty-first birthday in September or risk losing control of some profitable sugar estates in Jamaica. The prospect of immersing himself in such affairs terrified and depressed him. "Don't call me *illustre ami*, and *homme unique*," he would later plead; "I'm still in my cradle! Spare the delicacy of my infantile ears. Leave me to scamper on verdant banks — all too ready, alas, to crumble, but rainbow-tinted and flower-strewn."[8] He finally returned to England on April 14; but, just before he departed from Paris, he wrote to his friend, Lady Hamilton, the following confession: "I fear I shall never be . . . good for anything in this world, but composing airs, building towers, forming gardens, collecting old Japan, and writing a journey to China or the moon."[9] These were defensive and apologetic words, but they were remarkably prophetic. For the next

few years, he began fulfilling part of that prophecy by committing
himself to writing instead of politics.

I *Henley and the Composition of* Dreams

During the Grand Tour, Beckford kept with him a number of
notebooks in which he made abbreviated day-to-day entries. These
manuscript notes, only a small portion of which survive,[10] were
"very inefficient in themselves" (Left Florence — a sober Autumnal
Eve: — Thunder storm — Ruins of Castles in a Vale — shrouded by
poplars — with faded yellow leaves"), but they served as useful
skeleton material for most of the letters in *Dreams* — for his memory
and imagination supplied whatever material was wanting.[11] When
the process of transformation was complete, it was not an ordinary
book of travel filled simply with the "facts" of the journey; but it
was a visionary pilgrimage that occasionally revealed the inner world
of the author's own soul. The personal anguish investing his life at
the time of composition was generally masked and kept under control, but the root of the book's constant wavering between reality
and fantasy, combined with the persistent invocations to Morpheus,
was inevitably Beckford's aggravated psyche. "Shall I tell you my
dreams?" became the opening words of the volume. "To give an account of my time, is doing, I assure you, but little better. Never did
there exist a more ideal being. A frequent mist hovers before my
eyes, and through its medium, I see objects so faint and hazy, that
both their colours and forms are apt to delude me. This is a rare confession, say the wise, for a traveller to make; pretty accounts will
such a one give of outlandish countries: his correspondents must
reap great benefit, no doubt, from such purblind observations: —
But . . . with my visionary way of gazing, I am perfectly pleased."

Without discounting the possibility that Beckford could have
begun transforming his diary notes into finished letters sometime
during his extended stay in Paris in 1781, he more likely did not
begin serious work on *Dreams* until after his arrival in London on
April 20. It is clear, at any rate, that the work was well underway by
August 31, 1781, when he wrote to Lettice: "I am impatient to have
you look over my Italian Journal and will do my best to make it
worth looking at."[12] It is also evident that this effort was not a
literary exercise carried out merely to please a tutor; it was a serious
work for publication and one that they had already discussed. "You
know I have my heart set upon the success of my book," he wrote in

the same letter, "and shall not at all relish its being only praised as a lively, picturesque excursion." At this early stage, Beckford had also given some thought to the composition of Letter XXVII, a long, reflective essay on the political, economic, and artistic characteristics of the principal European countries he had seen. The decision to include a letter of this kind seems to have been the outcome of a certain self-consciousness about the potentially "luxuriant and sentimental" nature of the travelogue. Speaking metaphorically, he indicated to Lettice what role the reflective letter would serve in the book: "Unless there is a good solid trunk that cuts fair and sound in the grain I would not give a farthing for leaves and flowers, so I propose being wise and solemn in the Letter of reflections."

Most of the letters were written, though perhaps not in final form, by the Christmas season of 1781 when Beckford met the Reverend Samuel Henley, formerly a professor at William and Mary College, Virginia, who because of the American Revolution had returned to England where he served as a schoolmaster, private tutor, and, significantly, as editor of Henry Swinburne's *Travels in the Two Sicilies*. Henley's Oriental interests and his willingness to take on certain literary tasks undoubtedly recommended him to Beckford's attention. Before they parted, Henley had agreed to edit *Dreams* and to act as a professional go-between when the time came to approach a London publisher. The Reverend Lettice, who had occupied a similar role a year and a half earlier when *Biographical Memoirs of Extraordinary Painters* was being readied for the press, might have continued had it not been for Beckford's Christmas meeting with Henley. Thereafter Lettice's role as literary assistant diminished to providing aid with the preparation of a fair-copy manuscript, but Henley's assumed increasing significance.

Beckford was in constant communication with Henley in 1782–83 during the completion of the travel book. Numerous letters were exchanged; and a number of meetings between the two men were held to discuss editorial matters in detail. "There will be no proceeding in our work," Beckford wrote in January, 1782, "without long consultations."[13] One concrete result of this collaboration was the inclusion of the episode of the two Neopolitan lovers in Letter XXIII which Beckford began writing at Henley's urging. On Wednesday, January 16, 1782, Henley wrote the following to Beckford: "The situation of your mind at the time of your writing excited in me all the energy of sympathy. I have something to communicate analogous to what you perhaps refer to — but of this more on Saturday (January 19) when I hope to see you."[14] The proposed visit took place; and on Monday, January 21, Beckford wrote to his colleague: "The spirit has moved me this eve; and shut up in my apartment as you advised, I have given way to fancies and inspirations. What will be the consequence of this mood I am not bold enough to determine."[15]

The major outcome of this "romantic" mood of January 21 has often been identified as the creation of *Vathek*, but Henley's reply makes it clear that Beckford was referring to the episode in Letter XXIII of *Dreams:*

> I am not surprised to find that the Spirit hath moved you. I knew the moment of inspiration would come, and beheld the power herself descending, surrounded by an effulgence of glory. A splender of golden radiance kindled beneath her foot steps, and the fiery track that marked her way thro clouds of the saddest purple is still glowing from earth to heaven. Such was my vision! I conversed too, with your crone, visited the top of the chasm into which the unhappy fair one fell: noted the ivory that surrounded the sarcophagus which her lover was exploring; and beheld the earth still fresh, from whence the loosened crag broke beneath his weight. — But truce to visions! I shall wait with the most anxious impatience till I learn the story from yourself.[16]

This letter is undated; but, as a reply to Beckford's letter of January 21, it is reasonable to conclude that Henley had written it before the end of the month. The letter concludes with another reference to *Dreams*, specifically to Letter XIX that contains the description of Valombrosa and to "An Excursion to the Grande Chartreuse," which Beckford had already decided to incorporate as part of *Dreams*. Henley was busily engaged with both pieces: "The evening I returned I neither gave sleep to my eyes nor slumber to my eyelids till I had carefully transcribed Valombrosa, and transferred the remaining corrections to the Grande Chartreuse. I shall think every hour a century till I receive and we have prepared the whole."

On January 29, Beckford drafted another letter to Henley in which he explained that his inspirations concerning the "wild and terrible story of unbridled passion" had reached the point of being set down on paper. Using the language of the tale itself ("I tremble to relate what has happened"), Beckford wrote: "You are answerable for having set me to work upon a story so horrid that I tremble whilst relating it, and have not a nerve in my frame but

vibrates like an aspen."[17] Further words of encouragement came
quickly from Henley:

> My soul rejoices to know that your imagination hath been wrapped in the
> thickest gloom: never is the lightening so glorious as when it flashes from
> the darkest clouds.
> I will gladly answer for all the horrible imaginings that may have been
> suggested by my surly spirit, though the murder which so shakes your state
> of mind were more than fantastical.[18]

Two months passed before Beckford completed the episode and
wrote to Henley on April 25 that the "story is finished"; and, referring to the conclusion of Letter XXIII, he added that he had
brought himself "home pretty decently to Naples."[19]

By the middle of May, Beckford made his second journey to
Naples, the occasion for the seven additional letters that he later included in the volume. Still pressed by the prospect of assuming the
responsibilities of manhood in public life and of being continuously
badgered by his family, he sought once again the congenial society
of Sir William and Lady Hamilton. "I really am not able to blaze at
present in the political Hemisphere," he wrote to Lady Hamilton.
"Twelve months of leisure and tranquility may prepare me for as
many years of Torment and Illustration."[20] When he left for Dover
on May 16, he was traveling in sumptuous style with postilions, a
charge of servants, and spare horses. The Reverend Lettice accompanied him, along with a physician, Dr. Ehrhart; a musician, John
Burton; and the water-colorist, John Robert Cozens, the son of Alexander, who had agreed to sketch whatever scenery caught his
employer's eye. Beckford, who followed the same route as on his
previous journey, drove through Ostend and Brussels to Cologne, a
rough, tiring passage over some difficult roads; and he then went to
Augsburg, Innsbruck, and Padua, which he reached on June 11 or
12. Resting in Padua, after maintaining a grueling pace of travel, he
ran into his old friends Madame de Rosenberg and Count Benincasa
and indulged in the delights of their hospitality.[21]

All was not play, however. *Dreams* was very much on his mind,
but he still had not completed the long "Letter of reflections" which
he wanted to use as the conclusion to the first twenty-six letters of
the book. By June 18, he had made significant progress; for he told
Henley in a letter that the "strange Letter for the conclusion" was
"far advanced."[22] When a letter from Henley arrived a few days

later, pressing him to complete the remaining material and notifying him that Cipriani had completed two drawings for the travel letters, Beckford responded optimistically about bringing the work to an end. "I beg you will see Cipriani paid," he wrote on June 29, and then added: "I hope . . . you will have patience a fortnight longer when I shall have finished the conclusive Epistle."[23]

Beckford might have completed the task as planned had it not been for a severe fever after his arrival in Naples on July 8 that kept him bedridden or at least weak for the rest of the month. August at the Hamilton country house in Portici might have been better, but Lady Hamilton suffered a serious illness which may help to explain the further delay. He made an attempt to finish the letter, for on August 20 he wrote to Henley: "I have been spinning out my conclusive letter, & I flatter myself you will not dislike my web. As I bring it along with me, we cannot publish till after Xmas, the best moment, too, I believe."[24] Before the end of the month, however, Lady Hamilton died of a "bilious fever," a blow for Beckford considering the quality of their relationship; and he experienced within a matter of days another setback with the death of one of his traveling companions, John Burton, his favorite harpsichord player.[25] On September 10, he understandably left Naples for home. Not until Paris is *Dreams* mentioned again. By this time (October 28), the final letter was "almost finished."

By the winter of 1782–83, the final preparations for the publication of *Dreams* were underway. There were some last-minute revisions to be made, and Henley was close at hand to provide whatever aid Beckford desired. The decision was made to incorporate the seven letters of 1782 to complete the volume. On January 15, 1783, Beckford complained to Henley that "Mr. L[ettice]'s abominable amanuensis [had] committed a thousand errors in the concluding letter."[26] The following month he was still consulting with Henley about the book: "We must look over the last letter, so don't forget to bring it with you."[27] Very soon after their meeting on Saturday, February 16, the book must have been in the press with everything done to make certain that it would fulfill the original expectations of its ambitious author. By the end of March, or by the first part of April, *Dreams* was bound and ready for distribution. Then came the unexpected decision: Beckford wrote Henley on April 15, 1783, that the production of the travel book would have to cease but that his lawyer, Thomas Wildman, would pay for whatever expenses were incurred:

I have been considering & reconsidering, & *cannot* reconcile myself in the least with the idea of committing my *Dreams* to the wide world. Therefore must beg you will stop advertisements, entries, &c., at Stationers' Hall, &c., &c. Don't imagine I shall change my mind any more. This determination is as fixed as the Sun. As for the copies? I will have them locked up like my title-deeds, not one shall transpire, so Hamilton must go without his *large paper* for some years to come.

I have desired Mr. Wildman to settle everything concerning expenses. Seeing you upon my return from F. becomes now more necessary than ever. Give me that satisfaction, & believe me most.[28]

This letter was followed by another to Henley fifteen days later in which Beckford complained about not having received the copies that Joseph Johnson had printed: "Mr. Johnson has not yet delivered up the copies, to my great surprise, & I have desired Mr. Wildman to renew his application. I must entreat you will take care that none transpire. . . . Don't forget the original copy & the letters from Lucca and Padua."[29]

As for the reason Beckford suddenly decided to suppress a book he was once so eager to publish, part of the explanation lies in the fact that family pressure made it intolerable for him to do otherwise. This factor is evident from subsequent correspondence, particularly in a letter to Henley in November 1783. "How can I endure my book of *Dreams*," Beckford lamented, "when I reflect what *disagreeable waking* thoughts it has occasioned us? If you have a mind to reconcile me to it, let me be assured you are not less my affectionate friend than when you silenced the hiss of serpents at Fonthill. Neither Orlando nor Brandimart were ever more tormented by demons and spectres in an enchanted castle than William Beckford in his own hall by his nearest relations."[30] The specific objections the family had to the book are not really clear, but Beckford's biographers have offered several possible explanations. Such an effusive travelogue, it is usually said, could seriously compromise the author's political career in Parliament. The display of "lively imagination" and "quickness of sensibility . . . so opposite to common modes of thinking," wrote Cyrus Redding, could "prejudice him in the House of Commons, and make ministers imagine he was not capable of solid business."[31]

Another theory is that the family sought to dissuade Beckford from publishing the book because "beneath all its veneer of fine language there was a moral rottenness" that would lend credence to the ugly rumors that were circulating about Beckford's questionable

relationship with William Courtenay.[32] Still another theory is that
Beckford had consented to "abandon everything that was equivocal
in his life" because he had agreed to a family-arranged marriage, a
decision that was made about the time *Dreams* was to appear. In this
case, getting rid of a book "charged with all the dangerous tendencies his mother had feared" would serve as "one symbol of the
sincerity of his intentions."[33] One final theory, and perhaps the most
plausible, is that, if the book had been distributed, its severe
criticisms of the Dutch that filled its early pages would have offended
many prominent political figures, particularly at a time when the
English government was attempting to maintain good relations with
that country.[34]

Whatever the precise reason, Beckford consented to the sacrifice
and removed the whole edition — said to total five hundred copies
— from the publisher's hands.[35] Once in his possession, Beckford
destroyed all of the copies by fire save a small number which he kept
at Fonthill to display to friends and interested visitors. Never
secretive about its existence, he even distributed copies to a few fortunate individuals: to his bookseller, George Clarke; to his lawyer,
Richard Samuel White; and to Louise Necker, known later as
Madame de Staël, who expressed enthusiasm about the book in a
letter to the author:

I have not as yet finished the extraordinary work which you had the
kindness to entrust to me, Monsieur. It is difficult to tear myself away from
it, for you travel so rapidly from idea to idea, from scene to scene, that it is
impossible to find a moment's pause between one sensation and another.
You dream when you have nothing to describe. Imagination, which invents
or represents objects, has never been given more freedom. Nature has a
great hold on you. Your soul is carried away by all that surrounds it. You
should never forget the places that you have seen, for each one of them has
evoked thoughts that can never be erased. Your manner of depicting has
often made me laugh, but I believe that you never realized how spirited you
were, for you speak your natural language, while we, at the same time, find
you to be extraordinary. I do very much like the origin you attribute to the
Flemish. As for you, Monsieur, it is on Mount Etna that I will search for
yours, and I shall hasten to see if you speak of that volcano with gratitude.[36]

II   Dreams *and Its Followers*

While *Dreams* remained unavailable to the public for many years
following its suppression, it enjoyed a kind of notoriety among a
select group of writers, particularly Thomas Moore, Samuel Rogers,

and John Mitford. When Beckford considered putting it out in companionship with a volume of his Spanish-Portuguese letters as early as 1818, he asked Rogers to encourage Moore to visit Fonthill in order to discuss the possibility of preparing the book for the press. Rogers dutifully communicated the offer to Moore; he even suggested that Beckford might give him "something magnificent for it — a thousand pounds, perhaps."[37] But Moore quickly declined saying he had no taste for having his name forever coupled with Beckford's. It is usually said that Moore, though he disdained the idea of being Beckford's "sub," did not hesitate thereafter to borrow from the "unpublished travel notes" for parts of his poem "Rhymes on the Road" and for one of his songs in *Irish Melodies*.[38] But the resemblances normally cited between Moore's work and *Dreams* seem too slight to classify them safely as "borrowings." The possibility exists, however, that Moore had access to Rogers' copy of *Dreams* and was familiar with the book when he wrote *Irish Melodies*. Beckford believed that a copy of *Dreams* remained "several years in the holy keeping of Mr. S[amuel] R[ogers] and that "from this reservoir . . . many a little tinkling rill has found its way into some of our fashionable publications."[39] Rogers, it is certain, used material from *Dreams* for a few passages in his poem *Italy;* but, contrary to Beckford's biographers, he did acknowledge at least one of the borrowings in the notes appended to the 1830 edition.[40]

Dreams finally appeared in 1834, after extensive revisions by its author, as volume one of *Italy; with Sketches of Spain and Portugal.* With editions printed in London, Paris, and Philadelphia, *Italy* was reviewed at length in leading literary journals; and it was met, almost without exception, with unqualified enthusiasm. By then *Vathek* had made Beckford's name known in literary circles, but *Italy* established him as a travel writer of unsurpassed talent. "He is a poet, and a great one too," observed John Gibson Lockhart,

though we know not that he ever wrote a line of verse. His rapture amidst the sublime scenery of mountains and forests . . . is that of a spirit cast originally in one of nature's finest moulds; and he fixes it in language which can scarcely be praised beyond its deserts — simple, massive, nervous, apparently little laboured, yet revealing, in its effect, the perfection of art. Some immortal passages in Gray's letters and Byron's diaries, are the only things, in our tongue, that seem to us to come near the profound melancholy, blended with a picturesque description at once true and startling. . . . We risk nothing in predicting that Mr. Beckford's Travels will henceforth be classed among the most elegant productions of modern literature: they will be forthwith translated into every language of the Continent — and will keep his name alive, centuries after all the brass and marble he ever piled together have ceased to vibrate with the echoes of *Modenhas*."[41]

III *Psychological and Esthetic Interest*

To the extent that interest in Beckford's life and writings is sustained in the future, *Dreams* will be regarded as an important source of information about the author, especially since, in its unbuttoned fullness, it is a more open book than *Italy*. *Dreams* has a confessional character that wholesale deletions have, for the most part, erased in the revised work; it is also laced with passages that possess the intimate tone of a private letter, which sometimes has the effect of making the reader feel he is eavesdropping on confidences designed only for the eyes of a kindred spirit. The young Beckford, who comes into clearer view during these moments, reveals his feelings of isolation, his boredom, and his basic restlessness. Enough has been said in biographical terms about the origin of his emotional turmoil and its particular intensity during the period of the book's composition, but the apprehension he felt about the threats to his love of freedom and childish irresponsibility finds expression, even if only veiled, in various parts of *Dreams*. It can be detected in the escapist preoccupation with dreams and private fantasies, in the passages devoted to the pursuit of protective closure, in the evocation of paradisaical playgrounds, and in the kind of solipsistic longing evoked in his description of the fanciful globe he wished to construct beneath the dome of St. Peter's:

We would have all the space to ourselves, and to such creatures too as resemble us. The windows I should shade with transparent curtains of yellow silk, to admit the glow of perpetual summer. Lanterns, as many as you please, of all forms and sizes; they would remind us of China, and, depending from the roofs of the palace, bring before us that of the emperor Ki, which was twice as large as St. Peter's . . . and lighted alone by tapers; for his imperial majesty, being tired of the sun, would absolutely have a new firmament of his own creation, and an artificial day. Was it not a rare fantastic idea? For my part, I should like of all things to immure myself, after his example, with those I love; forget the divisions of time, have a moon at command, and a theatrical sun to rise and set, at pleasure.[42]

Aside from the psychological interest, *Dreams* remains one of the best illustrations of "literary picturesque" that was produced in the declining years of the eighteenth century. Among his devotees,

Beckford's descriptive powers have always been identified as his major strength as a writer; they are fond of citing the graphic richness
of the halls of Eblis in *Vathek*, where the carefully drawn descriptions flicker before the eye of the reader in the manner of an exotic
motion picture. *Dreams* exhibits the same interest in visual imagery
and pictorial composition, the character of which is perhaps best
defined in terms of the esthetics of William Gilpin, a theorist who
defined "the picturesque" as "that peculiar kind of beauty, which is
agreeable in a picture."[43] Chapman once complained that some of
the descriptive passages in *Dreams* were "not a little stiff and formal," that sometimes a "figure seems arrested in its pose as in a
painting."[44] But this characteristic — the analogy between prose
description and painting — is an essential feature in Beckford's
writing; it illustrates his training as an artistically conditioned
observer. Almost from the date of his relationship with Cozens, and
as a consequence of his training in the pictorial arts under this tutor,
Beckford was in the habit of making observations about the world
around him as if he were examining a painting in one of the galleries
at Fonthill. The young writer's letters to the water-colorist, especially those from Switzerland in 1777 and 1778, provide additional
evidence of his ability to structure a view, to reconstruct in prose his
general impression of a scene with all the elements required to fill
and frame a picture.

When Beckford came to write *Dreams*, therefore, he purposely
aimed for pictorial effect, just as he did later in *Vathek*. Page after
page of *Dreams* displays an eye eager for color, lights and shades,
surface textures, distant lines, perspectives, and picture-like views.
Beckford's picturesque orientation also explains why he reveals in
Dreams his partiality for seeing objects in the "dubious, visionary
light" of dusk, and why, in the fashion of the picturesque theorists,
he is consistently drawn to the paintable qualities of rough, rugged
surfaces and irregular lines. Nor is it a coincidence that his own
descriptions are frequently keyed to the works of famous painters, so
that irregular hills, clumps of cypress, and pastoral cottages become
the ingredients for a scene that "Zuccarelli loved to paint," or rocks
and grottoes, "half lost in thickets from which rise craggy pinnacles
crowned by mouldering towers" constitute "just such scenery as
Polemburg and Peter de Laer introduce in their paintings."
Beckford cultivated seeing as if it were an art form, and he used the
painter's guide book to learn how to see.

When the pictorial accent is combined with the poetic sensibility,

Dreams achieves a distinctive character that finds few parallels in the history of travel literature. If Beckford has the facility for portraying with accuracy the genuine aspect of things, he is also capable of conveying how they make him feel. There are times in the book when he does not stop with a mere literal transcription of objective reality but goes beyond to render the mood and the feeling associated with it. There is a sense, therefore, in which some of Beckford's pictures become "equally objective and subjective . . . brilliantly clear in outline . . . yet steeped in the rich hues of his own peculiar feeling."[45] His sunsets, in particular, partake of this combination of pictorial and emotional values. Whether the closing scenes of day are described in terms of a final blush of crimson in a darkening sky, or as the last sunbeams purpling the sails of ships at rest in the harbor, or as a glow lingering on the verge of a landscape, which slowly fades into a variety of warm hues, and then into deeper, more melancholy blue — these scenes take their meaning from the feeling observer, from a man who is obviously touched by what he sees. The same is true of the following scene in the Tyrol:

A goat-track . . . conducted me, on the brink of the foaming waters, to the very depths of the cliff, whence issues a stream which, dashing impetuously down, strikes against a ledge of grey rock, and sprinkles the impending thicket with dew. Big drops hung on every spray, and glittered on the leaves partially gilt by the rays of the declining sun, whose mellow hues softened the summits of the cliffs, and diffused a repose, a divine calm, over this deep retirement, which inclined me to imagine it the extremity of the earth, and the portal of some other region of existence; some happy world beyond the dark groves of pines, the caves and awful mountains. (102–03)

On these occasions, Beckford seems no longer concerned simply with the artistic analysis of pictorial effects. Color and form have been surpassed, and observation has been enriched and vivified by the power of emotion.

As a traveler, Beckford seems ever willing to allow experiences to operate on him, to remain freely exposed to the influence of whatever comes his way. In Mannheim, he indulges the repose of a cool garden where exotic birds sing, a tall poplar quivers in the wind, and jets of water rise above the foliage to spangle brilliantly in the sun. In Venice, his careful eye catches at dusk the innumerable tapers glimmering through the awnings of windows, the variety of shadowy figures "shooting by in their gondolas," and the play of lantern lights upon the water. In Arqua, he makes a pilgrimage to

Petrarch's house, sits in the poet's chair, and indulges a "train of pensive sentiments and soft impressions." "Who could sit in Petrarch's chair," he asks, "void of some effect?" In Florence, he visits the art gallery and runs "childishly by the ample ranks of sculptures, like a butterfly in a pasture, that skims before it fixes, over ten thousand flowers." The effect of this sensitivity on the reader is cumulative; but it is reinforced throughout by means of deliberately contrasting scenes that move "from the dark cathedral to the bright casino, from gay society to, 'wild spots where the arbutus flourishes;' and from the noisy mart to the lonely seashore."[46]

Dreams, in short, is a remarkable achievement for a young man of twenty-two; it is, in fact, a testimony to literary powers that were to be tested in the Oriental tales that followed. The book's psychological character and its "picturesque" esthetic became central features of the Beckfordian style of writing. Indeed, blended with the author's fascination with the Orient, they helped to give *Vathek* its peculiar interest and beauty.

CHAPTER 6

The Central Tale: Vathek

VATHEK, itself a kind of travelogue, is not unlike *Dreams,
Waking Thoughts and Incidents;* but its setting is the East
instead of Europe. The fact that Beckford continued to assimilate
Oriental geography, history, and literature in the four-year period
between his stay in Switzerland and the composition of *Vathek* helps
to explain his attempt to try his hand at writing an Oriental tale.
Like his contemporaries, Sir William Jones and Jonathan Scott, he
worked with the thoroughness of a scholar to understand his subject.
To skim the surface was not sufficient; immersion supplied the only
satisfaction. The important Oriental works of Barthélémi
d'Herbelot, Jean Chardin, and Charles Le Brun were already among
his familiar reading. Whenever time was available during these four
years, he not only devoured Eastern legends and customs but also
showed critical enthusiasm for the most seemingly insignificant bit
of Orientalia. As the following letter to his half-sister displays, his attitude toward the East represented a significant departure from his
English predecessors:

Don't fancy, my Dear Sister, I am enraptured with the orientals themselves.
It is the country they inhabit which claims all the admiration I bestow on
that quarter of the Globe. It is their woods of Spice trees, their strange
animals, their vast rivers which I delight in. The East must be better known
than it is to be sufficiently liked or disliked. If you would form a tolerable
judgment upon it not a single relation, not one voyage or volume of travells
must be neglected, whether in Portuguese, Spanish or any other language.
With this intent I am learning Portuguese and find great treasures indeed,
uncommon descriptions, marvellous Histories and perilous adventures. . . .
And why read such unmeaning Stuff? What matters it whether we are con-
versant with India or no? Is it not better to study the histories of Europe? I
answer — these I look upon as occupations, the others as amuzements. Such
is my taste; it may very easily be a lamentable one.[1]

Addison, Johnson, and Hawkesworth may have possessed a superficial knowledge of the East; Beckford was determined to know it better — even in the face of familial opposition.

I *In Search of the Authentic East*

Besides accumulating bits and pieces of information from the books he read on the subject, Beckford's visit to Venice in 1780, which was a watering-place for Orientals, brought him for the first time into contact with native Asiatics. Moving among Arabs and Turks on every street corner, he listened with fascination to the strange sounds of their respective languages: "Had St. Mark's church been the wondrous tower, and its piazza the chief square, of the city of Babylon, there could scarcely have been a greater confusion of languages. The novelty of the scene afforded me no small share of amusement, and I wandered about from group to group, and from one strange exotic to another."² In this atmosphere, even St. Mark's church, with its slender pinnacles, its semi-circular arches, and its gold, mosaic cupola, took on an Oriental aspect that enabled Beckford to imagine himself instantly transported to an Eastern city.

Prompted by an overwhelming desire to converse with the foreign inhabitants, Beckford willingly braved the stench of canals to venture into the byways and musky quarters of the city in search of infidels who could tell him about Damascus and Sunristan, "those happy countries, which nature had covered with roses." "Asiatics find Venice very much to their liking," he wrote in his notebook; "and all those I conversed with allowed its customs and style of living had a good deal of conformity to their own. The eternal lounging in coffee-houses and sipping of sorbets agree perfectly well with the inhabitants of the Ottoman empire, who stalk about here in their proper dresses, and smoke their own exotic pipes, without being stared and wondered at as in most other European capitals."³

The experience in Venice was important because it came at a time when he was, among other things, developing his interest in Oriental languages. Soon after, he directed his energies toward the mastery of Persian and Arabic. Although he had some previous knowledge of both languages, this time he sought the assistance of a native Arab by the name of Zemir. The exact date the two men came together is not known, but Chapman believed that "Beckford was working with Zemir in 1780, and also on both sides of Christmas, 1782."⁴ Zemir helped him to gain further insight into the nature of authentic Oriental literature. For, no longer satisfied simply with

French or English translations of Eastern tales, Beckford now desired firsthand experience with the originals themselves. He and Zemir examined together the Arabic manuscripts of Edward Wortley Montagu, which are now in the Bodleian Library; and, as a literary exercise, Beckford turned one tale after another not into English, as one might expect, but into French instead.

None of these translations has ever been published, but at least six of them are among the Beckford papers today. According to Chapman, they were all done between the years 1780 and 1783; and the following list provides some idea of the extent of the young student's labor:

1. *Histoire d'Elouard Felkanaman et d'Ansel Hougioud* (104 leaves)

2. *Histoire du Prince Ahmed, fils du Roi de Khoten et d'Ali Ben Hassan de Bagdad* (388 quarto pages)

3. *Histoire de Mazin* (219 quarto pages)

4. *Histoire d' Aladdin, Roi de Yémen* (112 quarto pages)
   a) *Histoire du Prince Mahmed* (29 quarto pages)
   b) *Histoire d'Abou Niah, Roi de Moussel* (51 quarto pages)

5. *Histoire de la Princesse Fatimah, Fille du Roi Ben Amer* (25 quarto pages)

6. *Histoire de Kebal, Roi de Damas, conté par Mamalébé, Nourrice de la Princesse Hajaia à la Chevelure blanche* (44 quarto pages)

7. Six folio exercise books in foolscap, containing translations from the *Arabian Nights* in English.[5]

Both the number of manuscript pages and the short time in which these translations were made testify to the energy with which Beckford applied himself to these studies. When we consider that much of his time was consumed by travel during these years — with a tour of England in 1779 and a Grand Tour of Europe in 1780–81 — his accomplishment as a translator becomes more considerable.

II *The Refuge of Oriental Exoticism*

There is little question that Beckford thoroughly enjoyed for its own sake the kind of research in which he was engaged. He had a passion for information; but, as we suggested earlier, his pursuit of the authentic East was likewise connected with his personal problems, with his being very much of a Romantic escapist. When he immersed himself in his work with excessive vigor, it was often because he found the world of fiction more tolerable than that of reality. As he neared majority, furthermore, he showed increasing signs of psychological imbalance over the thought of embarking on a political career as his father had done. Politics terrified him, and the resulting trauma was serious enough to provoke in him giddy notions of suicide. Ecstatic visions were therapeutic, and he indulged in them frequently. "My Imagination roams to other Countries," he explained, "in search of pleasures it no longer finds at Home. This Evening it has been transported to those immense unfrequented Plains of Tartary which are covered with Herbs and Flowers. . . . Such Delusions as these form my present felicity, without them I would be the most unhappy of mankind."[6]

Increasing his knowledge of the East to the extent that he had, it was inevitable that the usual setting for his dream-visions was placed in various Asiatic regions. Since these were the alien cultures with which he was most thoroughly imbued, he could therefore realize his presence there with more facility than he could with other parts of the world. Occasionally he would speak of wandering ecstatically into the interior of places like Africa, Peru, and Virginia, but he more frequently turned to Oriental scenery. Unlike later writers, such as Thomas DeQuincey and Samuel Coleridge, who used opium to produce Asian fantasies, Beckford could lapse into reverie almost effortlessly. "How pure! How truly oriental!" he wrote of one of Cozens' letters. "Indeed I believed it dated from *Sanna* or *Hism al mowâhab*, the Castle of Delights. This must be an Arabian Composition, said I within myself, it breathes all the odours of that happy Country and I inhale them, tho' surrounded by perfumes; for you must know I have left Fonthill sometime and have been transported to *Ginnistan*."[7]

In a rather detailed letter to his half-sister, he once explained how, after observing an exquisite Oriental room in the palace of Prince Charles, a "Chinese rage got uppermost" in his mind and produced one of these imaginative digressions:

The awful name of Quandacaendono was half out of my mouth when the instruments in P[rince] C[harles]'s Bedchamber, and the view discovered from his windows diverted my attention; but this calm was of short duration, for upon the opening of a door which discovered a very brilliant cabinet, the

Chinese rage got uppermost and you thought I should expose myself again by the ardour and vehemence with which I praised the room, running now to one group of hideous images and then to another exclaiming all the while. There's your Japan of the true rain, look at the delightful strange form of these artificial Rocks that bulge out of the panels, only see that dear mimping creature that fans herself on the side of a Lake covered with water flowers. Surely she is one of the ten Princesses that trim the hallowed whiskers of the sacred Dairo. Look, Sister, that great spreading bush is loaded with the fruit of the Mihisho near the Plains of Nagasaki, these corpulent reptiles that I confess look a little like toads are the Quoohucachi that hop in the profound fosses of the Castle of Azuchiyama. These blossoms I take to belong to the Mokurege of Molylmwha or at the farthest the Oudonge. In vain would you beseech me to defer all this out of the way learning for another time, in vain would you intreat me to check the career of such contemptible erudition. Nothing would hinder me from making eternal digressions about the Country in which these ornaments are fabricated and talking forever about the lofty Mountains of Fukenzosama, not forgetting the sixty Convents of Bonzes that are placed on its brow, with tedious detail of all the gardens amongst which they are situated and the cascades that tumble from the Rocks into the Valley below. You tried to make me observe the Cabinet in general, the rich effect of the glasses, the inlaid floor, the ivory house and in short the *tout ensemble;* but the Japan had touched that spring which never fails of sending me to China in the twinkling of an eye, so the same subject was continued all the way thro' the State Rooms and the Gold Salle de Campagnio whose elegant gilding and stately windows I scarce deigned to regard, but now since I have surveyed the whole Palace and am at present got out into the open air again the charm is broken, the illusion dissolved, all the splendid objects vanished and I find myself at a sad distance from you.[8]

A detailed knowledge of the Orient united with a volatile imagination and with an urgent need to articulate his sensuous life help to account for the concrete quality of Beckford's visions. Indeed, the sharpness and clarity of his images bear a resemblance to Blake in his quest for "stronger and better lineaments." But the exotic character of Beckford's imaginings seems to suggest an even stronger kinship with Keats. "I have lately committed myself to the guidance of Voyagers," he wrote, "and followed them over Oceans to distant Climates where my exotic Inclinations are satisfied."[9] His dreaming flights were seldom vague, abstract states of euphoria; they were almost always weighed down by a keen awareness of the senses. He did not seek the experience of the mystic, but transported himself imaginatively to a distant country in order to indulge his senses more fully.

III *"soaring . . . upon the Arabian bird roc"*

Beckford's mind was so thoroughly soaked with Oriental imagery that a tale like *Vathek* was bound to be developed; and, the transition from visionary letters to the "realization of romance" in sustained composition was an easy one. All Beckford needed was the proper stimulus, and it was provided by a Christmas party at Fonthill in 1781, an occasion of sumptuous pageantry and self-indulgence. The setting, his father's mansion, was appropriately equipped for "Orientalizing" with the existence of an Egyptian hall and a Turkish room. Philip de Loutherbourg, a master of lighting effects and a scene designer, was hired to display his talents in an arrangement of lighting that would bathe the rooms in an eerie glow. Italian singers contributed to the exotic background. The party was kept private, the doors were locked, and the windows shuttered. The guests were mostly young women and handsome boys. Alexander Cozens came, and so did Samuel Henley, who played an important role in the final production of *Vathek*. There were the daughters of the Earl of Dunmore, the notorious beauty Sophia Musters, and two daughters of Baron Pitt-Rivers, one of whom was Louisa. Also present was the young William Courtenay with whom Beckford was now intimately involved. Beckford later reconstructed the whole mood of the "voluptuous festival" that followed:

Immured we were *au pied de la lettre* for three days following — doors and windows so strictly closed that neither common day light nor common place visitors could get in or even peep in — care worn visages were ordered to keep aloof — no sunk-in mouths or furroughed foreheads were permitted to meet our eye. Our *société* was extremely youthful and lovely to look upon. . . . Through all these galleries — did we roam and wander — too often hand in hand — strains of music swelling forth at intervals — sometimes the organ — sometimes concerted pieces — in which three of the greatest singers then in Europe — Pacchierotti, Tenducci, and Rauzzini — for a wonder of wonders — most amicably joined. . . . Delightful indeed were these romantic wanderings — delightful the straying about this little interior world of exclusive happiness surrounded by lovely beings, in all the freshness of their early bloom, so fitted to enjoy it. Here, nothing was dull or vapid — here, nothing ressembled in the least the common forms and usages, the "train-train" and routine of fashionable existence — all was essence. . . . Even the uniform splendour of gilded roofs — was partially obscured by the vapour of wood aloes ascending in wreaths from cassolettes placed low on the silken carpets in porcelain salvers of the richest japan. The delirium of delight into which our young and fervid bosoms were cast by such a combination of seductive influences may be conceived but too easily. Even at this long, sad distance from these days and nights of exquisite refinements, chilled by age, still more by the coarse unpoetic tenor of the present disenchanting period — I still feel warmed and irradiated by the recollections of that strange, necromantic light which Loutherbourg had thrown over what absolutely appeared a realm of Fairy, or rather, perhaps, a Demon Temple deep beneath the earth set apart for tremendous mysteries — and yet how soft, how genial was this quiet light. Whilst the wretched world without lay dark, and bleak, and howling, whilst the storm was raging against our massive walls and the snow drifting in clouds, the very air of summer seemed playing around us. The choir of low-toned melodious voices continued to sooth our ear, and that every sense might in turn receive its blandishment tables covered with delicious viands and fragrant flowers — glided forth, by the aid of mechanism at stated intervals, from the richly draped, and amply curtained recesses of the enchanted precincts. The glowing haze investing every object, the mystic look, the vastness, the intricacy of this vaulted labyrinth occasioned so bewildering an effect that it became impossible for anyone to define — at the moment — where he stood, where he had been, or to whither he was wandering — such was the confusion — the perplexity so many illuminated storys of infinitely varied apartments gave rise to. It was, in short, the realization of romance in its most extravagant intensity.[10]

What happened shortly after this unusual Christmas gathering has been told many times: Beckford left Fonthill for his London residence at 12 Wimpole Street; and sometime in January, 1782, with the visions of the festival still swirling in his brain and while "soaring in my young fancy upon the Arabian bird roc," he composed *Vathek* in French in one sitting, or, as he later told Cyrus Redding, in "three days and two nights of hard labour." "I never took off my clothes the whole time," he explained; "this severe application made me very ill."[11] Although this statement has long been discredited by some Beckfordians, particularly by Guy Chapman, it is probable that *Vathek* was at least *substantially* finished in January, 1782, perhaps in the stage of a rough draft. In any case, it was revised, amplified, and finally translated by Samuel Henley before it was published in 1786.

IV *Henley and* Vathek

Behind the history of *Vathek* looms the mysterious Henley. Little is known about the man except that he was an impressive scholar and a minister with strong latitudinarian views. The correspondence between Henley and Beckford from 1782 to 1786 that relates to the development and the translation of *Vathek* and to the creation of additional Oriental tales strongly supports the view that Henley inspired Beckford to embark on not just a single work but a whole "Collection of Arabian Tales." *Vathek,* in other words, was originally designed to represent only a portion, albeit the central one, of a larger, more ambitious project that was to be written in the manner of the *Arabian Nights.*[12]

The whole scheme was aborted, however, by Henley's celebrated indiscretion. According to the modern reconstruction of events, Beckford left the manuscript of *Vathek* in Henley's hands in May, 1783, for transcription and then translation into English, while he himself set about writing *The Episodes of Vathek.* The task of translating proceeded slowly at first but was completed by April, 1785, at which time Henley suggested appending a series of notes to illustrate the more obscure Oriental allusions in the tale. He also recommended adding a preliminary dissertation about the tale's "machinery" and "costume." Beckford received the translation, made certain revisions of his own, and then returned it to Henley in June, 1785, presumably with the intention that in a short time it could be published with his sanction. But on February 9, 1786, he told Henley that on no account should the book appear in print before the publication of the original French edition:

The publication of *Vathec* must be postponed at least another year. I would not on any account have him precede the French edition. . . . The episodes to *Vathec* are nearly finished, & the whole work will be completed within a twelve-month. You must be sensible that, notwithstanding my eagerness to see *Vathec* in print, I cannot sacrifice the French edition to my impatience.

The anticipation of so principal a tale as that of the Caliph would be tearing the proudest feather from my turban. I must repeat, therefore, my desire that you will not give your translation to the world till the original has made its appearance & we have touched more on the subject. You may imagine how I long for the moment of enjoying your notes & the preliminary dissertation, which, I doubt not, will be received with the honors due to so valuable a morsel of *orientalism.*[13]

Later in the year, Beckford pushed the date of publication even farther into the future. He was grief-stricken over the sudden death of his wife, and he also had not finished the *Episodes.* "I fear the dejection of mind into which I am plunged," he wrote in August, 1786, "will prevent my finishing the other stories, & of course

Vathec's making his appearance in any language this winter. I would not have him on any account come forth without his companions."[14] Beckford was also expecting to receive and approve the manuscript of Henley's notes. What he did not know at this point was that Henley had already submitted the entire manuscript to a London publisher before June 1, on which date nine printed copies were entered at Stationers' Hall.

Moreover, *Vathek* was published anonymously and with its Preface suggesting that it was not an original tale but a translation of an extant Arabic manuscript. "The Original of the following Story," the Preface ran,

together with some others of a similar kind collected in the East by a Man of Letters, was communicated to the Editor about three years ago. The pleasure he received from the perusal of it, induced him at that time to transcribe and since to translate it. How far the copy may be a just representation, it becomes him not to determine. He presumes, however, to hope that, if the difficulty of accommodating our English idiom to the Arabick, preserving the correspondent tones of a diversified narrative, and discriminating the nicer touches of character through the shades of foreign manners, be duly considered; a failure in some points will not preclude him from all claim to indulgence: especially, if those images, sentiments, and passions, which, being independent of local peculiarities, may be expressed in every language, shall be found to retain their native energy in our own.

Needless to say, Beckford was shocked when he discovered Henley's breach of faith. Nor did Henley help matters when he insisted in an ambiguous letter to the *Gentleman's Magazine*, dated February 7, 1787, that "the said History [of the Caliph Vathek] is, as the preface declares, a translation of an unpublished manuscript."[15]

It is difficult to determine with any certainty why Henley went to press with his translation knowing, as he must have, how Beckford felt. The usual explanation given is that he feared the loss of the time he had devoted to the translation and to the compilation of the notes. Moreover, additional delays could continue for years; and Beckford could at some time in the future cancel all publication plans.[16] But these explanations are only conjectural. When it came to completing the translation for Beckford, Henley was himself dilatory; for he had taken almost two years to accomplish the task. Beckford's August 1 letter in which he re-affirmed his wish to postpone the appearance of *Vathek* certainly could not have had any bearing on Henley's decision since, when Beckford drafted the letter, the English version had been on the bookstalls for over two months. When Henley attempted to clear himself in a letter addressed to Beckford's solicitor on October 23, 1786, the content was vague and deliberately evasive. He claimed he had written Beckford to apprise him of the forthcoming publication and had forwarded a large paper copy of the volume once it was printed. He also tried to base his case on the grounds that he did not receive Beckford's letter of August 1 until August 18; but the fact remains that Beckford was equally firm about the same subject in his letter of February 9, 1786: "I must repeat, therefore, my desire that you will not give your translation to the world till the original has made its appearance."

Equally baffling is the additional explanation that Henley gave for his premature move. "In consideration of a late unhappy occurrence," he wrote, "it was my own wish to have intirely suppressed the work, but as I had been employed upon it prior to that event, and was known to be by some of my friends, I could not decline it without favouring a charge that I was unwilling to countenance, and therefore sacrificed my own inclination to what I considered as a positive engagement to Mr. Beckford."[17] The phrase "unhappy occurrence" in this statement may have meant something to Beckford, but it is not easily decipherable today. A plausible explanation might be that Henley's name had somehow become linked with Beckford's in connection with the public scandal of 1784 that involved Beckford's supposed immoral activities with the young son of Lord Courtenay. To suppress the book, would have been tantamount, in Henley's mind, to giving countenance to the charge against Beckford. But, supposing this explanation to be true, it does not acquit Henley of betraying Beckford's confidence.

V   *The French and English Editions*

The additional history of *Vathek* is sufficiently complicated to have baffled for years the most dedicated students of Beckford. The generally accepted theory, before the appearance of Parreaux's compendious study in 1960, was formulated originally by Marcel May in 1928.[18] May argued that Beckford, having no copy of the original French manuscript of *Vathek* with him in Switzerland, where he was residing at the time of the discovery of Henley's betrayal, prepared in haste, probably with some assistance, a re-translation into French of Henley's English version. He then identified himself in the Preface as the real author of the tale and published the edition in Lausanne before the end of 1786 (with a title page date of 1787).

The haste with which the translation was done, May felt, accounted for the many Anglicisms in the Lausanne text and for the subsequent appearance of a new, more refined French version in Paris the following year. The re-translation hypothesis was so seductively plausible that it convinced bibliographer John Carter, who in 1936 identified the clergyman-writer Jean-David Levade as Beckford's Swiss translator.[19]

The more authoritative research of Dr. Parreaux, however, has undermined Carter's and May's theory. By collating the Lausanne and Henley texts, he has demonstrated convincingly that substantial differences between the two make the re-translation theory a bit too ingenious. He has shown that an early unfinished translation of *Vathek*, extant in eighty-three manuscript pages, which was apparently done by the Reverend John Lettice in 1782, corresponds more closely to the Lausanne edition than does Henley's, which points to the existence of a French version of *Vathek* earlier than and in addition to the text used for the Paris edition. Furthermore, a careful examination of the manuscripts of Beckford's other tales and the discovery of an original draft fragment of *Vathek* in Beckford's own handwriting reveal that Beckford's French was far from faultless, as it used to be thought to be, and that Beckford himself was quite capable of producing the Anglicisms in the Lausanne text. In view of this evidence, it is possible to conclude that Beckford did possess a manuscript copy of an early French text *Vathek* in Switzerland, which after incorporating Levade's "corrections," he rushed into print before the close of 1786. Early in 1787 he submitted an "improved" version to Poinçot in Paris, and this text was published by June of the same year.

As for the first English edition, though it appeared in print without Beckford's approval, it was in general, a sound translation. Henley was not an overly scrupulous translator, however; he took needless freedoms to the extent, at times, of mutilating the original. He had the unfortunate tendency of blunting some of Beckford's most satiric edges; and he sometimes opted for cold abstractions when he should have retained the concrete vigor of the original French. His principal weakness, in H. B. Grimsditch's words, was his failure "to preserve the rapidity and epigrammatic force of the original."[20] Despite these faults, Beckford himself felt that, "as a whole, it did him justice."[21] On March 21, 1785, after reading a portion of the translation, he wrote to Henley: "You make me proud of *Vathek*. The blaze just at present is so overpowering that I can see no

faults. . . . I know not how it happens, but the original when first
born scarce gave me so much rapture as your translation. Were I
well and in good spirits I should run wild among my rocks and
forests telling stones, trees and flowers, how gloriously you have succeeded. My imagination is again on fire."[22] Beckford thought well
enough of Henley's effort, furthermore, to authorize a re-issue of his
edition in 1809 and on several occasions thereafter. To this day,
Henley's translation remains the standard work in English.

VI   *The History of a Willful Caliph*

The story of *Vathek* is uncomplicated. To a certain extent, it
depicts Beckford's interest in freedom; for the will finds full expression in the deliberate violation of law. It is the old story of the man of
power, in this case an Oriental superman, who, in clear knowledge of
his deed, defies both the gods and humanity; then, for a time, he
wantonly enjoys his enlarged freedom, only to experience the ultimate irony of having all control over his own will nullified in eternal damnation. The leading character in the tale, the Caliph
Vathek, is a man of vast excesses; for he is willing to use all of his
wealth and authority to feed his multifarious desires. A sybaritic
lover of pleasure, he builds five gorgeous palaces — the Palace of the
Eternal Banquet, the Temple of Melody, the Delight of the Eyes,
the Palace of Perfumes, and the Retreat of Joy — to gratify each of
his senses.

Fascinated with the occult sciences and astrology, he is Faustian
in his thirst for forbidden knowledge; and he is willing to sell his soul
to achieve it. It is from the "insolent curiosity of penetrating the
secrets of heaven," Beckford tells us, that the caliph constructed his
immense tower of fifteen hundred stairs:

His pride arrived at its height, when having ascended, for the first time,
the fifteen hundred stairs of his tower, he cast his eyes below, and beheld
men not larger than pismires; mountains, than shells; and cities, than bee-
hives. The idea, which such an elevation inspired of his own grandeur, completely bewildered him: he was almost ready to adore himself; till, lifting his
eyes upward, he saw the stars as high above him as they appeared when he
stood on the surface of the earth. He consoled himself, however, for this intruding and unwelcome perception of his littleness, with the thought of being great in the eyes of others; and flattered himself that the light of his
mind would extend beyond the reach of his sight, and extort from the stars
the decrees of his destiny.[23]

The insatiable caliph, having an evil eye that no person would dare to look upon, is an unusual creation for Beckford's day. Without a doubt, he is more outrageously evil than any of his Oriental forerunners; for in co-operation with his wicked mother, Carathis, a mistress of the black arts, he becomes a willing servant of infernal powers. A hideous giaour who visits the kingdom of Samarah has little trouble persuading Vathek to renounce his religion and his God in favor of accepting Eblis, the Oriental Satan. In return, the caliph is told he will be permitted to enter the Palace of Subterranean Fire beneath the ruins of ancient Istakhar, and there he will find the treasures of the pre-Adamite kings and the mysterious talismans that control the world. But he is first required to shed the blood of fifty children of his most faithful subjects, which he does with grim despatch. Meanwhile, his mother directs a second sacrifice to appease the giaour — an act that involves the brutal hanging and burning of additional inhabitants of Samarah. After the massacres have been accomplished, Vathek receives a parchment containing the directions for his journey to Istakhar. He then gathers a shimmering cavalcade of wives and servants for the expedition; but, before departing, he is warned not to enter any dwelling en route to his destination.

Only a few days of travel pass, however, before the sumptuous retinue is wracked by storms, attacked by wild beasts, and forced to seek refuge — in violation of the prohibition — in the valley of the good Emir Fakreddin. Here Vathek is given the opportunity to redeem himself by renouncing the giaour and by discontinuing his quest; instead, true to his nature, he violates the laws of hospitality by seducing the emir's beautiful daughter Nouronihar, who has been betrothed to her stripling cousin Gulchenrouz, "the most delicate and lovely creature in the world" (53). Fakreddin attempts to hide Nouronihar and Gulchenrouz in a distant retreat, but they are discovered accidentally by Vathek. Nouronihar is henceforth Vathek's mistress, and he then succeeds in poisoning her mind with his own uncontrollable ambition for superior knowledge, and they seek together the dark summits of the mountains of Istakhar.

To atone for his failure to pursue a direct course to the Palace of Subterranean Fire, Vathek commits as many crimes as possible during the remaining leg of the voyage. Upon reaching the beautiful valley of Rocnabad, he commands his men to level the oratories of a community of monks residing there, while the "horses, camels, and guards, wantoned over their tulips and other flowers, and made a terrible havoc amongst them" (82). When some leading citizens of nearby Schiraz visit his camp, bearing gifts and an offer of hospitality, Vathek responds to their petition by making them endure ludicrous and degrading punishment. One final effort to divert Vathek from pursuing his own destruction is made by an emissary of Mahomet in the disguise of a shepherd:

Deluded prince! to whom Providence hath confided the care of innumerable subjects, is it thus that thou fulfillest thy mission? Thy crimes are already completed; and art thou now hastening towards thy punishment? Thou knowest that, beyond these mountains, Eblis and his accursed dives hold their infernal empire; and, seduced by a malignant phantom, thou art proceeding to surrender thyself to them! This moment is the last of grace allowed thee: abandon thy atrocious purpose: return: give back Nouronihar to her father, who still retains a few sparks of life: destroy thy tower with all its abominations: drive Carathis from thy councils: be just to thy subjects: respect the ministers of the Prophet: compensate for thy impieties by an exemplary life; and, instead of squandering thy days in voluptuous indulgence, lament thy crimes on the sepulchres of thy ancestors. (85)

But Vathek's pride once again prevails: he rejects the shepherd's plea, but the words of warning prompt most of his attendants to escape from camp the following night.

The tale moves to a swift conclusion after the two lovers reach the realm of Istakhar, and incident gives way to vision at this point in the narrative. Beckford begins to paint his scenery with a graphic richness that continues to impress those who read the final section of the book. As Vathek and Nouronihar approach the ruins, a rock platform suddenly opens and discloses a staircase of polished marble lighted on both sides by brilliant torches. They descend until they arrive at an ebony portal where the malignant giaour is waiting with the golden key to admit them to the domains of Eblis. Passing through the portal, they view the following scene:

Their eyes at length growing familiar to the grandeur of the surrounding objects, they extended their view to those at a distance, and discovered rows of columns and arcades, which gradually diminished, till they terminated in a point radiant as the sun when he darts his last beam athwart the ocean. The pavement, strewd over with gold dust and saffron, exhaled so subtile an odour as almost overpowered them. They, however, went on, and observed an infinity of censers, in which ambergris and the wood of aloes were continually burning. Between the several columns were placed tables, each spread with a profusion of viands, and wines of every species sparkling in vases of crystal. A throng of genii, and other fantastic spirits, of which either sex, danced lasciviously at the sound of music which issued from beneath.

In the midst of this immense hall, a vast multitude was incessantly passing, who severally kept their right hands on their hearts, without once regarding any thing around them: they had all the livid paleness of death. Their eyes, deep sunk in their sockets, resembled those phosphoric meteors that glimmer by night in places of interment. Some stalked slowly on, absorbed in profound reverie; some, shrieking with agony, ran furiously about like tigers wounded with poisoned arrows; whilst others, grinding their teeth in rage, foamed along more frantic than the wildest maniac. They all avoided each other; and, though surrounded by a multitude that no one could number, each wandered at random unheedful of the rest, as if alone on a desert where no foot had trodden. (89)

Terrified by what they have seen, they soon meet the formidable Eblis himself, "a young man, whose noble and regular features seemed to have been tarnished by malignant vapours. In his large eyes appeared both pride and despair" (90). This Miltonic Satan sends them to the resting place of the pre-Adamite kings where they hear the history of Soliman Ben Daoud and discover finally their own nightmarish fate. Both Vathek and Nouronihar, like the other inhabitants of these regions, are condemned to conditions of despair. As punishment for their sins, they must wander aimlessly in eternal torment, their hearts engulfed in flames, their faces ever expressing hatred for each other. Stricken with fear, Vathek cries out his willingness to relinquish the rewards of presumption in the hope of returning to his former life; but he learns that no mercy exists in these abodes. The "awful and irrevocable decree" of their fate is then pronounced: "Their hearts immediately took fire, and they, at once, lost the most precious gift of heaven, — HOPE. These unhappy beings recoiled, with looks of the most furious dissatisfaction. Vathek beheld in the eyes of Nouronihar nothing but rage and vengeance; nor could she discern aught in his, but aversion and despair" (97).

Thus *Vathek* ends on a darkly tragic note, more tragic than any earlier tale of the East. According to Jorge Luis Borges, this stunning conclusion depicts "the first truly atrocious Hell in literature."[24] It has also been characterized by Lafcadio Hearn as an idea of Hell "so powerful and original that we can compare it only to the grand conceptions of the greatest poets."[25] And we agree that nothing in the first part of the story quite reaches the power and sublimity of this finale. By exposing the reader to such unearthly scenery and to such extremes of punishment, Beckford undertook to write the moral of the tale in large letters. "Such was, and such should be," he concludes, "the punishment of unrestrained passions and atrocious deeds! Such shall be the chastisement of that blind curiosity, which would transgress those bounds the wisdom of the Creator has prescribed to human knowledge; and such the dreadful disappointment of that restless ambition, which, aiming at discoveries reserved for beings of a supernatural order perceives not, through its infatuated pride, that the condition of man upon earth is to be — humble and ignorant" (97–98).

VII   *"sentiments of European growth"*

It must be admitted at the outset that there is much about *Vathek* that is European in nature, a fact that is as evident today as it was to some of its readers in Beckford's time. "There are in this work," observed a critic in 1787, "too many ideas and sentiments of European growth, to admit of its passing for a translation of an Eastern manuscript."[26] The reviewer failed to cite any specific provincialisms, but Beckford's overstated moral at the conclusion of the story might have provided one hint because it was needlessly explicit and reminiscent of Augustan art.

Vathek, it is usually said, shares the Neo-Classical penchant for clear portraits, precise outline, and lucid imagery. The mysterious vagueness of some of the nineteenth-century Romantics is lacking in the descriptive passages of this book, and a good example of this tendency to realize a scene with special clarity is the description of the spacious valley of Rocnabad:

The season of spring was in all its vigour; and the grotesque branches of the almond trees in full blossom, fantastically checkered with hyacinths and jonquils, breathed forth a delightful fragrance. Myriads of bees, and scarce fewer of santons, had there taken up their abode. On the banks of the stream, hives and oratories were alternately ranged; and their neatness and whiteness were set off by the deep green of the cypresses that spired up amongst them. These pious personages amused themselves with cultivating little gardens, that abounded with flowers and fruits; especially muskmelons of the best flavour that Persia could boast. Sometimes dispersed over the meadow, they entertained themselves with feeding peacocks whiter than snow, and turtles more blue than the sapphire. (82)

Edith Birkhead, after reading the tale, marveled at Beckford's accuracy of vision: "There are no vague hints and suggestions, no lurking shadows concealing untold horrors. The quaint dwarfs perched on Vathek's shoulders, the children chasing blue butterflies, Nouronihar and her maidens on tiptoe, with their hair floating in the breeze, stand out in clear relief, as if painted on a fresco. The imagery is so lucid that we are able to follow with effortless pleasure the intricate windings of a plot which at Beckford's whim twists and turns through scenes of wonderful variety."[27] In this respect, *Vathek* is linked inextricably to an older tradition.

Vathek has also been described as a book pervaded with the kind of wit and irony that characteristically belong to the eighteenth century. Critics have frequently cited the book's mixture of the sacred and the profane, as when, for example, the caliph during the course of a dinner suddenly grows pious and calls in the same breath in which he recited his prayers for "the Koran and the sugar" (43). They have also noted how frequently the prose exults in bizarre associations that are simultaneously shocking and grotesque, the effect of which often collapses the reader into nervous giggles:

Wherever the caliph directed his course, objects of pity were sure to swarm round him; the blind, the purblind, smarts without noses, damsels without ears, each to extol the munificence of Fakreddin who, as well as his attendant grey-beards, dealt about, gratis, plasters and cataplasms to all that applied. At noon, a superb corps of cripples made its appearance; and soon after advanced, by platoons, on the plain, the completest association of invalids that had ever been embodied till then. The blind went groping with the blind, the lame limped on together, and the maimed made gestures to each other with the only arm that remained. The sides of a considerable waterfall were crowded by the deaf; amongst whom were some from Pegu, with ears uncommonly handsome and large, but who were still less able to hear than the rest. Nor were there wanting others in abundance with humpbacks, wenny necks, and even horns of an exquisite polish. (50)

To William Hazlitt, these unexpected juxtapositions represented Beckford at his best. To maintain a tone of indifference, where "nothing surprises — nothing shocks," in the face of such grotesqueries constituted for Hazlitt a "masterly performance" in style. This posture gave *Vathek* the kind of odd appeal that irresistibly compelled a critic to favor it. *Vathek*, Hazlitt felt, deserved the attention of both poet and philosopher because few books could so effectively insult the reader into a sense of humanity.[28]

But Hazlitt's comment does not tell the whole story, for the humor of *Vathek* has a distinctive quality that is typically Beckfordian in character. The best satirists of the eighteenth century allowed their sense of the grotesque to be generated internally from the work itself; Beckford, on the other hand, generates his "outside" the context of the tale; and he allows it to intrude upon the general serious character of the work. The humor is fundamentally incongruous to the tale and seems more impulsive than purposeful. Thus, in the cemetery scene in which Carathis and her Negresses attempt to communicate with the dead, Beckford unexpectedly spoils its Gothic character with a comic statement:

A hollow noise was heard in the earth; the surface hove up into heaps; and the gouls, on all sides, protruded their noses to inhale, the effluvia, which the carcases of the woodmen began to emit. They assembled before a sarcophagus of white marble, where Carathis was seated between the bodies of her miserable guides. The Princess received her visitants with distinguished politeness; and, supper being ended, they talked of business. Carathis soon learnt from them every thing she wanted to discover; and, without loss of time, prepared to set forward on her journey. Her negresses, who were forming tender connexions with the gouls, importuned her, with all their fingers, to wait at least till the dawn. But Carathis, being chastity in the abstract, and an implacable enemy to love intrigues and sloth, at once rejected their prayer; mounted Alboufaki, and commanded them to take their seats instantly. (75)

Edmund Wilson seems to have had this deflationary humor in mind when he observed that "the cynicism and irony of Beckford do not imply a criticism of society; they seem merely to satisfy a perverse impulse. . . . Beckford's fancy has the slightly mad silliness that we also find in Firbank."[29]

Instead of society, Beckford's humor has a literary referent; for its appreciation relied on the reader's awareness of the conventions of his day for the joke. Stylistic parody and caricature become the usual means by which he achieves his bizarre comic effects. Carathis may be a wicked, evil woman in the novel, but she also becomes a caricature of the strong-willed, tyrannical mother of sentimental fiction. The Caliph Vathek may likewise be an image of depravity, but he is also subject to whimsical transformation. Without notice, Beckford converts him into a slapstick figure, showing him childishly beating his head and chewing his fingers when incapable of solving a problem, or joyously kissing at another time the "horrid mouth" of the ugly giaour, or being slung over the shoulder of one of his Ethiopian wives, "like a sack of dates." In addition to parodying character types, Beckford employs the use of understatement (Carathis' "antipathy to wine was by no means insuperable''); puns (Carathis says "There is nothing so pleasing as retiring to caverns: my taste for dead bodies, and every thing like mummy is decided''); euphemisms ("The camels, which had been left unmolested to make sal ammoniac''); and *double entendre* ("Vathek, reposing upon a mattress of down, and tolerably recovered from the jolting of the Ethiopian, who, to his feelings, seemed the roughest trotting jade he had hitherto mounted, called out for something to eat'').

What troubles the reader during these moments of disengagement is that Beckford seems to have such slight authorial regard for their effect either on the style of the work or on the way in which they tend to subvert its context. This recognition has led some readers to feel that Beckford was intentionally satirizing the conventions of the traditional Oriental tale. The problem with this interpretation is that neither the satire nor the comedy is sustained and that the work is, on the whole, fundamentally serious. Actually, this unevenness of tone recalls Beckford's stylistic problem in *Biographical Memoirs of Extraordinary Painters;* and perhaps it can best be understood in terms similar to those of that earlier work. Whatever *Vathek* is as a literary work, it shares a characteristic of Beckford's other writings in that it is inescapably his private fantasy; but, when the dream becomes too real, he pinches himself awake. The intrusive humor, in this sense, becomes a way of diminishing the intensity with which he becomes a part of the world he creates. But the comedy cannot hide the moral anarchy that the author finds so powerfully attractive. Beckford personally identifies with the sybaritic caliph — with his restlessness, his self-importance, and his abandonment of self-restraint; and he also sympathizes with Nouronihar's aspirations and with Gulchenrouz's childish innocence. At the same time, he feels compelled to let the reader know that he can detach himself from the fantasy, which he does by means of the arbitrary comic effects. There is, as Roger Lonsdale has already suggested, a psychological need to do so.[30]

VIII *The Allegory of Self*

The tendency to read the novel as a revelation of the author's personality has led some students to draw direct correspondences between the fictional characters and the actual. "The caliph's unscrupulous and insatiable ambition," writes Ernest Baker, "is Beckford's egoism and boundless curiosity pushed to the verge of monomania."[31] As for the other characters, Beckford is said to have drawn upon members of his family and upon intimate friends. Nouronihar, who joins Vathek in sin, is said to be a portrait of the delicious Louisa Beckford; the willful Carathis, an exaggeration of the overpowering Mrs. Beckford; the captivating Gulchenrouz, a translation of the fawn-like Courtenay boy. Also, in one or other of the many magicians and sorcerers who emerge here and there in the story, Chapman sees "a glimpse of the furtive and unknown Cozens."[32] Indeed, Beckford himself is partly responsible for encouraging this kind of reading since he once told Cyrus Redding that the hall of Fonthill, with its Oriental decorations, inspired the final scene of his story. "Old Fonthill," he explained, "had a very ample, lofty, loud echoing hall, one of the largest in the kingdom. Numerous doors led from it into different parts of the house, through dim, winding passages. It was from that I introduced the hall — the idea of the 'Hall of Eblis' being generated by my own. My imagination magnified and coloured it with the Eastern character." And he then added that "All the females in *Vathek* were portraits of those in the domestic establishment of old Fonthill, their fancied good or ill qualities exaggerated to suit my purpose."[33]

When we are aware of the extent to which writing is a form of self-realization for Beckford, it is difficult to avoid reading the caliph's journey as simultaneously a journey into the self. Samarah, in the end, is another one of Beckford's dream landscapes — a wish-fulfillment for a troubled and repressed young man. Just as internal evidence in *Biographical Memoirs of Extraordinary Painters*, in *The Vision*, in *Dreams*, and in his personal letters to friends demonstrates a marked struggle to translate himself into visionary lands to find release from the trammels of society, so does he convey himself into a realm of his own making in *Vathek* to rise above the better realities of his own life. In a dream creation, he was at liberty to express energies that were usually frustrated in the pale, conventional world; therefore, he indulged his caliph in a myriad of atrocities and pleasure-seeking activities as a means of finding an acceptable mode of self-expression. "In writing an oriental fantasy such as this," argues James H. Rieger,

one enters upon a realm of hallucination and daydream as surely as Coleridge claimed to have done with the aid of opium. In such a world anything can happen and usually, frighteningly does. The only limits to action, experience, and passion here are those of one's own personality. If the personality in question is as warped and tormented as Beckford's was, then the djinns and demons summoned from the depths will be those of neurotic nightmare. Beckford seems to have become aware that he had unleashed and embodied energies which had hitherto found no overt expression. . . . There is ample reason to believe that this "Arabian tale" was born in violence, in the bursting forth into symbols of a long-choked wellspring of association.[34]

It may be due to Beckford's unusual sympathy for his indulgent caliph that readers sometimes consider the finale inadequately prepared for; but such empathy surely explains why his villains are so much more attractively portrayed than those characters who live by society's laws.

IX Vathek *and the Orient*

Vathek holds a unique place among eighteenth-century romances of its kind for additional reasons: it is a prose tale which achieves a certain faithfulness to the Orient. This Orientalism does not mean, of course, that Beckford's knowledge of the East is always accurate or that it is always based upon reliable sources. The scholarship of the period, as we noted earlier, was too erratic to be authoritative. Nevertheless, his imaginative use of information gleaned from much reading does invest the composition with an Eastern character which is sufficient to make *Vathek* a distinctive achievement in this genre. We have already seen evidence of Beckford's serious concern for the real East in *The Long Story*. At the writing of *Vathek*, with five years of study behind him, he possessed a broader, deeper knowledge of the Orient which he had filed away in his memory. For *Vathek* he consistently relied on material from source books about the East to produce a work of which it would ultimately be said that it "might appear without disadvantage in the *Arabian Nights*, with Aladdin on the right hand and Ali Baba on its left."[35]

The leading character in Beckford's story is actually based upon the historical figure Vathek, the ninth caliph of the Abassides, the son of Motassem and Carathis, and the grandson of Aaroun al Raschid. Eighteenth-century readers could find him documented in d'Herbelot's encyclopedia, *Bibliothèque Orientale*, a primary source for *Vathek*.[36] Vathek's impatience with orthodoxy, his dedicated sensuality, his heretical opinions on matters of religion, his profound love of astrology and science in general, and even his killing glance, "l'oeil si terrible," all could be found in the biographical sketch entitled *VATHEK Billah.*[37] Beckford does, however, enlarge his character by giving him a Faust-like drive for forbidden knowledge. According to d'Herbelot, the historical Vathek died from the excesses of debauchery — from his eating and drinking even without appetite and from his indulging in the pleasures of women without discretion. The fate of Beckford's caliph is grander; it is more the result of a restless ambition that fails to recognize the limits of man's earthly condition.

The son of Motassem is also more cruel in Beckford's work and his associates in crime are blacker than they are in the *Bibliothèque Orientale;* and this modification represents a significant departure from the traditional view of the Orient in the eighteenth century. Both French and English writers had a tendency to idealize Orientals by exaggerating their virtues as well as the wisdom of their government and their customs. Most often this form of Oriental utopianism was employed as a means of satirizing Western man and his institutions. Beckford's vision opposes the tradition; he transforms the Oriental world into a nightmare by infusing it with wickedness and evil and by painting a Promethean hell at its conclusion.

The *Bibliothèque Orientale* provided a wealth of additional and different types of material which Beckford borrowed for the creation of his work. The Caliph Omar Ben Abdalaziz, who was supposedly favored by Mohammed because of his temperance and self-denial; Samarah, the city of the Babylonian Irak, founded by Vathek's father Motassem, who erected the palace of Alkoremi on the hill of Pied Horses; the celebrated artist Mani, whom Inatulla of Delphi styled the "far-famed"; the dives, the afrits, the genii, the peris, the horrible mountains of Kaf surrounded by a dark and cheerless desert; Simurgh, the wonderful Oriental bird; the fortress of Aherman; the halls of Argenk — all came from d'Herbelot's learned volumes.[38] The same source book afforded Beckford detailed accounts of the pre-Adamite sultans — Soliman Raad, Soliman Daki, Soliman Di Gian Ben Gian — of Istakhar with its "ruined and defaced columns and its forty watch-towers" and of Eblis himself, the fallen apostate angel "exiled to the infernal regions for refusing to worship Adam at the command of the Supreme."[39] For details of Eastern customs and etiquette which Beckford incorporated for greater authenticity in *Vathek*, the *Bibliothèque Orientale* once again contained ample material.

The breadth of Beckford's reading in the Oriental field becomes

strikingly apparent when we discover the resemblances between
Vathek and the many other source books on the East which were
available in his day. Marcel May described in 1928 a considerable
number of the background materials for *Vathek*. He illustrated, for
example, how closely Vathek's visit to Istakhar followed the description of the ancient Persepolis by the French traveler, Jean Chardin,
in his *Voyage en Perse et autres lieux de l'Orient* (1711).[40] Chardin's
book described the two rocks forming the portal to the valley of
Istakhar, the royal mausoleums on the mountainside, the terrace of
black marble, the gloomy watch towers, the colossal forms of
animals in stone, the tall columns, and the fragments of the wrecked
palace. Marcel May has also shown how Beckford's minute descriptions of the ruins themselves could have been inspired by the
engravings of the actual site in Le Brun's *Voyage par la Moscovie en
Perse, et aux Indes Orientales* (1718).

Of course, not all of the Oriental literature Beckford absorbed
before creating his own Arabian tale was authentic. One of his most
well-known borrowings — the episode of the flaming hearts — came
from a pseudo-translation, Gueullette's *Mogul Tales* (1736). The
relevant passage in *Mogul Tales* begins when Aboul-Assan spies a
bright light at the foot of a mountain in Persepolis:

I was a good deal surprised at this unexpected sight, yet I rose and ran
towards it; when I came up, I found it proceeded from a flambeau, which
was carried by a little man, towards whom as I drew near, I perceived that
he was entering a subterraneous passage, . . . He beckoned to me to follow
him, which, when I had a little recollected my spirits, I did; we went down
together for some time into the mountain, at last we traversed a long alley of
black marble, but so finely polished that it had the appearance of a looking-
glass; having passed this in the space of a quarter of an hour, we reached a
large hall, where we found three men standing mute, and in posture of sorrow. . . . The little man whom I had followed had not hitherto broke silence,
but now bid me sit down by those three persons; I heard him with surprise,
but obeyed him. I wish, said I to one of them, that this peace may continue
always among you. Peace is banished from these sad places, replied the
eldest of the three, with an air of sternness. If peace be not here, answered I
affrighted, what are you, and what do you here? We wait, said the second, in
this sepulchre, for the just judgment of God. You are then, continued I,
great sinners. Alas! cried the third, we are continually tortured for the evil
actions we have done, see what a wretched state we are in; then they unbuttoned their waist-coats, and through their skin, which appeared like crystal,
I saw their heart compassed with fire, by which they were burnt without
ceasing, yet they were never consumed.[41]

Other revealing reference works may be found in Henley's notes to *Vathek* — over two hundred in all — that were written in collaboration with Beckford and appended to the first English edition. Almost all of the prominent sources of information on the East that were available in the eighteenth century were cited and frequently quoted to document Beckford's work — to make it appear, as Henley indicated in the Preface, that *Vathek* was an "Original" Arabian tale "collected in the East by a Man of Letters" and "communicated to the Editor." John Richardson's *Dissertation of the Languages, Literature and Manners of Eastern Nations* (1777) is included for providing material on Eastern customs and mythology. George Sale's translation of the *Koran,* together with his famous *Preliminary Discourse,* is mentioned as supplying some of the factual matter regarding the faith of Islam and the Mohammedan peoples. Bernard Picart's *Cérémonies et coûtumes religieuses de tous les peuples du monde* (1723–43) is noted as documenting material dealing with Eastern deities and religious sects. Even Lady Mary Wortley Montagu's *Letters from Turkey* (1763) found a place among the voluminous collection of notes as a principal source book for the domestic details of *Vathek.*

The reviewers of *Vathek* in the summer of 1786 were impressed by the learning and critical knowledge displayed in the notes.[42] Little did they realize, however, that this new tale, with its realism of local color, supported by the evidence of travelers and learned Orientalists, actually looked forward to a similar use of Oriental material in the works of later authors and even to a whole new era of genuine Oriental studies in the mid- and late nineteenth century.

CHAPTER 7

Voices from Eblis:
The Episodes of Vathek

THE nouvelles which were to form the tail-piece to Vathek's history, *The Episodes of Vathek*, were written during Beckford's most fertile and, at the same time, most frustrating years. Never again did he write at such a productive pace. Besides devoting some time to refining Vathek in 1782, he was at work on the *Histoire de Darianoc, jeune homme du pays de Gou-Gou*, a long unfinished narrative about a young rebel who denies Allah's existence and, as a consequence, undergoes a series of excruciating trials until he repents and acknowledges the Deity. In the same year, Beckford readied *Dreams, Waking Thoughts and Incidents* for the press; he scribbled happily to Henley in August that additional "Arabian Tales" were springing up like mushrooms all over the downs of Fonthill; and, before the winter season was ended, he had embarked on *The Episodes of Vathek*.

By now it must have seemed to those who knew Beckford that he was seriously committed to writing. Preferring to be master of himself, he was, in addition, showing some signs of success in resisting the blandishments of his family. But, when he attempted to place five hundred quarto copies of *Dreams, Waking Thoughts and Incidents* on the market in March, 1783, Mrs. Beckford and several members of the family, as we have seen, forced him to order their withdrawal and to confiscate most of the copies. The suppression of a work of art, however, was not enough to satisfy Mrs. Beckford; she took even sterner action to ensure her son's entrance into the political world by arranging his marriage to Lady Margaret Gordon, the daughter of the fourth Earl of Aboyne. On May 5, 1783, the couple recited their vows under the mother's watchful eye.

Beckford's marriage was a triumph for the family; and it seemed for a time that Beckford was ready to settle down to the practical affairs of life. He wrote to his friend Lord Chancellor Thurlow in the following spring that he was inclined to sit in Parliament; and, before the year was over, he had obtained the seat for Wells. But the romance with politics was shortlived; for, after a few sittings through the tedious proceedings of the House, he sought freedom from these responsibilities by means of a comfortable peerage with the title "Lord Beckford of Fonthill." He tried to obtain it through Thurlow and might have been successful had it not been for the scandal in which he became involved after a visit to Powderham Castle, Devonshire, where his young friend William Courtenay resided. Following his stay there in 1784, a series of stories began to circulate about a sexual liaison between Beckford and Courtenay which spread to the London newspapers by the end of November.

Throughout the furor of these reports, Beckford protested his innocence. He solemnly declared to both friends and relatives that the sordid tales were groundless. But, as word of the "Courtenay affair" spread throughout England, Beckford plunged into despair, finding only temporary relief in the birth of his first daughter in 1785. After passing a few months in despair, his depression gave way to contempt. Reaching a breaking point, he finally decided, at the suggestion of his wife, to return to the "tranquil pure atmosphere" of Vevey on the shores of Lake Geneva where he had found solace once before. He was there less than a year, however, before he suffered another serious setback: the death of Lady Margaret on May 26, 1786, after she had given birth to their second child. To Beckford, her death was a severe shock because he had grown to love and respect her and because she had been one of the few individuals who had stood by him during the scandal. To make matters worse, when the news of her death reached England, a few newspapers claimed that it was due directly to his brutal treatment of her.

These years that span the composition of *Vathek* and the death of his wife were, therefore, the most emotionally feverish of Beckford's lifetime. He would never again experience the same depth of psychological strain that he had had during this troubled period. Yet, despite the turmoil, these years mark a particularly fruitful literary phase of his life; and from or during this vortex of conflict — perhaps as a way of finding his stay against confusion — he created *The Episodes of Vathek*.

I   *The Creation of Vathek's Companions*

It is difficult to fix the precise composition date of the three inset pieces — the tales of Prince Alasi, Prince Barkiarokh, and Princess

Zulkaïs — which Beckford was planning to work into the framework of *Vathek* after the manner of the *Arabian Nights;* for allusions to these tales in the surviving Beckford letters are infrequent and sometimes vague. An ambiguous reference appeared, for example, as early as January 13, 1783, in the Beckford-Henley correspondence: "I go on bravely with the episodes of *Vathec*, & hope in a few days to wind up his adventures."[1] But the likelihood, considering the early date of the letter, is that the "episodes" referred to here really belong to the Caliph Vathek and not to the three characters who relate their own moral tales in the subterranean regions of Istakhar.

The first clear indication that Beckford had begun to compose the companion-pieces to *Vathek* can be found in a letter he wrote to Henley from Cologny, Switzerland, on November 18, 1783: "I shall bring you some Caliphs not unworthy to succeed your beloved Vathec."[2] The following month Beckford suggested in a letter of December 29 that at least one of the stories had been completed and was ready for Henley's perusal. Henley seems, however, to have refused to allow Beckford to send it, for Beckford wrote to Henley that "I grieve to think that you refuse me the satisfaction of communicating to you Vathec's kindred as soon as born."[3] A third allusion was made by Beckford in a letter from Paris on January 25, 1784;[4] and on May 6, 1784, Beckford disclosed that he had advanced to a second story: "I am far gone in another episode."[5] Nothing more was said about his progress by Beckford until October 13, 1784, when the Beckford-Courtenay scandal was about to explode: "I spend many an hour in dreaming abt my unfortunate princes (Vathec's companions), & contriving reasonable ways & means of sending them to the Devil."[6]

On March 31, 1785, he informed Henley that another episode, perhaps the second, had been written and that still another was well on its way: "I have been giving the last evenings to one episode, & sown the seeds of another which I trust will bring forth fruit in due season."[7] The last episode mentioned was almost completed by the opening of the following year, as is evident from the letter of February 9, 1786, in which Beckford announced that "The episodes to *Vathec* are nearly finished, & the whole work will be completed within a twelvemonth."[8] But the sudden death of his wife in May halted all work, so that on August 1, 1786, without knowing that Henley had already published the translation of *Vathek*, Beckford declared: "I fear the dejection of mind into which I am plunged will prevent my finishing the other stories, and of course *Vathec*'s making his appearance in any language this winter. I would not have him on any account come forth without his companions."⁹ It seems reasonable to conclude, with all the available evidence marshalled, that the three episodes known today were written sometime after January 1783, and before the death of his wife in May 1786, and that a fourth one remained to be done.

It is clear also from both the London (1786) and the Lausanne (1787) editions of *Vathek* that the fourth episode was in preparation or was at least planned during this same period. The Lausanne *Vathek* announced near the conclusion of the story that three additional histories were to be given and a portion of an unnamed fourth:

Le Calife et Nouronihar consentirent à cette proposition, et Vathek prenant la parole, se mit à leur faire, non sans pleurs et gémissemens, un sincère récit de tout ce qui lui étoit arrivé. Lorsqu'il eut fini sa pénible narration, le jeune homme qui avoit parlé commença la sienne de la manière suivante.
Histoire des deux princes amis, Alasi et Zironz, enfermés dans la palais souterrain.
Histoire du prince Kalilah et de la princesse Zulkaïs, sa soeur, enfermés dans le palais souterrain.
Histoire du prince Berkiarekh enfermés dans le palais souterrain.
Histoire du prince . . . enfermés dans le palais souterrain.
Le quatrième prince en étoit au milieu de son récit, quand il fut interrompu, etc.¹⁰

The translation of 1786, without mentioning the specific names, reported the same number of episodes: "When the afflicting narrative was closed, the young man entered on his own. Each person proceeded in order, and when the fourth prince had reached the midst of his adventures, a sudden noise interrupted him."¹¹ But, when Beckford published the Paris edition (1787), he finally trimmed the plan to two histories and a fragment of a third.¹² The unnamed fourth episode in the Lausanne edition could well have been "The Story of Motassem" which he did not finish until 1815 and which he then destroyed as being "too wild" to appear in print.¹³

The idea of publishing *Vathek* with interlocking episodes remained firm in Beckford's mind for years. He hinted at the possible publication of the *Episodes* in the Preface to the 1815 edition of Vathek, and he even prepared an "Advertisement for the edition of *Vathek* with the *Episodes*," which was to be affixed to the confederated edition. This advertisement (in French) is still preserved among the Beckford papers in the author's hand:

> For some time we have been advancing, with rapid strides, towards universal toleration. Horace Walpole's famous drama, founded on the most revolting incest, is, at last, published without any scruple. "Don Juan" is devoured by innumerable readers. People throw themselves headlong into the novels of Madame du Devant and Victor Hugo. No one is stricken dead with surprise and indignation on reading the blasphemous rhapsodies of Edgar Quinet. I make no pretence of rivalling, even approximately, the effervescent lubricity of literary productions such as these; — but, as in the Golden Age of the Society of Jesus, its learned members regarded all means as justifiable in a view of the end to be attained, even so do I dare flatter myself that the *moral* of my tales is sufficiently apparent to produce upon the reader a salutary effect. Let him, therefore, peruse these stories in full confidence, bearing in mind, the while, a truth which religion itself inculcates, and which he cannot do better than ponder in his innermost conscience, viz: — that those who, like the Caliph Vathek, and his unhappy companions, abandon themselves to criminal passions, and deeds of infamy, will, by a terrible but just retribution, have their abode for ever in the regions of eternal vengeance.[14]

In time, the *Episodes* became unpublished literary curiosities which Beckford guarded with jealous care but relished showing to the curious who visited Fonthill and, during the later years of his life, Lansdown Crescent in Bath. Samuel Rogers listened to a reading of two of the tales and later concluded that they were "extremely fine, but very objectionable on account of their subjects. Indeed, they show that the mind of the author was to a certain degree diseased."[15] On February 8, 1818, Rogers gave an account of this visit in a letter addressed to Lady Byron: "I . . . paid a visit to the Abbot of Fonthill. . . . He read me his travels in Portugal, and the stories related in that small chamber in the Palace of Eblis. The last were full of unimaginable horrors, but of those delectable personages, of Zulkais and Kalilah — more when we meet."[16] This bit of information so tantalized Lord Byron, who was already an avid admirer of *Vathek*, that he expressed by return mail a strong desire to see these curious stories.

> Your account of your visit to Fonthill is very striking: could you beg of *him* for *me* a copy in MS. of the remaining *Tales?* I think I deserve them, as a strenuous and public admirer of the first one. I will return it when read, and make no ill use of the copy, if granted. Murray would send out anything

safely. If ever I return to England, I should very much like to see the author, with his permission. In the meantime you could not oblige me more than by obtaining me the perusal I request, in French or English — all's one for that, though I prefer Italian to either. I have a French copy of "Vathek," which I bought at Lausanne. I can read French with great pleasure and facility, though I neither write nor speak it.[17]

Rogers carried out Byron's request, but Beckford, "hesitated, half consented, and concluded with saying that he hoped they [the *Episodes*] would induce [Byron] to venture within the walls of his Abbey — the place of their birth, and from which they had never wandered."[18] Byron never voyaged to Fonthill, and in his later years Beckford expressed relief that that interview never took place. "Oh! to what good," he declared, "could it possibly have led! We should have met in full drill — both talked at the same time — both endeavoured to have been delighted — a correspondence would have been established, the most insufferable and laborious that can be imagined, because the most artificial. Oh, gracious goodness, I have the opportunity of enjoying the best qualities of his mind in his works, what more do I require?"[19]

In 1833, Beckford corresponded with publisher Richard Bentley concerning the printing of the *Episodes,* but Bentley was unwilling to pay the amount of money that Beckford was attempting to extract from him. Beckford's reactions that were expressed were that "unless Bentley can persuade himself and feels inspired to give a sum as round as the great globe itself, nay rounder, for the globe we know is flatter at the poles than my *Episodes,* I hope, will be found to be in any part of them, we are not likely to deal. As you are more and more convinced . . . that he will never think of thousands, he had better give up the point and cease fidgetting himself upon the subject. As to me, I am fidget proof."[20] Bentley made a proposal to bookseller George Clarke, but Beckford rejected it as inadequate; consequently, this material remained in manuscript form until 1909 when Lewis Melville discovered it among the papers of the Hamilton family and published two of the three episodes for the first time in the original French in three issues of *The English Review* in 1909. The French text of all three tales, combined with an English translation by Sir Frank T. Marzials, was subsequently published in 1912.[21]

II   *Tales from the Small Chamber*

Beckford planned to interlock the *Episodes* with the master tale by introducing near the conclusion of *Vathek*, the caliph and Nouronihar to the narrators of the *Episodes:*

> After issuing these orders, the caliph and Nouronihar continued walking amidst the silent crowd, till they heard voices at the end of the gallery. Presuming them to proceed from some unhappy beings, who, like themselves, were awaiting their final doom, they followed the sound, and found it to come from a small square chamber, where they discovered, sitting on sofas, four young men, of goodly figure, and a lovely female, who were holding a melancholy conversation by the glimmering of a lonely lamp. Each had a gloomy and forlorn air; and two of them were embracing each other with great tenderness. On seeing the caliph and the daughter of Fakreddin enter, they arose, saluted, and made room for them. Then he who appeared the most considerable of the group, addressed himself thus to Vathek: "Strangers! who doubtless are in the same state of suspense with ourselves, as you do not yet bear your hand on your heart, if you are come hither to pass the interval allotted, previous to the infliction of our common punishment, condescend to relate the adventures that have brought you to this fatal place; and we, in return, will acquaint you with ours, which deserve but too well to be heard. (94)

The caliph and Nouronihar agreed to relate the story of their previous crimes. Vathek was the first to give his "sincere recital" and then, according to the plan, Prince Alasi, the narrator of the first episode, followed.

III   *Constructing a Credible Oriental Tale*

As Beckford did in *Vathek*, he incorporated in the first episode, the story of Prince Alasi, realistic Oriental details and wove threads of historical verisimilitude through the whole fabric of the narrative. "I have truth to work upon in my dreams," Beckford once said, "and some truth I must have."[22] For Beckford, as we have observed, fiction writing was a form of dreaming — the "realization of a romance in its most extravagant intensity." In the case of the Oriental tales, however, any credibility they may have as representations of the genre derives from the underpinning of factual truth. In *Vathek*, Beckford used the *Bibliothèque Orientale* as a primary source book

for the Oriental material; the same compendious work provided the
historical and geographical documentation for *Prince Alasi*.[23] Ron-
dabah, in this episode, for example, is princess of Ghilan, which is
described by d'Herbelot as a "province of the Persian empire extending along the banks of the Caspian Sea." (II, 115); and Firouz's
home country, Shirvan, is identified as a "province of the realm
which today we call Persia, which is found on the western side of the
Caspian Sea, and which is separated from Adherbigian and
Daghestan, by the rivers Aras and Kura" (s.v. "Schirvan," 3: 272).

Beckford's description of Filanshaw, the king of Shirvan and the
father of Firouz, as a man beseiged by the troops of the "Calif
Vathek" was historically accurate and was based upon d'Herbelot's
notation that "Filanschah reigned in Schirvan, during the time
when the Caliph Vathek of the Abassides added this province to the
empire of the Moslems" (*ibid.*). Samakhie, the capital city of
Shirvan where King Filanshaw is held captive by rebellious subjects,
and Cheheristan, the city which Alasi mistakenly identifies with the
mage's fabulous cave, are found in the same source book; so also is
the name of Firouz, which "signifies good fortune and victory"
(2:44). Finally, d'Herbelot's encyclopedia included information
about the kingdom of Kahrezme, over which Alasi presides in
Beckford's tale (s.v. "Khouarazem," 2: 451).

Another of the new episodes, *The Story of Prince Barkiarokh*, is
for the most part poured from the cauldron of Beckford's own
imagination. Yet, as with the first episode, he continued the method
of deepening the Oriental character of the tale by borrowing in-
cidental material from prominent Eastern source books; and André
Parreaux has already identified three of these sources. "The History
of the Second Old Man and the Two Black Dogs" from *The Thousand and One Nights* provided it seems, a point of departure for
Beckford's second episode.[24] Ridley's *Tales of the Genii* (1764) contained a description of the "cave of Falri . . . surrounded with unhal-
lowed swine," which most likely inspired Beckford's "Miry Desert
. . . inhabited by an Afrite" in "The Story of Barkiarokh's Younger
Sister-in-Law."[25] The most fruitful reference document, upon which
Beckford seems to have relied most heavily, was once again the
Bibliothèque Orientale. In this collection, he evidently found some
of his leading characters in embryo form as, for example, the dervish
Alsalami who is developed in Beckford's tale as "a man of peace, as
his name suggested." According to d'Herbelot, the same name
signified a native of the city of Bagdad, a city "which was called by

its founder Caliph Abou Ciafar Al Mansor, *Daralsalm*, the resting place, or the City of Peace, in imitation of Jerusalem, which means in Hebrew, Vision of Peace" (s.v. "Salami," 3: 185). Homaïouna appears under the form of "Homaioun" in the *Bibliothèque Orientale*, and the name signifies appropriately "blessed, royal, and august" (2: 254). In Barkiarokh's history, she comes from "the delightful country of Shaduka," which d'Herbelot defines under the name "Schadukiam" as meaning "pleasure and desire." It is a Persian word, explains d'Herbelot, "a fabulous province in the country of Ginnistan" said to be peopled "by dives and peris" (3: 222). Homaïouna, in Beckford's story, once lived in the "superb city of Gianhar" the capital of Shaduka; and this fact was also documented in d'Herbelot's work as "Ghevher," or the "city of joy" (*ibid.*). Finally, the father of Homaïouna, Asfendarmod, the most powerful of all peris, is also described as the "name of a genie who presides over and gives his name to the twelfth and last month of the year, according to ancient Persians in the calendar Iezdegiridque" (1: 266).

The final episode, *The Story of the Princess Zulkaïs and the Prince Kalilah*, which concerns, in part, the incestuous relationship of a young Prince and his beautiful sister, seems to be based on an episode in "The First Kalandar's Tale" of *The Arabian Nights*.[26] In the original narrative, an uncle describes to his nephew how his son and daughter met their fate:

O son of my brother, this youth from his boyhood was madly in love with his own sister; and often and often I forbade him from her, saying to myself: — They are but little ones. However, when they grew up sin befel between them; and, although I could hardly believe it, I confined him and chided him and threatened him with the severest threats; and the eunuchs and servants said to him: — Beware of so foul a thing which none before thee ever did, and which none after thee will ever do; and have a care lest thou be dishonoured and disgraced among the Kings of the day, even to the end of time. And I added: — Such a report as this will be spread abroad by caravans, and take heed not to give them cause to talk or I will assuredly curse thee and do thee death. After that I lodged them apart, and shut her up; but the accursed girl loved him with passionate love, for Satan had got the mastery of her as well as of him and made their foul sin seem fair in their sight. Now when my son saw that I separated them, he secretly built this souterrain and furnished it and transported to it victuals, even as thou seest; and, when I had gone out a-sporting, came here with his sister and hid from me. Then His righteous judgment fell upon the twain and consumed them with fire from Heaven.[27]

In the broad lines of Beckford's tale, which are similar, Zulkaïs rebels against her father and indulges in forbidden love with her twin brother, Kalilah. Her father, Emir Abou Taher Achmed, attempts to separate the two lovers — a step which has the effect of forcing them to meet clandestinely in the recesses of a nearby forest. Taking more severe steps, the emir banishes his daughter Zulkaïs to the Isle of Ostriches, whereupon she arranges with an emissary of Eblis to be reunited with Kalilah in the heart of a subterranean cavern. But, before the reunion takes place, the tale ends. It is clear from the existing fragment, however, that, like their counterparts in "The First Kalandar's Tale," righteous judgment will fall upon their heads; and they too will suffer by fire.

All this material is admittedly fragmentary, and it would be misleading to foster the view that Beckford's tales were designed principally to depict authentic Eastern manners and customs. It is true, as we have noted, that Samuel Henley attempted to present *Vathek* as a genuine Arabian tale in the Preface to his translation. The learned notes that accompanied this first edition also reinforce the impression of an "imitative" Oriental tale. It is likewise not surprising that many contemporary readers, including Byron, admired the mother tale "as the only modern composition which has seized the genuine spirit of the Arabian tales."[28] But the "truth" of Beckford's Oriental tales cannot be restricted to the factual information that may have been gleaned from a study of the Orient. For Beckford's fiction, as we have shown, — in fact, almost everything he wrote in the 1770's and 1780's — is almost always and irrevocably autobiographical: in a sense, an allegory about himself.

IV   *Confessions of an Artist Voluptuary*

`Beckford seems, for example, very close to his subject in *The Story of Prince Alasi*. In the Vathekian mode, Alasi, the narrator of the tale, displays, like Beckford, the same restless craving for the forbidden. He is betrothed to Rondabah, Princess of Ghilan, for reasons of state; but, with an "almost misanthropic repulsion from the ordinary ways of men," he finds the whole idea of marriage distasteful. Alasi, who is in many ways a portrait of Beckford, is a perpetual dreamer and a man of taste and refinement; and he is more impressed, it seems, by a "superb collation" than by public duties that he regards as "a burden very heavy to be borne." Instead of the woman he is about to marry, his interests are directed toward winning the affections of a young boy named Firouz, the son of the King of Shirvan. Initially,

Alasi appears blind to the true nature of his feelings for his new friend; but, before long, he finds them perplexing. "The fascination he exercised upon me," Alasi confesses, "was extraordinary, to myself, quite inexplicable" (15–16). In effect, Firouz becomes a fictional counterpart for William Courtenay; and the story itself becomes an opportunity for Beckford to explore his own ambivalent relationship with the young heir of Powderham Castle. "What is there in common between the affection I shall owe to my wife," he asks of Firouz, "and the affection I shall ever entertain for yourself?" (7)

The subject of the tale is homosexual love. Love, which in its own shape would have been repelled, according to Alasi at the opening of the narrative, "took Friendship's shape, and in that shape effected my ruin." As the relationship develops, however, innocent friendship gives way to sexual feelings so strong that Alasi is even willing to become a partner in Firouz's crimes: "The sound of Firouz's voice, his words, his looks, seemed to confuse my reason, and made my speech come low and haltingly. He perceived the tumult raging in my breast, and, to appease it, abandoned a certain languour and tenderness of demeanor that he had so far affected, and assumed the childish gaiety and vivacity natural to his years; for he did not appear to be much more than thirteen" (6).

The sudden reversal half way through the story which changes Firouz's sex is unconvincing, but it does no violence to the theme since "she" dons male clothing at the end. This deliberate blurring of sexual identity simply suggests Beckford's own uneasiness in dealing with such a delicate subject. That Firouz becomes an expression of evil, one of the more arrogant and perverse characters of the *Vathek* cycle, likewise does not diminish the possibility that this tale, in its treatment of aberrant love, represents a vehicle for the projection of Beckford's own private predicament. From one point of view, Firouz's evil can be considered an expression of Beckford's own guilt; but evidence in his biography indicates that, in time, he actually viewed Courtenay as "the meanest traytor and the blackest enemy."[29] Admittedly, it is slippery activity to become too literal in establishing a relationship between the fictional and the actual world; but, in this case, the correspondences are too significant to overlook.

In the Beckfordian dream, the self inevitably becomes the central object of contemplation; and the ego is projected and in a sense realized in a way that it could never be in the conventional world.

This characteristic is no less true of his Oriental tales; indeed, since he readily admitted that he portrayed real persons in *Vathek*, we have tried to make a case for the revelations the book contains about his own tormented life. The allegory of the self continues in *The Story of the Princess Zulkaïs and the Prince Kalilah*, the episode of the cycle that has not survived in its complete form. At the moment when the narrative begins to reach a climax — with the entrance of Zulkaïs into the domain of Eblis — it suddenly ends but may have once existed as a completed tale. Samuel Rogers, who singled it out for particular attention in a letter to Byron, made reference to "your commission with regard to certain unimaginable fancies in the shape of an Eastern Tale, the Loves of Kalilah and Zulkaïs," seems to suggest that it was complete as late as 1820.[30] According to Beckford in a letter of October 20, 1817, Rogers was "in a delirium" when he read it and "swears that Kalilah is better than anything of Byron's."[31]

There is much about Beckford's tale which suggests details of his own life. Like Lord Mayor Beckford, Abou Taher Achmed is a ruler who achieves fame in his own time; and he also speculates heavily in trade and in commerce and, as was true of Beckford's father, exaggerates the extent of the wealth accumulated from such ventures. The subjection of Prince Kalilah to a "course of study rigorous and above his years" in order to satisfy his father's desire to possess a child of extraordinary nature recalls the discipline of Beckford's early education and the same nervous concern of his own family. Another parallel can be found in the emotional bond between Zulkaïs and Kalilah, the result of "the ardent elixir of a too exquisite sensibility," which seems to mirror Beckford's traumatic involvement with William Courtenay. Finally, Beckford's childhood wish to live in his own euphoric dreamland, instead of dutifully accepting the responsibilities of a conventional world, finds expression in the remonstrances of Abou Taher Achmed:

Must the sun, as it rises and sets, see you only bloom and fade like a weak narcissus flower? Vainly do the Sages try to move you by the most eloquent discourses, and unveil before your eyes the learned mysteries of an older time: vainly do they tell you of warlike and magnanimous deeds. You are now nearly thirteen, and never have you evinced the smallest ambition to distinguish yourself among your fellow-men. It is not in the lurking haunts of effeminacy that great characters are formed; it is not by reading love poems that men are made fit to govern nations! Princes must act; they must show themselves to the world. (184)

Another unifying relationship between this tale and the others in Beckford's Oriental ensemble — particularly *Vathek* — exists in the theme of ambition. This theme which dominated *Vathek* reasserts itself here, less dramatically in the character of Emir Abou Taher Achmed. In a quest resembling that of the insatiable caliph, he searches for "the mysterious tablets" that bear the hieroglyphics which would accord him the forbidden knowledge that he desires and the power that he believes would forestall the decrees of Providence. As a ruler, he cares little for the real needs of his subjects; his primary concern is with his commercial speculations, the success of which is deliberately inflated. In violation of the Koran, he is seldom particular "with regard to religious observances, and often forgot to perform the ablutions ordained by the law" (167). He is also impetuous like Vathek; for, when he first sees Ghulendi Begum, the lovely daughter of the venerable Iman Abzenderoud, he orders that the "nuptial chamber be got ready, and all necessary preparations for our marriage be complete within one hour" (168). Abzenderoud's condition for giving his consent and approval to the union is that the emir abandon his interest in the unholy search for the tablets. But, even after the wedding, the emir's mind is "always dwelling on the magnificence of the ancient Pharohs"; and, as Vathek had erected his tower, he orders built "a palace with twelve pavilions — proposing, at an early date, to install in each pavilion a son" (171).

The emir's punishment for this kind of idolatry manifests itself in two forms in the fragment of the story that has survived: the sudden death of his wife, while giving birth to Kalilah and Zulkaïs; and the incestuous relationship which subsequently develops between the son and the daughter. The ambition of the emir does not, however, subside with the birth of two children; it is simply translated into an overwhelming desire to control the destinies of his offspring. In spite of the shift of interest then to the new characters, Kalilah and Zulkaïs, the emir remains a principal villain in the tale. "His sole end," Zulkaïs explains, "was to see his son become a great warrior, and a potent prince, and with regard to the character of the means by which that end was to be obtained, he cared not one twittle. As for me, he regarded me only as an instrument that might have its use" (190).

With the focus of attention in the story on the emotional relationship between Zulkaïs and Kalilah, Beckford returns to the theme of forbidden love. The image of the persecuted lovers who seek nothing more than exclusive happiness from a hostile society persists throughout the story. "Come," beckons Kalilah, "Let us bury ourselves among the trees. Let us, from our retreat, listen, disdainful, to the tumultous sound of music and dances. I will cause sherbet and cakes to be served on the moss that borders the little porphyry fountain. There I shall enjoy your sweet looks, and charming converse, till the first dawn of the new day" (p. 188). These soft, insinuating words are a call to move beyond "common day light" and "care worn visages" and to immure the self in a private realm beyond space and time where the light is warm and has the perpetual glow of summer.

This amoral world of Romantic estheticism is what Beckford strives to achieve — the world of Keats' nightingale or Edgar Allan Poe's artist-monarch. "Immure," a word that Beckford frequently used, expressed his solipsistic longing for seclusion and private happiness. This achievement inevitably involved shedding an old consciousness, symbolized by Shamelah in this tale, for a new visionary consciousness. "We will take into our veins the soft distillation of the flowers of the stream," Kalilah says to Zulkaïs, "which the Sages have so often vaunted in our hearing. That essence will lull us painlessly to sleep in each other's arms, and so bear our souls imperceptibly into the peace of another existence!" (189).

It matters little to the final interpretation whether Kalilah and Zulkaïs are seen as fictional representatives of Beckford and Courtenay or as two dramatized human beings that constitute a single personality — Beckford's. The two interpretations ultimately become one since the self for Beckford is the center of the universe; since even his relationship with Courtenay might be accurately described as self-devouring, an effort to discover his own image in his young friend; and since the same narcissistic tendency is characteristic of his art. The tragedy is that he can never sustain the vision in the water: it is inevitably disrupted by the intruding mundane world.

The concluding section of the manuscript of *The Story of the Princess Zulkaïs and the Prince Kalilah* has never been found among the Beckford papers, but what it contained can be gleaned from a reference among the unpublished notebooks of John Mitford to a Beckford tale in which a prince "had carnal connection with his sister, in the center of the great Pyramid."[32] That the two lovers remain victims of self-gratification to the end is apparent from their residence in Eblis. Indeed, the Vathekian character, like Ambrosio in Matthew Gregory Lewis' *The Monk*, inevitably loses his soul in a struggle to realize a fundamental self. It is the frustration of this great effort in the Kingdom of Eblis that provides the best image of Beckford, the artist-voluptuary, who, subjected inexorably to the furies of time and reason, must witness a failure of imagination and the ultimate collapse of his palace of art.

V   *Beyond Right and Wrong*

The Story of Prince Barkiarokh was announced in the Lausanne *Vathek* (1787) as the third history to be recited; the order was changed, however, to the second position in the Paris edition of 1787. Guy Chapman suggested that Barkiarokh's tale was very likely the first episode written after *Vathek:* "It is impossible to say which of the three surviving tales was written first; that of prince Barkiarokh may be suggested, since it is the least finished, the least 'experienced' of the three, and in which the grim humour is best woven into the texture of the tale."[33] Vaster in size than the other two episodes combined, it mirrors in structure Beckford's scheme of forming an ensemble of interlocking tales. Into the major framework of Barkiarokh's history, in other words, are interwoven three other secondary lives: "The Story of the Peri Homaïouna," "The Story of Barkiarokh's Younger Sister-in-Law," "The Story of Leilah, Barkiarokh's Daughter." From the standpoint of structure, therefore, this episode is much more complex than *Vathek.*

The Story of Prince Barkiarokh is darker, more cynical and pathetic, in tone than *Vathek.* A sense of evil pervades a good portion of the tale, but the somberness of *Vathek* is often relieved in it by the grotesque humor. Undoubtedly the same tale which Samuel Rogers described to Byron in 1818 as "full of unimaginable horrors," it is still regarded as "the most horrifying thing that Beckford ever wrote," horrifying because "the Prince has no redeeming feature and revels in evil."[34] Unlike the Caliph Vathek, Barkiarokh is not only always conscious of his own criminality but even views it as a mark of his superiority: "My crimes are even greater than those of the Calif Vathek. No rash and impious counsels hastened my ruin, as they have hastened his. If I am here, in this abode of horror, it is because I spurned the salutary advice oft repeated, of the most real and loving friend" (51). If Beckford could never achieve a sense of independence during the early years of his life in the real world of "little bustles and paltry concerns," he could at least create fictional characters who, in the world of imagination, indulged their emancipated egos. Beckford must have viewed the rational choice of evil in the face of all known laws and conventions as representing a maximum expression of the will. For Barkiarokh seeks this kind of freedom; and, in the process, he perhaps fulfilled the long-suppressed wish of his inhibited creator.

The story opens with a description of Barkiarokh's early life. He was born in Daghestan on the Caspian Sea and was the son of a fisherman named Ormossouf. He and two brothers are educated by the dervish Alsalami until they reach the age they can assume the responsibilities of manhood. Alsalami's teachings have little effect upon Barkiarokh, however; his unregenerate nature finds early expression in the form of dedicated hypocrisy. He decides to employ devious means to gain access to a cupboard in his father's house which contains a treasure promised to the most worthy son. To please his father, and thereby secure for himself the cupboard's treasure, Barkiarokh even agrees to become married. He selects for the sake of expediency the unknown woman Homaïouna whom he met accidentally on a street in Daghestan, and who turns out to be an exceptional being. Although modest in appearance, Homaïouna is of celestial origin, the daughter of the peri Asfendarmod. Homaiouna is Barkiarokh's guardian, his conscience in the story; but he resists her advice at every turn.

Moral law has no relevance for Barkiarokh: "We laughed at all restraints, holding that they had not been invented for people of our condition." He lives beyond the conventional distinctions between right and wrong. In crime after crime, he affirms this freedom of his self-seeking will. He seduces the beautiful Princess Gazahidé, daughter of the reigning king of Daghestan and then brutally suffocates the King to gain the throne. When Princess Gazahidé falls into a fit "that seemed to be accompanied by every symptom of death," Barkiarokh revels in necrophilia. "So dire an accident," he admits to the reader, "ought to have been as a curb to my passion; on the contrary, it acted as a spur." Other debaucheries include adultery, which he enjoys with the wife of Iman of the Great Mosque and others, until "pleasures so facile at last brought satiety" (128). Recognizing nothing as sacred or as forbidden, he convinces his two sisters-in-law that they must persuade their husbands to commit parricide. Then, in concert with the two women, he surprises the husbands at the very moment they have consummated their reckless act; and he orders that they be beheaded. Later, he murders his two female accomplices and casts their bodies into the sea.

Perverted self-will finds its most dramatic expression when Barkiarokh meets, for the first time, his daughter, Leilah, in a forest near Daghestan. She is guarding the body of her dead mother, Gazahidé, when he discovers her in a dwelling of caves and palm leaves. Concealing his true identity, Barkiarokh gains entrance to help with the burial proceedings; but, instead of remorse at the sight of the cadaver, he experiences sentiments of an entirely different order: "I experienced, at that terrible moment, nothing but wild, ungovernable passion, and vowed that my daughter, my own daughter, should ere long become my prey! I called on Eblis to give me success in this my sinister design; and immediately set to work to carry out Leilah's filial wish with regard to the interment of her mother's body, so as thus to gain her confidence, and ultimately bring her into my arms!" (150). Barkiarokh's incestuous designs are ultimately thwarted by Homaïouna, however, who rescues Leilah at the moment that she and her father begin the descent into the subterranean halls of Eblis. Barkiarokh then receives the fate of Vathek, "I was hurled down into the crowd of the damned — with whom I am destined, like yourselves, O my wretched companions, to be whirled about for ever, bearing in my heart the fearful furnace of flame which I have myself prepared and ignited" (161).

Much in *The Story of Barkiarokh* anticipates the dark side of Edgar Allan Poe. Beckford's own preoccupation with morbid subjects, his temperamental concern about malice and perversity, and the sometimes unearthly character of the tale would doubtless have led him to have had a keen appreciation of "The Fall of the House of Usher" had he ever received the opportunity to read it. Poe, like Byron, admired Vathek; and he even cited in "Landor's Cottage" the "infernal terrace seen by Vathek, [which] était d'une architecture inconnue dans les annales de la terre."[35] Poe's other allusions to Beckford in "Thou Art the Man," "The Domain of Arnheim," and "Ligeia" suggest that Beckford had clearly excited Poe's imagination. Poe would have found in Barkiarokh a reflection of his own sense of the grotesque as well as the "fascination of the abyss." Baudelaire once said of Poe that he had revived "the great forgotten truth — the primordial perversity of man."[36] Beckford's fascination with this "primitive irresistible force" in *Barkiarokh*, clothed in the formula of an exotic genre, represents an earlier resuscitation of this dark truth.

VI   *The* Episodes *and* Vathek

Taken as a whole, the *Episodes* pale in comparison to *Vathek;* for its opulent imagery, its picturesque detail, its richly atmospheric qualities, though not lacking in the companion-pieces, are considerably toned down in these later tales. Yet, at the same time, a deepening of interest appears in these later works in the subject of evil that is united with the dominant Beckfordian theme of ambition. Following in the footsteps of the insatiable Caliph Vathek, the leading characters in the *Episodes* demonstrate the same hunger for forbidden pleasures; and their ruthless egotism leads similarly to a renunciation of all that is orthodox in a civilized world. Beckford's goal seems to be to give full play to the repressed passions of Western society — to allow untrammeled indulgence in a variety of excesses in spite of his occasional salutes to morality. To a more intense degree than in *Vathek*, furthermore, Beckford seems interested in exposing the appeal of evil, a radical commitment that he has in common with the Gothic novelists of his day. Consequently, evil is revealed in these tales with such energy and power that it is convincingly embraced for itself with only token regard for frustrating law or custom.

If the virtuous characters and the orthodox believers are seen in the fantasy world of the *Episodes* as insipid weaklings in contrast to the followers of Eblis, they seem so because Beckford, living momentarily in a world of his own making, deliberately reverses the traditional scale of values. With sudden abandon, he gleefully highlights the impotency of virtue against the virility of vice through the major portion of these additional tales; but as if aware that the fiction of freedom cannot be sustained, he makes his villain-heroes submit in the end in a token way to conventional justice. In a kind of horrible irony, of which Beckford himself may not have been conscious, there is even a Beckfordian luxury in such damnation — a luxury which is ultimately denied the faithful.

CHAPTER 8

The Light of Maturity

BECKFORD'S literary output diminished in the years that followed the writing of *The Episodes of Vathek.* Early discouragement — depression over the death of his wife, the Powderham scandal, the frustrating suppression of *Dreams, Waking Thoughts and Incidents,* and the premature publication of *Vathek* — explain in part his reluctance to take up the pen as often as he had in the past. Furthermore, between 1786 and 1796 he was frequently on the Continent in virtual exile from England. Aside from fragmentary notebooks he kept at hand, to which he returned in later life to revise and publish, his literary muse seldom stirred at this time. Whatever creative energy he had was dissipated quickly in a weary cycle of balls and banquets in Portugal, Spain, and France and in collecting rare books and paintings throughout his travels.

Beckford's creative energies took a different turn in 1796, however, when he began to devote his time to landscape gardening on the family estate at Fonthill. This was not an unusual pastime for a writer. Alexander Pope, William Shenstone, and Horace Walpole, to name a few, had carried out garden experiments on their own estates before him, and landscape architecture ranked high as one of the "sister arts" in eighteenth-century England. The Fonthill property was extensive, and its woods, hills, and water served as a stimulus to a man with an eye for naturalistic design. Throughout the countryside of this large estate Beckford could find another challenge to his artistic imagination, and he could live in exile from a society that had turned its back on him. "In their deep fastnesses," he wrote of Fonthill's woods and groves, "I will hide myself from this world, and never allow its glare to bicker through my foliage."[1]

With a scheme in mind that rivaled the epic gardens at Stourhead and Longleat, Beckford began the serious business of bringing to life all the latent beauties of 519 acres of natural landscape. More than one million trees were planted, avenues were laid out, vistas were opened, paths were cut through the dense woods, and a twenty-seven mile ride, encircling the entire estate, was created to provide the necessary points of view. From 1796 Beckford personally directed over one hundred laborers working by day and sometimes by torchlight at night to realize his vision of a "picturesque garden composition." He also engaged a prominent British architect, James Wyatt, to erect a massive neo-Gothic abbey as the central feature in the general design. For the next twenty-six years Beckford devoted his imaginative powers to laying out the grounds immediately surrounding this exotic building and produced in the end what was called "the most remarkable seat in the West of England."[2]

I *Excursions into Satire:* Modern Novel Writing *and* Azemia

Overseeing the activities of the Fonthill Abbey estate consumed much of Beckford's time, but there was a sudden resurgence of literary activity in the late 1790's. Nine years had passed since his work on *The Episodes of Vathek,* and then in 1796 he published *Modern Novel Writing, or the Elegant Enthusiast* under the pseudonym of Lady Harriet Marlow. This volume was followed almost immediately by *Azemia: A Descriptive and Sentimental Novel* (1797) which Beckford published under the name of Jacquetta Agneta Mariana Jenks. No information exists as to the composition history of either book. The identification of Beckford as the author, in fact, rests on the testimony of the poets Thomas Moore and Samuel Rogers and that of Beckford's first biographer Cyrus Redding. The only evidence from Beckford himself that he wrote *Modern Novel Writing* is his hand-written statement in a personal copy of the book, which reads: "W. B. Presentation copy from the divine authoress."[3]

Reminiscent of the satiric style of *Biographical Memoirs of Extraordinary Painters,* both books were designed in part to ridicule the sentimental and sensational novels of the day. Elizabeth Hervey, Beckford's half-sister, is usually identified as the principal object of the attack for her works in the sentimental vein, particularly *Louisa; or the Reward of an Affectionate Daughter* (1790). It is more likely, however, that Beckford was thinking of the general proliferation of sentimental and even Gothic novels in the 1780's and 1790's, particularly if they were authored by women. At the end of *Azemia,* in fact, he provided a list of the authors parodied, including Fanny Burney, Ann Radcliffe, Sophia Lee, Charlotte Smith, Helen Maria

Williams, Elizabeth Inchbald, Elizabeth Gunning, and Maria Robinson. And in 1821 Beckford revealed how he felt about such authors. "It might be as well," he wrote, "if instead of weaving historical romances the super-literary ladies of the present period would pass a little more of their time at cross stitch and yabble stitch. We should gain some pretty chair and screen covers and lose little by not being tempted to pore over the mazes of their interminable scribbleations."[4]

In *Modern Novel Writing* Beckford manages to highlight almost all of the most flagrant excesses of the fashionable novelists of the day. Instead of a carefully articulated plot, for example, he presents the reader with a patchwork of incidents — poorly constructed and crowded with irrelevant detail. As in the novels he parodies, the characters tend to appear and disappear without purpose or meaning. Bombast replaces natural speech for the purpose of giving expression to the false sentiment and overstrained emotions that pervade the book. An exquisite type of poetry, which is interspersed throughout the novel, is also in keeping with the conventions of the sentimental school:

> Love is a soft, involuntary flame,
>   Beyond the pow'r of language to express;
> That throws resistless magic o'er the frame,
>   And leads to boundless pleasure or distress.[5]

There is a painfully familiar heroine, Arabella Bloomville, who, like Pamela, can swoon in the face of indecency. Lord Mahogany, the pursuing villain, is an exaggerated version of Samuel Richardson's Lovelace who ultimately expires while giving a speech. The hero, Henry Lambert, with his bright hazel eyes, a nose "inclined to the Grecian" and a complexion "fair as alabaster," is the stylized Man of Feeling. "O matchless effervescence of human happiness," he confesses to Arabella, "divine empress of my soul, I have languished for ages to behold thee, I have been burnt up and consumed by the unquenchable fire of exhaustless passion" (2:145). Henry's problem is also not without precedent: he finds it impossible to propose marriage to Arabella because of her exalted rank. But the deterrent is removed before long, and the two lovers are allowed to unite in marriage to live happily ever after as "Lord and Lady Laughable." In these ways Beckford demonstrates the flaws of sentimental fiction.

Modern Novel Writing has a much wider scope, however, than its title suggests. A great deal of space is devoted to political satire against the Tory Party and its leader William Pitt. Interspersed among the nonsense in this book are moments of lucidity given over to attacking the government's policy of war against France. Lord Mahogany's speech in the throes of his final illness illustrates this point: "I might have given my vote for peace! but O! 'twas war, war, war! how they bleed! thousands, ten thousands dead! Such a waste of murder! . . . O! this cursed war — I voted for it — how it burns my brain. . . . O conscience, conscience! — the troops march — alas! — the war is mine. . . . murder, war, murder cannot go unpunished. . . . Bottle up the war in a cornfield, and put my vote in hell" (2:39, 42, 44, 46, 48). In another section, Beckford satirizes Pitt's government for such repressive measures as the Treasonable Practices Act and Seditious Meetings Act of 1795 which aimed at frustrating "just remonstrances" of the people. These acts ensured "a dead silence throughout the nation," which Beckford identifies as "THE ISLAND OF MUM" (2:99–101). Finally, at the conclusion of the novel, he lodges a devastating attack against the writers in *The British Critic* and against other supporters of Pitt by ironically approving their point of view:

> To your virtues, liberality, and candour, the whole nation can bear testimony, for I defy the most impudent of your detractors to shew a single instance amongst all your writings, where you have spoken favorably of any work that was base enough to vindicate the hoggish herd of the people, that was mean enough to object to any measures of the present wise and incorruptible administration, or that was cowardly enough to censure the just and necessary war in which the nation is now so fortunately engaged. No, ye worthy magistrates of the mind! You have exerted your civil jurisdiction with meritorious perseverence, and if at any time you have stepped forth as warriors to defend the exclusive privileges of the *FEW*, against the vulgar attacks of the *MANY*, your demeanor has been truly gallant, you have thrown your lances with a grace, becoming the most renowned Knights of chivalry, and have hurled your anathemas at the murmuring multitude with a dignified fury that would have done honour to Peter the Hermit, or to the chief of the Holy Inquisition. (2:229–30)

The second novel, *Azemia*, expands the personal and political satire of *Modern Novel Writing*. Beckford's liberalism — his fundamentally humanitarian spirit — comes into full play in an attack on antidemocratic ideas. Once again William Pitt is the main object of the political satire. In a mock ode Beckford castigates the Prime Minister:

All he does is grand and daring,
    All he says is right and fit;
Never let us then be sparing
    In the praise of Mister Pitt.

Who, like him, can prate down reason,
    Who so well on taxes hit?
Who detect a plot of treason
    Half so well as Mister Pitt?

. . . .

He the multitude is humbling,
    Britons that doth well befit:
Swinish crowds, who minds your grumbling?
    Bow the knee to Mister Pitt.

Tho' abroad our men are dying,
    Why should he his projects quit?
What are orphans, widows, crying,
    To our steady Mister Pitt?[6]

Inflation, repressive legislation, rising debt, decline of the farmer, mistreatment of the poor, and the apathy of the rich are also objects of Beckford's concern in the book. "I would not have the rich live much worse than they do," he writes, "but I would have the poor supported a great deal better" (2:160). These liberal political views were unusual for a member of the English landowner class in 1797 and seem more appropriate for William Godwin than Beckford. But the Whig tradition of Beckford's father had apparently some measure of influence on him, while the personal tragedies Beckford had suffered in the 1780's, and particularly his ostracism from English society, also help to explain his unorthodox political opinions at this time.

The parody of the sentimental novel also continues in *Azemia* but with little variation. A better written and more coherent book than *Modern Novel Writing*, *Azemia* is a tale of a Turkish girl captured by a British man-of-war and brought to England where she becomes separated from her lover, a handsome sailor, and, after a number of misadventures, is finally united with him. Beckford gives his heroine a Turkish background, but she is still the English stereotype of what is referred to in the novel as "soul dissolving tale[s] . . . printed at the

Minerva press" (1:20). "Take something from . . . the Pamela of Richardson," Beckford writes, "borrow a little from the Sophia of Fielding, and the Narcissa of Smollet, and a feature, a look, an air, from what thou canst imagine of the favourite heroines of the inferior and more modern schools: and having done so, and composed a figure and face . . . thou mayest then, peradventure, furnish thyself with some resemblance of my attractive Mussulman, my charming Azemia" (1:27–28).

What is apparent from both *Azemia* and *Modern Novel Writing* is that in Beckford's mind Richardson's form of sentimentalism had now become the province of second- and third-rate novelists. Furthermore, these new sentimental novels were being aided by the proliferation of circulating libraries near the end of the century. Beckford feared that by making such inferior novels readily available the circulating libraries were fostering a taste for them. Particularly troublesome to Beckford was that the sentimental view of reality seemed an absurd defense against the harsh realities of war, poverty, and political oppression in the 1790's. Sensibility carried to such extremes seemed strangely unrealistic at a time when more realism and good sense were needed. And it is on this point that the political and sentimental strains of these two novels come together. For Beckford, circulating-library novels provided a vision of life that was equivalent to the political schemes of Pitt's government — both were equally irrational.

As a novelist with a taste for the bizarre, Beckford, of course, had been guilty of his own kind of extravagances. But *Modern Novel Writing* and *Azemia* mark a period in his life when the child was finally giving way to the man. Close to forty, he was no longer quite willing to abandon himself to all the wildness of his imagination as he had done so often in the past.

II *Fonthill Abbey and the Beckford Legend*

In spite of their importance in the light they shed on Beckford's character, *Modern Novel Writing* and *Azemia* seem more like digressions compared to his obsession with building and landscaping at this time. The two novels fell quickly into obscurity, while Fonthill began adding to his celebrity. The British newspapers reported in 1807 that Beckford had ordered the demolition of the family mansion, after having taken up permanent residence in his self-appointed monastic structure, Fonthill Abbey. The whole was a remarkable private dwelling in its day, much more sublime and mysterious than the "Gothic mousetrap" of Strawberry Hill. Situated on the brow of a hill, Fonthill Abbey took the shape of a huge cross in its final form, 312 feet long from north to south and 270 feet from east to west, in the center of which rose the octagonal tower 276 feet high. As the building continued, the rumors spread rapidly that Fonthill was the scene of nightly revelries and sexual orgies organized by Beckford and his disreputable servants, one of whom, it was said, was a mad dwarf. But this kind of gossip made Fonthill even more irresistible as an object of curiosity. As Guy Chapman pointed out, rumor actually nurtured the growing Beckford legend: "By the curious processes of rumour, Beckford was emerging from that long period of oblivion, from which no earlier effort had been able to extricate him. Now his ostentatious seclusion brought him celebrity, the illusion of greatness, which the antics of five-and-twenty years in the public eye had failed to win him. The legend that was to recreate him in the forty years of life still left, was beginning; the millionaire and his incredible Gothic building became by-words, were improved on and enlarged."[7]

The interest in Fonthill and Beckford reached such a fever pitch in England within the next few years that it became increasingly difficult to discuss either the building or its master in prosaic terms. Samuel Rogers' impressions of his visit to Fonthill, as they were conveyed by Lady Bessborough in a contemporary letter, illustrates this point:

He was received by a dwarf who, like a crowd of servants thro' whom he pass'd, was covered with gold and embroidery. Mr. Beckford receiv'd him very courteously, and led him thro' numberless apartments including precious stones; another the finest pictures; another Italian bronzes, china, etc., till they came to a gallery that surpass'd all the rest from the richness and variety of its ornaments. It seem'd clos'd by a crimson drapery held by a bronze statue, but on Mr. B's stamping and saying, "Open!" the statue flew back, and the gallery was seen extending 350 feet long. At the end an open arch with a massive balustrade opened to a vast Octagon Hall, from which a window shew'd a fine view of the park. On approaching this, it proved to be the entrance to the famous tower — higher than Salisbury Cathedral: this is not finish'd, but a great part is done. The doors, of which there are many, are violent velvet covered over with purple and gold embroidery. They pass'd from hence to a chapel, where on the altar were heap'd golden candlesticks, vases, and chalices studded over with jewels; and from there into a great musick room, where Mr. Beckford begg'd Mr. Rogers to rest till refreshments were ready, and began playing with such unearthly power that Mr. Rogers says he never before had any idea how delighted one might be

with him, that he thinks Lady Douglas fails in the comparison. They went
on to what is called the refectory, a large room built on the model of Henry 7
Chapel, only the ornaments gilt, where a verdantique table was loaded with
gilt plate fill'd with every luxury invention could collect. They next went
into the park with a numerous cortege, and horses, and servants, etc., which
he describes as equally wonderful, from the beauty of the trees and shrubs,
and manner of arranging them, thro' a ride of five mile. They were met at
setting out by a flock of tame hares, that Mr. Beckford feeds; then phea-
sants, then partridges; and lastly came to a beautiful romantick lake, transparent as *liquid Chrysolite* cover'd with wildfowl. Mr. R. was hardly arrived
at the Inn before a present of game follows him, and a note beginning the
unfortunate Vathek was too sensible of the favour conferr'd upon him by
Mr. Rogers's visit not to keep something back to allure him to a repetition of
it, and then pressing him so strongly to return next day that he did so, and
then was shewn thro' another suite of apartments, filled with fine medals,
gems, enamell'd miniatures, drawings old and modern, curios, prints, and
manuscripts, and lastly a fine and well furnish'd library, all the books richly
bound, and the best edition, etc., etc. An old abbe, the librarian, and Mr.
Smith, the water colour painter, who were there, told him there were 60 fires
always kept burning, except in the hottest weather. Near every chimney in
the sitting rooms there were large gilt fillagree baskets fill'd with perfum'd
coal that produc'd the brightest flame.[8]

As Beckford's legend grew so did his literary reputation. In 1809
the English version of *Vathek* was reissued and then followed by the
appearance of the French edition in London in 1815 and in Paris in
1819. With the new reprintings *Vathek* became more widely known
and, once linked with the name of Beckford, sufficiently popular to
merit three separate London issues in 1816 and a printing in
America in the same year, where it was sold in Boston and
Philadelphia for the first time.[9] The subduing eye of Vathek and the
flaming Hall of Eblis were now beginning to become firmly fixed in
the minds of the reading public.

The 1820's were difficult financial years for Beckford. Never one
for money matters, he was unaware until too late that his fortune
was dwindling. For many years his coffers were full. Indeed, Byron's
label, "England's wealthiest son," was not without some justifica-
tion. But Fonthill was a drain, costly to build and costly to maintain.
And there was Beckford's passion for collecting books, paintings,
and objets d'art which seemed to grow in intensity when the financial strain was most acute. What income he could expect from the
family sugar plantations in Jamaica had been diminishing rapidly
after 1799, particularly when the slave trade in the West Indies was

abolished. Threatened with ruin, he moved desperately to recoup by mortgaging the estate for £70,000, but the 5% annual interest only increased his indebtedness and further drastic measures were forced upon him.[10] The inevitable result, one he long tried to avoid, was to sell Fonthill, with its buildings, land, and superb works of art. Thus to the astonishment of English society, the newspapers announced suddenly in 1822 that Fonthill was up for auction, and in a matter of weeks the deed passed to a gunpowder manufacturer, John Farquhar, for £300,000. "The pleasing vision is now past," the *Gentleman's Magazine* reported; the caliph had relinquished his palace.

III   Bath: The Final Phase

The spa of Bath became Beckford's new home: there he remained writing, gardening, and collecting for the concluding twenty-one years of his life. He acquired two houses in Lansdown Crescent and a considerable portion of the adjacent land, where he proceeded to create a miniature Fonthill. Still ardent in his pursuit of the picturesque, he began to change the barren grounds into woodlands and gardens and on the summit of Lansdown hill ordered the erection of a 130-foot tower in the Classical style, which would be crowned by a model of the Choragic monument of Lysicrates. This became his retreat for study and contemplation and a vantage point from which he could observe the distant scenery in the light of day and, like Vathek, the configurations of the stars in the dark of night.

He intended a secluded life in Bath, but he enjoyed more notoriety than ever before. The continued public interest in Fonthill, even after the dramatic sale, helped to make him one of England's most talked-about men. He was in his sixties now, a man both despised and respected, sought after and shunned. Stories of the Courtenay affair revived, and, when these no longer satisfied the taste for gossip, new tales were manufactured about the bevy of dwarfs who were said to inhabit Beckford's Lansdown house. Curious travelers to Bath inevitably inquired about him; sometimes they found their way to "Lansdown Bagdad" in the hope of catching a glimpse of the strange owner. Capitalizing on this popularity, William Clarke, the bookseller, brought out a new English edition of *Vathek* in 1823. This time William Hazlitt reviewed it in a London paper, calling it a "masterly performance" with "extraordinary power of thought and facility of execution."[11] The following year the second edition of *Biographical Memoirs of Extraordinary Painters*

was published, further assurance that Beckford's name would not
fade from public consciousness.

The 1830's were changing times for England. The march of
science, industrialism, and democracy in the previous century had
profoundly altered national ways and ideals, and the arts were affected as seriously as the other extensions of man. Shelley, Byron,
and Keats were dead; their works would be revived much later as
part of a golden era in the history of literature. William Hazlitt died
in 1830, followed shortly thereafter by other contemporaries who
made art synonymous with feeling: Sir Walter Scott, Samuel T.
Coleridge, and Charles Lamb. The citadels of the Romantic Age
were falling one by one. Only William Wordsworth lived on until
1850, but his voice had grown thin and strangely out of tune with a
world "seared with trade; bleared, smeared with toil."

The poets and authors in vogue in the new age were those who
found significance in seams of iron and beds of coal. The Romantic's
interest in the colorful past and private confessions of the heart, gave
way to a deep social consciousness of contemporary problems and a
more practical regard for the calloused hand of labor. Gradually the
factory town replaced the shepherd's field as the Victorians felt the
need to give a strong voice to the urban industrial worker.

For Beckford himself, the 1830's foreshadowed national ruin.
"For want of judgment," he wrote of the times, "the day of judgment is drawing terrifically near."[12] He was sixty-nine years of age
when the decade began, old enough to have observed the change
brought about during the whole cycle of the Industrial Revolution
— old enough to lament the passing of the old aristocratic society of
the eighteenth century and the birth of the machine-dominated
nineteenth. He witnessed with dismay the development of a railway
system in England, and when the Reform Bill was passed in 1832,
giving direct political power to the middle class, he felt it invited
anarchy and bloodshed, the downfall of the government. As he
wrote to the son of a Swiss friend, these so-called "symptoms of
progress" were really signs of decay:

Nowhere is there any Country — the forests are being cut down, the mountains violated — one only sees canals for the rivers are disregarded — Gas
and steam is everywhere — the same smell, the same puffs of dreadful
smoke, thick and foetid — the same common and commercial view on every
side: a deadening monotony and an impious artifice spits every minute in
the face of Mother Nature, who will soon find her children transformed to
Automata and Machines.[13]

In spite of the ominous clouds gathering on the national horizon, Beckford continued to lead an active life in the 1830's. He was seldom idle; he had his many interests — his books, his prints, his gardens — to fill his days. Although he rarely indulged himself in the pleasures of writing, he did take up his pen, if only for a brief period, to produce two travel books based upon his early tours in Europe. The first was a diluted version of *Dreams, Waking Thoughts and Incidents*, bearing the title of *Italy; with Sketches of Spain and Portugal;* the book came out in 1834 and quickly ran through more editions before the year end.

The decision to sell *Dreams* in an expurgated form was Beckford's. He revised heavily as he read through one of the few surviving copies, touching page after page with a careful editor's hand. In the end most of the changes were omissions: he pared the text of *Dreams* closer to the bone and in the process changed its character. He cut away the personal allusions and the anecdotes that might in any way make the persistent rumors about his homosexual nature more credible; he slashed passages brimming with sentimentality; he eliminated the dream machinery along with the excessive flights of imagination; the art criticism, which bulked large in the book, he qualified and made less rhapsodic. In short, he gave the book a general toning down in an obvious effort to avoid extravagance of any kind. The result was that the 1834 volume became cooler in tone, more Classical in character, exhibiting greater restraint of imagination and propriety of expression and a more formal decorum throughout. *Dreams,* on the other hand, was freer, more spontaneous and more passionate. It reflected the young Beckford, spoiled, undisciplined, eager to display his artistic sensibilities, an artist absorbed with his own image. *Italy* reflected the seventy-three-year-old man whose youthful ardor had cooled, whose tastes and spirit had tempered with age.

Italy was almost an immediate sensation on the Continent and in America. In fact, the enthusiastic reception was more than Beckford had anticipated. Tallyrand dubbed it "The Book," while John Gibson Lockhart predicted that "Mr. Beckford's Travels will henceforth be classed amongst the most elegant productions of modern literature."[14]

Stirred by the recognition, Beckford brought forth his last travelogue, *Recollections of an Excursion to the Monasteries of Alcobaça and Batalha,* in the following year. This book was based on a visit to Portugal in 1794 and specifically to the two great monasteries of Alcobaça and Batalha. Beckford, as was his habit,

kept at the time some some "slight notes of this Excursion" in a
small journal. Forty years later he "invoked the powers of memory
and up rose the whole series of recollections."[15]

The *Excursion,* covering as it does a period of only twelve days, is
spare in content. But critics have found it to be one of Beckford's
most impressive literary compositions — a "masterpiece of experience," as Charles Whibly called it.[16] It contains none of the com-
placent, tedious material which was the usual fare for most travel
books of the period; nor does it bear any similarity to their style and
manner of presentation. Rose Macaulay, one of the most perceptive
judges of Beckford's travel writings, admired particularly the sup-
pleness and ease of Beckford's prose, "so unlike the prim, stilted,
ponderous, didactic style of most of his fellow travellers."[17]

In the *Excursion,* Beckford is always the perceptive guide, drawing the reader's attention to the kind of minute and particular objects of experience that are usually only unconsciously received by
the traveler. The artistic eye is ever present; the detail sharply
delineated. The same taste for pageantry and amusing interest in
pampered luxury, so evident in *Vathek* and in *Italy,* revives in the
Excursion. Each page provides a scene along the journey that arrests
the reader's attention as if newly and freshly recognized. The conversation in the book, so often touched by irony, sparkles with the
fullness of life. And there is, as in *Italy,* those moments when a
Wordsworthian love for Nature is in evidence, as when, on the
eighth day, Beckford records: "I pant like a hart for living waters: I
am determined to follow the course of the river I noticed yesterday,
winding its fresh sparkling stream between aromatic thickets."[18]

But the *Excursion,* at the same time, differs significantly from *Italy* in tone and in the degree of Classical self-effacement the author
tried to achieve. The *Excursion* is Beckford's most light-hearted
work, filled with the humor and detachment that he could not
achieve in his younger days. The light of maturity penetrates more
deeply; the personal frustration and uncertainty of the past has sub-
sided. Guy Chapman admirably summed up this essential quality in
his observations about the work: "In the *Excursion,* for the first time
and only time all the contradictions of his character are harmonised.
There is no conscience pricking, nothing morbid. It is a happy book,
a book of remembered pleasures, written by an old man with all the
fire, exuberance and vivacity of youth, with an eye that recalls each
detail of a scene, a voice, an attitude, a gesture, which relishes every

incident whether it be beautiful or melancholy or grotesque. It is as if he had experienced these joys but yesterday."[19]

The remaining years of Beckford's life were relatively quiet and without serious interruption. Age gained on him, but in spite of it, he remained remarkably fit. He had outlasted all of his friends. Death, he frequently quipped, had overlooked him. Still slender and in good form he looked more like a man of fifty than one of seventy-five. He still had handsome features: a sharp, aquiline nose, lightening gray eyes, and hair the color of frost. Moreover, the passage of time had failed to impair his physical and mental energy. "A day with him," writes H. A. N. Brockman, "must at this time have been somewhat of an ordeal. His rapid, staccato conversation, his bustling energy, his endless knowledge of his own collections, all contributed to the mental and physical exhaustion of his guests. The heaviest volumes he would hoist from their places and bear to the light so as to show them, refusing aid and brusquely demanding visitors' interest. . . . The profusion of furniture he disregarded in his perambulations, leaping over the ebony stools and benches that were in his way. In showing off his tower he would mount the stairs with the greatest energy. Providing carriages for his guests, he himself would take horse and in a fast gallop down his mile-long turfed ride, he would outstrip the vehicles and be waiting to receive the visitors on their return to the house."[20]

Faithfully once a year Beckford traveled to London, where he renewed acquaintances and rummaged through the shops of selected picture dealers and booksellers. The result of these visits was the sizeable collection of fine books and pictures which was stored in the house and tower at Lansdown. His private library was one of the largest in all of England, and when it was auctioned during the famous Hamilton Palace sale of 1882–83, it brought £73,551. The collection of pictures he gradually accumulated ranked among the finest of his day. Sixteen of his paintings are hanging in the National Gallery today; and they include such important items as "Agony in the Garden" by Giovanni Bellini, "Poulterer's Shop" by Gerard Dow, "St. Catherine of Alexandria" by Raphael, "Adoration of the Kings" by Fillippino Lippi, and "Calling of Abraham" by Gaspar Poussin. Hazlitt was indeed mistaken when he once said that Beckford had "no picture of remarkable eminence that can be ranked as a heir-loom of the imagination."[21]

When the 1840's came, Beckford, now in his eighties, began to

prepare for the inevitable. "Certain twitches of Rheumatism —
pains in the eyelids and other effects of sharp humours," he wrote at
this time, "remind me that I am mortal. . . . for my part I am
perfectly resigned — perfectly ready to quit the moment proper
notice in the shape of acute disease is given."[22] Proper notice would
not be given until 1844; in the meantime, he drew up the designs for
his own sarcophagus, a large piece of rust-colored granite for which
he paid £511. Why leave this work to some tasteless executor who
might easily botch the job? He ordered it to be erected near his
tower in the adjoining garden — near his other creations — where
its quiet color would be "in perfect harmony with the surrounding
vegetation."

By the end of 1843 he fell ill with serious attacks of gout and
rheumatism. His eighty-three-year-old body fought back during the
bitter cold months that followed. Confined to his house most of the
time, he brooded, spoke bitterly of the changing times, and grew
morose over his feelings of isolation and loneliness. He longed for
the presence of his daughter, the Duchess of Hamilton, but she lived
too distant from Lansdown to make frequent trips. When spring approached without signs of relief, he wrote to his son-in-law:

At length it has pleased Heaven to grant us a few indications of Spring —
a light greenish gauze begins to extend itself over my miniature forests upon
Landsdown — the grass awakes — the breath of violets is no longer repressed — the lambs have found their delicately thin nourishment — I hear
on all sides upon the sod the almost imperceptible sound of their nibblings.

> Gia riede primavera
> Now spring returns, but not to me return
> Those thrilling joys my vernal years have known.

In the midst of this sweet revival, and of this pastoral charm I remain — alas
— sad and sickly — I am not tired of life, but life is tired of me.[23]

Finally on May 2, 1844 after a bout with influenza Beckford died in
an unadorned truckle bed — an odd contrast to his life of luxury and
refinements. At his side lay an open book, the last he read —
Nicholas Wiseman's *Lectures on Science and Revealed Religion* —
with marginal notes in Beckford's hand on almost every page.

IV   *Beneath the Mask*

From any survey of Beckford's life and works, the character of the
man only dimly emerges. He was a complex personality, an elusive

figure to pursue, and it may be a fruitless task to attempt to completely understand him from the traces that remain. He was an enigma even to those who might be called his friends. Yet of all the contemporary accounts of Beckford, and there were many, one stands out as at least representative of the many personal impressions recorded by those persons admitted to his circle. Published anonymously in the *New Monthly Magazine* shortly after his death, an article entitled "Conversations with the late W. Beckford Esq. Contributed by Various Friends" described Beckford in this way:

Every thing he talked upon was made interesting, either from not being generally known, or from its being instructive by the judicious keenness of his observations. It appeared to me that he elaborately studied every thing, so as to permanently fix in his mind an honest and decided view — that when called upon, he had not, like the generality of mankind, to deliver a judgment which is formed upon the demand of the moment. His opinion was the offspring of reflection. He had the courage to be honest, and his being free from the trammels of personal friendship, enabled him to speak without fear of offending. He has often said severe and reproving things to me, but in such a kind and ingenuous manner, that I felt he truly esteemed me by so doing. If the author of "Vathek" could be chilling and severe, where conceit and folly were conspicuous, his praise could likewise swell into bursts of the sincerest admiration at what was truly good. . . . His mind stood alone, like a splendid firmament, extending over the vast worlds of intellect; but that mind was not to be won by the worship of false idolatry. Woe to him who offered adulation to the author of "Vathek," for sure was his insight into the workings of the heart.[24]

Thus it was as a man of mature intelligence and taste that his friends and acquaintances in Bath knew him. This view of Beckford depicts him in his later years after time had contributed much to quiet the anguish of his youth. The recession of days poignantly associated with the early domestic storms, the scandal, the loss of his wife — the days of blasted promise — produced on the whole a more sober, reflective man. But this surely is not all that he was.

There was another Beckford; there was the discontented artist, suffering from the painful recognition that he had not fulfilled his destiny. The resulting malaise was submerged beneath the aged mask in Bath, but occasionally it broke through, the same bitterness reminiscent of bygone days — the 1780's and 1790's. The little description printed in the *New Monthly Magazine* fails to portray, in other words, the Beckford of *The Vision*, of *Vathek*, of the *Episodes*, a man engaged in a complicated struggle with himself. As early as

1793 Henri Meister perceived in Beckford a vitiated talent, spoiled by wealth and fortune, excessively given to the old and the whimsical. Swinburne in 1876, looking back over Beckford's life, spied the same canker of unfulfillment. The melancholia and consuming malaise, the bitterness and cold cynicism so often seen in Beckford's character may well have been the products of an ever-deepening belief that he had aborted his genius and trifled away his existence and that he had in the end fulfilled the sad prophecy of his youth. "I fear I shall never be . . . good for anything in the world," he wrote when he was only twenty, "but composing airs, building towers, forming gardens, collecting old Japan, and writing a journey to China or the moon."[25]

Beckford as a personality will always be a tantalizing subject to pursue. But what about his literary achievement? Doubtless his output was small, for it must be measured in pages, not in volumes. Yet today, more than one hundred years after his decease, he is recognized as a "standard author" and occupies a significant place in the literature of his age, and this was accomplished largely on the strength of his masterwork *Vathek*. There is little doubt that his literary reputation has been firmly anchored in this book in spite of the excellence of his neglected travel writings. The question remains, therefore, what influence, if any, did *Vathek* have on the imaginative literature of the nineteenth century?

CHAPTER 9

The Haunting Image

THE kind of Oriental awareness which contributed to the exotic quality of *Vathek* and gave it credibility as a relative of the *Arabian Nights* became widespread in British culture by the opening of the nineteenth century. A significant number of major writers of the Romantic period used the themes and the coloring of the Orient with as much zest as Beckford had. These writers also continued to deepen the realistic trend of this genre by endeavoring to be faithful to the style, the language, and the literature of the Orient. When Coleridge came under the sway of the East, he manifested the tendency of his era to translate raw fact into the world of fiction. It is almost superfluous to recall that the original inspiration for *Kubla Khan* (1798) was Samuel Purchas' *Pilgrimage:* "In Xamdu did Cublai Can build a stately Palace, encompassing sixteen miles of plaine ground with a wall, wherein all fertile Meddowes, pleasant springs, delightful Streames, and all sorts of beasts of chase and game, and in the middest thereof a sumptuous house of pleasure."[1]

Poets like Southey, Byron, and Moore experienced an even greater need than Coleridge to be Orientalists. Southey's *Thalaba* (1801) drew heavily from several books on Mohammedan religion, and the mythology of India served as the basis for his *The Curse of Kehama* (1810). Knowledge of Eastern legends and modes of thought clearly fascinated Byron and helped him to produce such works as *The Giaour* (1813), *The Corsair* (1814), and *Sardanapalus* (1815). So familiar was Thomas Moore with Sir William Jones' translations and with various encyclopedias of the East that it has been said of his Oriental tales, particularly *Lalla Rookh* (1817), that they have "the appearance of being written by a man who has spent a great part of his life in these regions."[2]

I *Beckford's Influence*

To what extent, it might be asked, did Beckford influence these or, perhaps, other writers of the nineteenth century? *Vathek*, of course, is the only work in his Oriental canon that could have left a mark on this age; and Beckford scholars have long claimed that the peculiar circumstances surrounding its initial publication in 1786 prevented it from creating any immediate stir. Beckford, himself, made the book an excessively rare item on the market; for, after discovering that Henley's translation had been published, he bought up the remaining sheets of the edition from Joseph Johnson before it had a chance to circulate widely. Three French and three German editions followed within two years, but no new English edition appeared until 1809. This delay of twenty years is responsible for conclusions, such as the one drawn by Guy Chapman, that *Vathek* had "lost its power to influence." "Had *Vathek* had its chance in 1786," Chapman wrote, "it is conceivable that it might have had a considerable following among the novelists of the day."[3]

Considerable or not, *Vathek* had its following during Beckford's lifetime. The *Gentleman's Magazine* in 1790 published a lengthy versification of the book in three issues.[4] Even before Byron gave added public recognition to its worth in 1813, Isaac D'Israeli and Robert Southey were indebted to it. D'Israeli, who read it before 1799, used it as a source book for details of local color in *Mejnoun and Leila* (1799); but he limited his direct borrowings to Henley's notes.[5] Southey was reading it during the composition of *Thalaba* (1801), which could well have been responsible for the incorporation of his own formidable array of explanatory notes in this verse tale. Marie de Meester believed in 1915 that the name "Sasar, the Icy Wind of Death," used in *Thalaba*, came directly from *Vathek*.[6] Southey's more substantial reliance upon *Vathek*, as Richard Garnett noted in 1893, is strikingly apparent near the end of *The Curse of Kehama* (1810):

> He did not know the holy mystery
> Of that divinest cup, that as the lips
> Which touch it, even such its quality,
> Good or malignant: Madman! and he thinks
> The blessed prize is won, and joyfully he drinks.
>
> Then Seeva open'd on the Accursed One
> His Eye of Anger: upon him alone

The wrath-beam fell. He shudders . . . but too late;
   The deed is done,
The dreadful liquor works the will of Fate.
   Immortal he would be,
Immortal he is made; but through his veins
   Torture at once and immortality,
A stream of poison doth the Amreeta run,
And while within the burning anguish flows,
   His outward body glows.
Like molten ore, beneath the avenging Eye,
Doom'd thus to live and burn eternally.

   The fiery Three,
Beholding him, set up a fiendish cry,
   A song of jubilee;
Come, Brother, come! they sung; too long
   Have we expected thee,
   Henceforth we bear no more
The unequal weight; Come, Brother, we are Four!

   Vain his almightiness, for mightier pain
Subdued all power; pain ruled supreme alone;
   And yielding to the bony hand
The unemptied cup, he moved toward the Throne,
   And at the vacant corner took his stand.
Behold the Golden Throne at length complete,
And Yamen silently ascends the Judgement-seat.[7]

"Part of Kehama's penalty," wrote Garnett, "is perpetual im-
mobility, part of Vathek's perpetual unrest, but the thought is the
same — the fruition of the sinner's desire is the sinner's punishment
— and the virtual identity of the catastrophe is obvious. . . . The
three upholders of Yamen's throne, moreover, are manifest though
far from servile copies of Soliman ben Daoud and the pre-Adamite
sultans."[8]

Byron encountered *Vathek* sometime before 1813. It is not possible to be more accurate about the date, but Thomas Medwin
reported that Byron's was "a very early admiration."[9] The quality of
that admiration was surely profound; to some, it carried almost
religious overtones.[10] Although we have already cited letters revealing Byron's eagerness to read the unpublished *Episodes* after being
so impressed by the master tale, we find it interesting that Medwin
recorded that, when Lady Caroline Lamb found a copy of *Vathek* ly-

ing in a prominent place on a table in Byron's quarters, she felt the volume had been of sufficient importance to the poet for her to write on its first page, "Remember me!"[11] It is also significant that a few months before Byron's death in 1824 he directed his banker, Charles Barry, to dispose of all the books he left in Geneva, with the exception of a few favorites, including "a copy of *The Caliph Vathek*."[12]

In Byron's final note to his Turkish tale, *The Giaour* (1813), he first paid public tribute to *Vathek*. Speaking of the notes to his own tale, he wrote:

For the contents of some of the notes I am indebted partly to D'Herbelot, and partly to that most Eastern, and, as Mr. Weber justly entitles it, "sublime tale," the "Caliph Vathek." I do not know from what source the author of that singular volume may have drawn his materials; some of his incidents are to be found in the *Bibliotheque Orientale;* but for correctness of costume, beauty of description, and power of imagination, it far surpasses all European imitations, and bears such marks of originality that those who have visited the East will find some difficulty in believing it to be more than a translation. As an Eastern tale, even Rasselas must bow before it; his "Happy Valley" will not bear a comparison with the "Hall of Eblis."[13]

If we rely on what is said here, it would seem that Byron limited his use of the book to Henley's notes. This procedure would have been in keeping with Byron's desire to insure that the "costume" of his poetry was correct in all matters of detail. As he once told John Murray, "I don't care one lump of sugar for my *poetry;* but for my *costume* and my *correctness* . . . I will combat lustily."[14]

However, Harold Wiener's research on the Eastern background of Byron's Turkish tales clearly indicates that Byron used not only the notes to *Vathek* in the composition of *The Giaour* but also the story.[15] Wiener cites the resemblance between Byron's description of the blue-winged butterflies of Kashmir and Beckford's reference to the same insects in his tale. Byron was also relying upon Beckford's text when he wrote the following lines:

> But thou, false Infidel! shall writhe
> Beneath avenging Monkir's scythe;
> And from its torments 'scape alone
> To wander round lost Eblis' throne;
> And fire unquenched, unquenchable,
> Around, within, thy heart shall dwell;
> Nor ear can hear nor tongue can tell
> The tortures of that inward hell! (11.747-54)

Byron's indebtedness to *Vathek* went beyond *The Giaour;* for reminiscences of Beckford's tale can also be found in *The Bride of Abydos* (1813), particularly in the resemblance between Byron's leading character, Selim, and Nouronihar's cousin, the delicate Gulchenrouz. "The essential situation in both stories," Weiner observes,

is the same. A young boy, raised in his uncle's court, spends most of his time in the harem, playing with his cousin, a beautiful young girl. The two children fall in love and pass many pleasant hours in the garden, reciting poetry and singing songs. It is significant that, in both tales, one of the songs in the repertoire is Sadi's story of Megnoun and Leila. Furthermore, because of this cloistered existence, the boy is unskilled in the attributes becoming the youths of the East — hurling the dart, curbing the steeds, and, for Selim, at least, bending the bow.[16]

For the *Siege of Corinth,* which was published in 1816, Byron again used *Vathek* and acknowledged its aid in a note to the poem: "I have been told that the idea expressed in this and the five following lines [11.643–48] has been admired by those whose approbation is valuable. I am glad of it; but it is not original — at least not mine; it may be found much better expressed in pages 181-2-3 of the English version of "Vathek" . . . a work to which I have before referred; and never recur to or read, without a renewal of gratification."[17] Additional echoes of *Vathek* have been discovered in Byron's later poems — in the conception of the leading character and in selected incidents of *Manfred* (1817) and in selected passages of the fifth canto of *Don Juan* (1819–23) — all of which suggests that Beckford's influence on Byron was more profound than has been generally recognized.[18]

Beckford seems to have resented the fame Byron had achieved with his Oriental verse tales, partly because he genuinely believed *Vathek* to be superior to any of Byron's Oriental verse tales. He used to say sneeringly that, if the *Episodes* ever saw the light of day, Byron's giaours would pale in significance. Among the unpublished manuscript notes in Beckford's personal copy of Thomas Moore's *Letters and Journals of Lord Byron with Notices of his Life,* Beckford left behind some revealing remarks on this subject.[19] Encountering Byron's letter to Samuel Rogers in which a reference was made to the Lausanne edition of *Vathek,* Beckford scrawled the following statement:

Rather cool after all — considering the red hot partiality he professed for
Vathek — a book, I know, he used to carry about in his pocket, & which lay
sometimes I have been told, under his very pillow — happy for him that he
never saw these episodes — they would have roused him to frenzy — & have
shortened the little rest he ever enjoyed — the most original of the set as full
as it could glare of Hell & the Devil, I have since thrown into the fire — the
two which remain are quite sufficiently Satanic — Your Corsairs & Don
Juans are milk & water Puritans compared with Barkiarokh, whose atrocities
shamelessly worked up & rhymingly paraphrased in the style of the passage
about the moon & the cloud in his Siege of Corinth, might have furnished
the material of half a dozen poems & extracted as many thousands from the
coffers of absolute John [Murray].

[Signed] W.B.

Other pencilings in the same volume disclose that Beckford knew
full well that Byron owed more to *Vathek* than he ever openly admitted:

It is rather melancholy to observe with what *ingenuous, unpoetical* caution,
the fashionable author of this volume abstains from even the most distant allusion to Vathek, a book well known to have engrossed no small share of Ld
Byron's attention, from which that great poet condescended to borrow
largely & some others to pilfer in their little way — which might easily be
proved, were it worth while to convict for such sneaking offences, or point
out instances of *petty larceny*.

[Signed] W.B.[20]

It is difficult to determine the effect of Byron's tribute to *Vathek*,
but Beckford's publishers seldom failed to extract his words of praise
and to print them on the fly leaves of the various editions which followed. At any rate, *Vathek* was made continuously available after
1815. Indeed, in the twenty-nine-year period preceding Beckford's
death, seventeen editions of the book appeared; and these included
English, French, and American editions as well as translations in
German, Dutch, and Russian.

Thomas Moore, who seems to have read *Vathek* before he wrote
Lalla Rookh (1817), makes no reference to Beckford in the plentiful
notes associated with the tale, probably because of the fact that he
had little taste for a man of Beckford's character. He once told
Rogers that he would never allow his name to be associated openly
with Beckford's. When Beckford tried to entice him in 1818 to edit

one of his travel books, Moore coldly declined. "I would not have my name coupled with his," he wrote in his notebook. "To be Beckford's *sub* [is] not very desirable."[21] So the omission in *Lalla Rookh* of any frank reference to such an important forerunner to the Oriental verse tale is not surprising, but there is little doubt that *Vathek* was firmly impressed on the mind of the author when he was writing *Lalla Rookh*.

In 1816, at about the same time that Moore submitted the manuscript of *Lalla Rookh* to Longmans, Moore wrote Francis Jeffrey, the editor of the *Edinburgh Review*, and offered to review "the original French edition of Vathek."[22] Jeffrey accepted the offer, but, mysteriously, the article never appeared — or was written. Moore liked *Vathek* well enough to describe it later as a "very striking and powerful production."[23] Among recent authors who have noted parallels between the two works, Fatma Mahmoud is convinced that "Moore utilised the romantic picture of the East it evoked."[24] Robert Birley, in his essay on *Lalla Rookh*, finds the frequent references in the tale to "Eblis" significant.[25] We might add that Moore's "vast illuminated halls" with their "long corridors," where "ranged in cassolets and silver urns, Sweet wood of aloe or of sandal burns" too closely resembles Beckford's descriptions to be idly dismissed.[26]

In addition to Byron and Moore, some evidence exists that Beckford influenced the poet Keats. *Vathek*, indeed, figured "among Keats's familiar reading."[27] His appreciation of the book, furthermore, is attested to in a letter he wrote to J. H. Reynolds in 1818, in which he expressed disgruntlement with the curator of the cottage where Robert Burns was born by saying, "I should like to employ Caliph Vathek to kick him."[28] Indirect allusions to *Vathek* have already been found among Keats' important poems, including "Ode to a Nightingale" and "The Cap and Bells."[29] Sidney Colvin, in his *John Keats, His Life and Poetry*, pointed to a resemblance between the mysterious caverns in Book II of *Endymion* and the Halls of Eblis, but the comparison seems rather strained.

More convincing has been the case Robert Gittings recently made for the influence of *Vathek* upon "Hyperion." Gittings cites several significant similarities between the two works to establish Keats' indebtedness to Beckford. He shows how details of imagery in Keats' work are remarkably close to Beckford's, including the description of the blazing Hyperion, portrayed sitting on his "orbed fire;" and

Hyperion's palace, with its thousand courts, arches, and fiery galleries; and even the imprisoned Titans, whose hearts have been turned to fire,

> Heaving in pain, and horribly convuls'd
> With sanguine, feverous, boiling gurge of pulse.
> (Bk. II, 11.27–28)

The relationship between "Hyperion" and *Vathek* does not end with verbal parallels. Keats, it seems, even relied upon Beckford's sequence of events for sections of his poem, as Gittings explains:

What connects Keats's picture of the Titans so closely with Beckford's vision is the particular sequence in which both lead the reader. In both, and in the same order, there are two regions, one of brilliant, metallic light, music, attendant spirits, and long vistas of architecture, the other dark, damp, cramped, rocky and soundless, except for the continual pouring of unseen waters. The connecting figure in each case, is a sad, tarnished, and godlike giant, whose keynote is not energy, or defiance (as with Milton's Satan) but much more of an uneasy melancholy.[30]

One final nineteenth-century author should be mentioned as owing a debt to *Vathek* — Benjamin Disraeli. Disraeli, a thorough admirer of Beckford, recognized him as a man of the "greatest taste." Disraeli was a young man of thirty when he first appeared on the literary scene equipped with a fascination for the East that easily made him a spiritual relative of the Caliph of Lansdown. "He is an Oriental Voluptuary," George Clarke wrote to Beckford, who "concocts his scenes with great effect."[31] When Disraeli's *Contarini Fleming* made its appearance in 1832, Beckford was among the very few to receive it with enthusiasm: "How wildly original! How full of intense thought! How awakening! How delightful!"[32] In 1833, when Disraeli's *Alroy* was published, a copy was immediately dispatched to Beckford. As he read this book, Beckford discovered Disraeli's reliance on *Vathek:* "What appears to be hauteur and extreme conceit in Disraeli is *consciousness,* uncontrollable consciousness of superior powers, and most proud I am to perceive that he is so strongly imbued with *Vathek* — the image it presents haunts him continually — the halls of Eblis, the thrones of the Sulimans are forever present to his mind's eye, tinted with somewhat different hues from those of the original, but partaking of the same awful and dire solemnity."[33]

One year later, after Beckford had read Disraeli's *The Infernal Marriage*, which was printed in the *New Monthly Magazine*, he remarked that,

Though D[israeli] is perpetually galloping over Vathek's manor of hell, it is no trespass. The Caliph and Alroy were born co-lords of that appalling region; its gloom, its vastness, its undefined horrors are their own, and the dreadful game they may start from its coverts belongs to them by prescription, as much as it did in his day to Dante. Who dares deny it was decreed from the beginning of time that Eblis should be pourtrayed reigning supreme on his globe of fire, and the burning hearts of his misguided followers displayed as beacon-lights to ward off the perpetrators of crime and the wallowers in sensuality? There is a nice moral for you![34]

Disraeli's works of this kind did not enjoy any wide degree of popularity; for by the 1830's, the taste for the colorful world of romance had been markedly diminished by the greater concern for the cold realities of ordinary life. Thomas Hope and J. H. Morier, who were already busy lifting the misty veils which had hidden the squalor and poverty of those Orientals who had never been inside a caliph's palace, increased the trend toward realism which was only suggested in *Vathek*. More and more in the nineteenth century, fidelity to the actual manners and vices of Eastern nations was insisted upon; and, as we have observed, the insatiable travelers and scholars of the period were in part responsible for this trend. As they boasted a more detailed knowledge of the lands so long misunderstood, the sentimental dream of the Romantic East passed away. Beckford, who sensed the condition of the times, predicted the indifferent reception of Disraeli's books; and he wondered how could they be appreciated by the "gross rattling readers of the present cold-hearted period."[35] The age of grinding machines and sooty factories must have diminished his own appeal, too, in spite of the fact that his tale continued to be reprinted, so that it might be said that the interests and concerns of an era prevented *Vathek* from achieving any wider span of influence.

II *A Final View*

As for what interest Beckford's Oriental tales have for us today, part of our concern with them is obviously historical. We regard Beckford as a key participant in an age of expanding intellectual horizons — an age that was successfully breaking through the insularity of Classicism. As is well known, the rationalistic art of the eighteenth century had well-defined boundaries: it catered to the *beau monde*, the society of fashion, the court and town, the club and coffee houses. In fact, "It was as indifferent to Venice, Switzerland, the Alhambra, the Nile, the American forests, and the islands of the South Seas as it was to the Middle Ages."[36] From the historical point of view, then, Beckford's tales of the East and his direct participation in the development of Orientalism in England through *Vathek*, constitute another manifestation of the growing democratic spirit of an era which aimed at familiarizing the remote and the distant, at bringing England into a more intimate association with other cultures, and at demonstrating that people of other lands were more than mere abstractions: they were flesh-and-blood identities with distinctive features and peculiar customs.

Indeed, the shift from the abstract Orientalism of the eighteenth century, represented in particular by Hawkesworth and Johnson, toward the more concrete, historical Orientalism, which became apparent for the first time near the end of the century in *Vathek*, can also be seen as part of the larger revolution in taste which helped to bring about a democratization of letters in England and to promote the view that specific facts and unusual experiences had a dominant role to play in art. As we have observed, the business of English literature during the first quarter of the nineteenth century was "the rediscovery and vindication of the concrete"; and Beckford's Oriental tales represent an early reflection of this movement away from the ordering, generalizing tendency of the Augustan age. He sought, instead, the reality of particulars, the vitality of concrete detail, and the excitement of his own special imagery.

We do not say, however, that Beckford was entirely free of eighteenth-century influences. The precise outline of his imagery, the heavily ironic strain, and the moralistic tendency of his work bind him to the older tradition. Nonetheless, his affinities with the age that followed are stronger; for, by assimilating countless books on the East and by absorbing a wealth of Oriental allusions, names, and imagery in the process, Beckford managed to conceive a work of art in *Vathek* which was more richly Oriental than any previous imitation and which was also more intimately connected with its successors. No fictional work of the time contained the accessories of Oriental costume, the local color, legends, historical detail so admirably distilled in composition as *Vathek*. These features anticipated Byron, Southey, and Moore; and they foreshadowed the new Orientalism of the nineteenth century.

That Beckford accomplished this feat without ever having experienced *directly* the Orient was a considerable achievement. He was a receptive, probing reader and a sensitive writer; and he could mingle reality and unreality with ease. Fantasy, he found, could be harmonized with glimpses of genuine Oriental customs and beliefs without disturbance. He selected real places for the tale's setting, but he then stretched the limits of the imagination in his descriptions of hell. The coloring of his tales is brilliant throughout, partly because he believed in the resources of the imagination, but also because to his mind the Orient was picturesque. The carefully staged succession of pictures, the exuberance of detail, the richness of texture, and the profusion of objects became the hallmarks of his composition. In modern terms, they gave his works the quality of visual happenings.

Beckford was so awed by the elaborate mythologies, institutions, and customs of Eastern cultures that they whetted his antiquarian appetite. He believed deeply that the "East must be better known than it is to be sufficiently liked." But the Orient was also capable of stimulating the puerile impulses in him — the love of exhibition and of erotic fantasy. The "magical atmosphere" of Eastern lands, conveyed as it was through books, aroused in him a childlike desire for vicarious participation in mystery and adventure. The Orient became the playground for his imagination. It seemed to him to celebrate the life of the senses because it was a land of feeling — gorgeous, voluptuous, and sometimes cruel. If it formed the substance of his art and his dreams, it also allowed him freedom to indulge feelings of delight and horror too long inhibited by his own society. As we have indicated about Beckford's early life, his longing for imaginative identification with half-known Eastern cultures began with his own reactionary tendency to seek a return to a newer, fresher world, one without responsibilities and one in which he could live the role of a perpetual child. "Don't call me *illustre ami,* and *homme unique,*" he wrote when he was twenty. "I'm still in my cradle! Spare the delicacy of my infantile ears. Leave me to scamper on verdant banks — all too ready, alas, to crumble, but rainbow-tinted and flower-strewn."

Beckford's Oriental tales have a more permanent value, however, in addition to their association with a moment of history and their illumination of Beckford's personality. These works evolved from a similar point of departure that has received the second emphasis in this study. Beyond their specific historical situation, their connection with an episode in the Romantic movement, they reveal, in a more universal context, the perpetual struggle of the self against the restraining forces of the outside world. Beckford's leading characters — Vathek, Carathis, Alasi, Firouz, Barkiarokh, Abou Taher Achmed, Zulkaïs, Kalilah — all rebel against the impositions of law and order. In their world, the free self, the liberated ego, is more important than the community. They are individualists whose freedom of expression takes on the quality of heroism, even though they all meet with tragedy in the end.

It is true that, according to one set of standards, they are criminals; but they are also heroes, whether good or evil, in their striking roles and postures and in their dramatic pursuits. They have, after all, the ultimate satisfaction of experiencing themselves for a time as uncircumscribed personalities. Part of the explanation for the creation of this kind of fictional personality, of course, lies, as we have stressed, in Beckford's own circumscribed youth and in the constant threat he endured of being forced to assume civic responsibilities he preferred to shun. Because this personal agony was naturally translated into his art, Beckford's Oriental tales successfully bring the modern reader face to face with a dilemma that always has significance; for personal freedom has to have some meaningful relationship with community life and its obligations. This conflict may never reasonably be resolved, but the types of solutions that may be found either by the community or by an individual are of concern today.

The ideal of the totally free personality remains an enduring and pleasurable image, in spite of its distance from actuality. Admittedly, it is a vision which can only be achieved through an escape from the present — a flight of only temporary pleasure which will nevertheless continue to be taken by certain restless souls. For this reason, there will always be some who will turn to *Vathek*, and even to the lesser-known *Episodes of Vathek*, to indulge in the fiction of freedom — to escape momentarily from the burdens of the ordinary world, just as Beckford himself did almost two hundred years ago.

Appendix

Mr. Urban,

Having often admired the latter part of the Romance of Vathek, and thinking it a subject more adapted to Poetry than to Prose, I have attempted it in verse; and conscious as I am, that I have not done Mr. Beckford that justice he might have received from an abler hand, yet, as I think it may not be unacceptable to some of your numerous readers, such as it is, I take the liberty of inclosing *The Palace of Istaker*, which I shall be happy if you think worthy of a place in your excellent Magazine. For its great length, the original must be my excuse; if you refer to that, you will see I could not shorten more than I have done.

Yours, etc. A. V.

The Palace of Istaker

The Caliph Vathek, with Nouronihar, daughter of the Emir Fakreddin, whom he had seduced from her father, after a long series of crimes, are led by the promises of a Demon to seek for pleasure, riches, and knowledge, supposed to be concealed in the Palace of subterranean Fire; and having violated the Holy Valley of the Santons, are pursuing their journey.

> NOW the fierce Caliph, and his impious
>   bride,
> Of ravage tir'd, forsake the mountain's side;
> Fatigued with slaughter, leave the calm retreat,
> Where pure Devotion fix'd her hallo'd seat;
> Where in long robes the peaceful Santons clad,
> Enjoy'd the limpid streams of Rocnabad.
> O'er the wide plain their journey they pursue,
> 'Till Istaker's vast rocks close in the view;
> Barren and bleak their craggy summits rise,
> And frown tremendous on the neighbour-skies: —
> Fir'd with delight, they quit their splendid car,
> And hail the long-sought object from afar.

"Have we not now," they cry, "each joy in sight?
"Gardens of bliss! and palaces of light!
"Above all prejudice, above all care,
"Knowledge, to man denied, awaits us there.
"O Mahomet, thy promis'd raptures keep!
"Let dreaming priests o'er the dull Koran sleep;
"For future bliss neglect the present hour,
"Trust to their Prophet, and implore his power!
"For us the fiery Genii ope their bowers;
"Wealth, boundless rule, and endless joy, is ours!"
     From the seventh heaven the holy Prophet saw
His mad Viceregent to his ruin draw;
Pitying he saw him to destruction run,
Nor to himself resign'd his guilty son.
"Save, gracious Allah! save this wretch!" he cried:
"Let one attempt to save at least be tried!"
Mercy divine, indulgent to the prayer,
A Heavenly Being sent, to warn and spare.
A mortal form conceals from human eyes
The bright inhabitant that quits the skies;
And, all-obedient to the high command,
To erring man presents a saving hand. —
Rais'd by his power, a greyish vapour grew,
And in the mist the glaring sun withdrew;
The lakes, depriv'd of the all-cheering light,
Chang'd to a bloody hue their crystal white.
Where near the flood a verdant mead extends,
The seeming swain a fleecy charge attends;
From his soft flute melodious air proceed,
Which rouse remorse for every guilty deed.
By secret impulse led, the Prince drew near,
And heard with wonder, mix'd with awe and fear,
The mournful sounds repeat his subjects' groans,
Of slaughter'd innocents the dying moans;
Whilst, to the ear of his astonish'd bride,
The notes proclaim her recent parricide.
     The musick ceas'd. — The Angel thus begun:
"Whither, ill-fated Caliph, dost thou run?
"Dost thou not know where ends thy destin'd road?
"Dost thou not know where Eblis makes abode?
"Behind yon mountain is his dark retreat:
"Ah, stay in time! nor aid his dire deceit.
"Stay, ere too late! thy fatal progress stay!
"Nor give thy last, thy only hope away.
"Devote to penitence thy future life; .

"Send to her father's grave thy guilty wife;
"Dismiss thy mother from thy tainted throne;
"Lament thy crimes; and worship God alone.
"If, when the sun emerges from yon clouds,
"Whose sable gloom th'enlivening radiance shrouds;
"If then thy mind its dreadful purpose hold;
"If then obdurate, obstinate, and bold,
"Thy heart remain, — the hour of grace is o'er;
"An hour, if scorn'd, which shall return no more."
  He ceas'd. — The Caliph's eyes those thoughts express,
Which with loud voice he hastens to confess.
With looks indignant, smiling as he spoke,
From his proud lips this impious answer broke:
"Shine forth, bright sun! I ask but for thy ray,
"Unaw'd and fearless to pursue my way."
The boon despis'd, the gracious Spirit mourn'd,
From the black cloud the darken'd orb return'd:
The warning vision vanish'd from his view,
And with a lamentable shriek withdrew.
Fear-struck and chill'd th' attendant train appear,
And still the musick and the voice they hear;
Anxious they wait for the approach of night,
Then quit their Prince, and save themselves by flight.
Undaunted still the guilty pair press on,
Eager for fate, in haste to be undone:
As nearer to their journey's end they drew,
Proud Istaker itself appear'd in view.
Between two frowning hills the palace lies;
Proud mausoleums on the mountains rise,
Which, hardly seen by the last streaks of light,
Deepen the shadowy horrors of the night.
Black as its gloom, a marble terrace lay
Against the rock, which now obstructs their way.
In death-like silence heaven and earth repose.
At length the moon in full-orb'd glory rose;
On the vast platform lofty columns made,
By her pale beams, a long terrific shade.
The gloomy watch-towers, open to the sky,
Harbour each noxious bird that knows to fly;
Screaming they rise, struck with a new dismay,
And from th' advent'rous strangers haste away:
In vain the omen calls him to desist,
Th' unfeeling Monarch, practis'd to resist,
Eager press'd on, and closely by his side
With equal ardour came his wretched bride.

Ascending now of many a step the flight,
They gain'd the sable terrace' utmost height:
Smooth was its surface as the tranquil lake,
When not a breeze the sleeping waters shake.
There to their sight the countless watch-towers rose,
And palaces their ruin'd fronts disclose;
Where stern colossal forms of beasts unknown,
And dreadful figures, rose from out the stone.
By the pale moon-beams, characters they
        view,
Shifting their forms, and changing shape and hue;
Till, fix'd at length, the darting meteors
        stood,
In large Arabian letters, mark'd in blood:

"Vathek, by prejudice and weakness sway'd,
"Oft from the path thy devious steps have stray'd;
"Yet for th' attempt thou well deserv'st the meed,
"Thou, and thy partner. — To your wish succeed:
"Eblis shall bid each obstacle retire; —
"Enter, and hail the subterranean fire!"

They read: and straight an earthquake rocks the ground,
The massy watch-towers shake and tremble round;
The solid mountain yawns, and gives to sight
A vast descending stair-case, large and light;
For on each step two flaming torches glare,
Whose sulph'rous smoke, high-curling, fills the air.
Th' ambitious Pair, with joy transported, gaze;
Their glittering vests shine brighter by the blaze;
Their eyes new lustre from the flame acquire,
And added beauty kindles new desire;
With pride thy nature's milder charms forego,
And plunge impetuous to th' abyss below:
Yet with amazement as they downward tend,
The dire descent appears without an end:
With eager pace as onwards still they move,
They feel a force impel them from above,
Attractive pow'rs below their aid supply,
They seem no more to walk, but fall from high.
At length their weary footsteps find a floor,
Their way impeded by a lofty door:
An ebon portal meets the Caliph's sight,
Oft seen before, in visions of the night:
The well-known Demon, prompt and ready, stands,

The pondrous key he poises in his hands:
"Welcome!" he cry'd, "ye long expected Pair!
"In spite of Mahomet, ye enter there."
   He said — and to the lock apply'd his hand;
With thund'ring roar the brazen gates expand.
The Pair now enter'd with an equal roar;
Recoiling quick, they close, to part no more.
So high the roof, so wide the walls were spread,
They think a plain's unmeasur'd length they tread;
But soon the objects more familiar grown,
Long rows of columns and arcades are shown.
To length beyond belief their lines extend,
Till in a radiant point they seem to end.
Gold-dust and saffron strew the marble floor,
Dazzle with brightness and with sweets o'erpow'r:
Censers surround them, whereso'er they turn,
Where ambergrease and fragrant aloes burn:
O'er high-spread banquets tempting odors roll,
And the wine sparkles in the crystal bowl:
Genii, of either sex, in airy ring,
Now dance lascivious, and now wanton sing.
But in the midst a strange promiscuous throng,
With diff'rent gestures constant mov'd along:
Some with slow steps seem'd gazing on the ground;
Some, torn with anguish, striking ran around;
Some, like the frantic Maniac rag'd with pain,
While dumb Despair in others seem'd to reign.
But o'er them all a livid paleness spread
Bespoke the wan complexion of the dead:
Deep in their sockets sung, their haggard eyes
Seem'd Meteors which o'er marshy graves arise:
By thousands press'd, each seem'd to be alone,
Unconscious of all suff'rings but his own;
And writhing with intolerable smart,
Each kept his hand fix'd steady on his heart.
   With terror struck, at such a sight of woe,
Vathek enquir'd the cause, yet fear'd to know.
"Cease vain demand," the sullen Demon cry'd;
"Thy wish to know shall soon be gratify'd.
"But come, and seek with me the inmost bow'rs,
"There bend to Eblis, now your Lords, as ours."
Forward they move; yet discompos'd in mind,
They leave unmark'd, stupendous scenes behind.
On either hand long perspectives extend,
Large Halls, and galleries that never end.

By gloomy embers, or by torches bright,
The polish'd walls reflect a ruddy light.
At length their journey's limit they behold,
Clos'd by long drapery, crimson streak'd with gold:
Here ceas'd the dances, and the songs were o'er,
The lights from far but glimmer'd on the floor:
Behind the veils a gleaming brightness glows,
They part, and all the inner scene disclose.
Now the vast tabernacle opens round,
With leopards' shaggy spoils was spread the ground:
Elders, and warriors, monarchs, genii, there
Prostrate on earth, their master's pow'er declare. —
Upon a globe of fire, and plac'd on high,
The formidable Eblis met the eye;
Beauty and youth once in his form had shone;
Now tarnish'd was their grace, their lustre gone:
In curling ringlets hung his flowing hair,
While his large eyes glar'd pride, and deep despair.
His hand, tho' blasted by the bolts of God,
To curb the fiends sustain'd an iron rod.
The Prince's heart sunk at the awful sight,
Then first he bent to Earth, in dire affright.
Eblis his prostrate votaries survey'd,
Nor with tremendous voice their souls dismay'd;
As the fall'n angel still his form confest,
The angel's mildness still his voice express'd;
Not sweet, as when, in heavenly courts above,
He breath'd the notes of harmony and love;
Yet not terrific, did his accents sound,
Tho' spreading deepest melancholy round.
  "Creatures of clay! who bend before my throne"
He said, "well pleas'd I claim ye as my own:
"Enjoy of all your toils the destin'd meed,
"In ev'ry wish, in each pursuit succeed:
"Does wealth delight? in mines of riches live,
"Does pleasure charm? go revel in those bow'rs;
"In music, feasting, love, employ yours hours.
"Does pow'r invite? the Demons shall obey;
"And beings more than human own your sway.
"Does knowledge please? here, in the realms below,
"Go learn what mortal man can never know.
"But, when each doubt is to your wish explain'd;
"Say not, ungrateful! 'tis too dearly gain'd." —
The impious pair felt dying hopes renew;
Eager they wish to gratify their view:

"O! Genius, lead," they cry, "to those bright stores;
"The talismans of wealth and power are ours!"
Th' insulting fiend, with eyes that wildly glare,
Bade them "Come on, and more than promis'd share."
Thro' a long aile their hasty steps he led;
Lightly they follow his more pondrous tread.
They reach at length a long-extended court,
Whose marble walls a lofty dome support;
And fifty brazen gates are seen from far,
Secur'd with many a bolt and massy bar:
The place was darkened by a murky gloom,
Long biers of cedar stood athwart the room;
On each lay fleshless forms of kings long dead,
Tho' still some ray of light their eye-balls shed,
And, only living to a sense of pain,
Some melancholy motion still retain;
Dejected looks they on each other dart,
With each right hand fix'd steady on the heart.
Beneath were grav'd the stories of their times,
Their names, their pow'r, their actions, and their crimes.
Great was their fame, and greater was but one,
Greatest, as wisest, David's matchless son:
Rais'd from the rest, beneath the dome he lay;
More life appear'd to animate his clay;
Frequent he sigh'd, transfix'd by sorrow's dart;
And, like the rest, his hand still press'd his heart:
He seem'd to listen to the sullen roar
Of a vast cataract's incessant show'r,
Which visible, a portal's grates between,
In part was jointly and at distance seen.
Its doleful murmur was the only sound
That broke the silence which prevail'd around.
"Seest thou," the Demon to proud Vathek cry'd,
"Those vases rang'd the Monarch's tomb beside?
"There lie the Talismans, ordain'd by Fate,
"To burst the bars of ev'ry brazen gate;
"Seize them! be master of their treasur'd store!
"Their magic Guardians then shall own thy pow'r."
Th' ill omen'd objects which attract their view,
Struck o'er the trembling Pair, a chilling dew;
With fault'ring step the Caliph ventur'd near,
Then at the Prophet's groans retir'd with fear.
As yet once more he strove to seize his prey.
From the dead lips these accents found their way —
"Whilst yet I liv'd, I fill'd a lofty throne,

"The wealth, the wisdom of the East my own;
"On my right hand twelve thousand seats of gold
"Grave Prophets fill'd, to hear my proverbs told;
"And on my left an equal band appear'd,
"Who, thron'd on silver, my decisions heard.
"My people flourish'd; I subdued my foes,
"My tow'ring palace to the skies arose;
"To the Most High I rear'd a stately fane,
"Nor did he the imperfect work disdain;
"But mov'd by restless wishes more to know,
"I scorn'd the Wisdom of the world below.
"To Pharaoh's daughter fatal trust was giv'n,
"Fire I ador'd, and all the host of Heav'n:
"Asham'd of scenes, where once respect I knew,
"From the bless'd city, blushing, I withdrew;
"The Genii, then obedient to my call,
"Rear'd Istaker's stupendous magic wall;
"The watch-tow'rs from the terrace shone afar,
"Each watch-tow'r sacred to a different star.
"Mankind to rule, did not my pride suffice;
"The Genii own'd me than themselves more wise;
"Like these, who round me their offences weep,
"I thought the eye of Heav'n was clos'd in sleep;
"When all at once its thunders roll'd around,
"My structures burst, my turrets strew'd the ground;
"All Nature shook — yes, Nature shook with fear,
"Till the foul cause was struck, and rooted here;
"Yet not, like all the rest, of hope bereft,
"One distant comfort to my soul is left.
"In pity for some good before I fell,
"My Guardian-angel has vouchas'd to tell
"That when yon cataract shall cease to flow,
"Then, and ah! not till then, shall cease my woe;
"But, till that hour, what unrelenting smart!
"What cruel flames consume my erring heart!"
    He said, his hands in humble prayer he rais'd:
The Caliph shudd'ring, now with horror gaz'd;
For, thro' his bosom as the crystal clear,
He saw his heart all wrapt in flames appear.
Silence alone at first his dread express'd,
Th' affrightened pair sunk trembling on his breast.
At length to horror rous'd by waking sense,
He shrieking cry'd, "O! Demon, take me hence!
"Where hast thou brought me? I my hopes forego,
"Thy gifts relinquish, — let me scape this woe!

"Does there no mercy, Mahomet, remain?"
"None, Vathek, none" the fiend return'd again.
"Thou soughtst the realms of Vengeance and Despair,
"Threw off thy prophet, and he leaves thee there.
"Soon shall thy kindled heart like others burn:
"The voltaries of Eblis ne'er return;
"Yet a few days enjoyment shall be thine,
"Employ them well, on heaps of gold recline.
"Command at will th' infernal potentates,
"Range at thy pleasure subterranean states,
"Thy boundless curiosity extend;
"No bar shall stop thee, no repulse offend.
"But, when each doubt is to thy wish explain'd,
"Think not such knowledge is too dearly gain'd."
    He said, and rising thro' the dusky air
Malicious laugh'd, and left them to despair.
Struck with a deep, unutterable woe,
No sound they breathe, no tear had pow'r to flow.
They hand in hand the fatal dome forsake:
Without design their random course they take;
Each portal opens as they turn that way;
The prostrate Genii ask but to obey;
Each reservoir of wealth is full in view,
But wish of wealth or power no more they knew:
With equal apathy the songs they heard,
And saw the sumptuous feast in vain prepar'd.
Thro' the long galleries, still wand'ring, roam,
And only fly from the tremendous dome;
For still in thought the Prophet's voice they hear,
The Demon's words still thunder in their ear,
Myriads like them thro' the funereal gloom
In ceaseless torture rove from room to room;
Their looks too plain their burning hearts betray,
Each from his fellow suff'rer turns away:
They too avoid the rest, and trembling wait
The hour when they must share an equal fate.
The wretched Princess first impassion'd cry'd,
"What! shall I ever wish to quit thy side?
"Shall this right hand, fix'd steady on my heart,
"Quit thy fond grasp, and from thy pressure
        "Part?
"Q! give some comfort to my woe-struck breast."
"Comfort!" the Caliph cry'd, "is for the blest;
"Yet from thy face can e'er my eyes retire,
"Nor drink from thine long draughts of sweet desire?"

But, as he spoke, he felt his words were vain;
He saw in all his own approaching pain;
Conscious of misery, expecting more!
Abject with pow'r! poor midst unbounded store!
At length, from the cold icy vaults of death,
There rose a blast of pestilential breath:
A solemn voice was heard beneath the floor;
All is accomplish'd, and ye hope no more.
At once, they sep'rate with convulsive start,
Each right hand fix'd upon the kindled heart.
In those bright eyes, with Vathek's Soul engag'd,
Now burnt Revenge, and fiery Passion rag'd;
While in his looks, where once reign'd am'rous care,
She saw fix'd Hatred, Malice, and Despair;
Flying each other, yet disturb'd alone,
Seeking repose which never can be known,
Single midst millions, who as lonely roam,
Ceaseless they wander thro' the spacious dome.
Such was the punishment in former times
Of passions unrestrained, and Vathek's crimes.
Such is, and such shall be in time to come,
Of blind Ambition the appointed doom;
The end of those, who, lur'd by Pleasure, run
Thro' flow'ry paths by which they are undone;
Of those, who scorn the surer influence
Of laws design'd to govern human sense;
Who, madly pleas'd, and ignorantly proud,
Despise the wisdom to mankind allow'd,
And, taking erring Reason for their guide,
Aspire to know what God to man deny'd.
When form'd of clay the hapless wretch he made,
Who soon, too soon, his Maker disobey'd,
And, on the word entailing foul disgrace,
With thirst of *useless* knowledge curs'd his race.

Notes and References

Chapter One

1. W. Beckford to Lady Hamilton, February 20, 1781, Lewis Melville, *The Life and Letters of William Beckford of Fonthill* (London, 1910), p. 103.

2. The first French edition of *Les Mille et une Nuits, Contes Arabes* consisted of twelve volumes, of which the first six appeared in 1704; the seventh, in 1706; the eighth, in 1709; the ninth and tenth, in 1712; the eleventh and twelfth, in 1717.

3. M. L. Dufrenoy, *L'Orient Romanesque en France, 1704–1789* (Montreal, 1946), I, 343.

4. The exact date of the first English edition of the *Arabian Nights* seems to be a subject of dispute, but the second edition appeared in 1712.

5. Martha Pike Conant, *The Oriental Tale in England in the Eighteenth Century* (New York, 1908), p. xxii. For a portion of this introduction, I have drawn on this invaluable study.

6. *Ibid.*, p. 229.

7. Ernest Baker, *The History of the English Novel* (New York, 1950), V, 56.

8. For a chronological list of Franco-Oriental works published in England in the eighteenth century, see Conant, pp. 267–93.

9. *Ibid.*, p. 233.

10. Joseph Addison, *Spectator*, No. 512, October 17, 1712; also in *The British Essayists*, ed. Lionel T. Berguer (London, 1823), XIII, 259.

11. Addison, *Spectator*, No. 535, November 13, 1712; also in Berguer (ed.), XIV, 91–92.

12. John Hawkesworth, *Adventurer*, No. 4, November 18, 1752; also in Berguer (ed.), XXIII, 20.

13. Baker, V, 56.

14. Quoted in Joseph Spence, *Anecdotes, Observations, and Characters of Books and Men, a Selection*, ed. John Underhill (London, n.d.), p. 169.

15. B. Sprague Allen, *Tides in English Taste (1619–1800): A Background for the Study of Literature* (New York, 1937), I, 234–35.

16. William Whitehead, *The World*, No. 12, March 22, 1753; also in Berguer (ed.), XXVI, 63–64.

17. Sir James Marriot, *The World*, No. 117, March 27, 1755; also in Berguer (ed.), XXVIII, 66–67.

18. Joseph Warton, *The World*, No. 26, June 28, 1753; also in Berguer (ed.), XXVI, 143; 146.

19. *Collected Works of Oliver Goldsmith*, ed. Arthur Friedman (Oxford, Eng., 1966), II, 144–45.

20. See Conant, pp. 207–20.

21. Wallace C. Brown, "The Popularity of English Travel Books About the Near East, 1775–1825," *Philological Quarterly*, XV (October, 1936), 71–72.

22. John Richardson, *A Dissertation on the Languages, Literature and Manners of Eastern Nations, Originally Prefixed to a Dictionary, Persian, Arabic and English* (Oxford, Eng., 1778); the dictionary was published in two volumes by the Clarendon Press, Oxford in 1777–80; Jones' early works include: *Poems, consisting chiefly of translations from the Asiatick languages. To which are added two Essays: I On the Poetry of the Eastern Nations. II On the Arts Commonly called Imitative* (Oxford, Eng.; 1772); *The Moallakatt, or the Seven Arabian Poems which were suspended on the Temple at Mecca* (London, 1782); *The Asiatic Miscellany, consisting of Original Productions, Fugitive Pieces, Imitations and Extracts* (Calcutta, 1785–86).

23. Mahmoud Manzalaoui, "Pseudo-Orientalism in Transition: The Age of *Vathek*," in *William Beckford of Fonthill, 1760–1844: Bicentenary Essays*, ed. Fatma Mahmoud (Cairo, 1960), p. 125.

24. *Ibid.*, p. 127. See also Imdad Hussain, "Oriental Elements in English Poetry 1784–1859," *Venture: A Quarterly Review of English Language and Literature*, I (June, 1960), 158–59.

25. André Parreaux, *William Beckford, Auteur de Vathek (1760–1844): Etude de la Création Littéraire* (Paris, 1960), pp. 331-32.

Chapter Two

1. W. Beckford Esq., to Pitt, January 7, 1761, *Correspondence of William Pitt, Earl of Chatham*, ed. W. S. Taylor and Capt. J. H. Pringle (London, 1838), II, 12.

2. Guy Chapman, *Beckford* (London, 1952), p. 36.

3. J. W. Oliver, *The Life of William Beckford* (London, 1932), p. 11.

4. Boyd Alexander, "Introduction," *Life at Fonthill, 1807–1822* (London, 1957), p. 10.

5. Oliver, p. 6.

6. Unpublished footnote to a copy of a letter Beckford wrote to his cousin's wife, Louisa Beckford, March 17, 1782, made by himself about 1838. See the "Photostats of Typescripts of the Correspondence between

William Beckford and Louisa." Beinecke Rare Book and Manuscript Library, Yale University.

7. Lady Hamilton to W. Beckford, March 19, 1781, quoted in Oliver, pp. 63–64.

8. Lady Hamilton to W. Beckford, January 9, 1781, quoted in Oliver, p. 55.

9. See Boyd Alexander, *England's Wealthiest Son* (London, 1962), pp. 36–37.

10. Oliver, p. 5.

11. P.R.O. 30 8/9. Both letters, in Mrs. Beckford's hand, are addressed to the Countess of Chatham. The first is dated September 19, 1772; the second, November 21, 1772. Portions of these letters are cited in my unpublished doctoral dissertation, "William Beckford and the Picturesque: A Study of Fonthill" (Syracuse, 1967), pp. 10–12.

12. Quoted in Joseph Farington, *The Farington Diary*, ed. James Greig (London, 1924), IV, 242.

13. The Reverend John Lettice to Chatham, December 11, 1773, in Taylor and Pringle, IV, 315.

14. *Ibid.*, 314.

15. Melville, pp. 20–21.

16. Taylor and Pringle, IV, 315.

17. Alexander, *England's Wealthiest Son*, p. 42.

18. Taylor and Pringle, IV, 290.

19. Chapman, p. 38.

20. W. Beckford to A. Cozens, November 24 [1777], quoted in Melville, p. 37.

21. Chapman, p. 39.

22. Anonymous, "Conversations with the late W. Beckford, Esq.," *New Monthly Magazine*, LXXII (November, 1844), 419. The presentation copy of Chambers' *Dissertation on Oriental Gardening* was lot 1788, first portion of the Hamilton sale of 1882.

23. Richard Garnett, "William Beckford," *Dictionary of National Biography*, IV, 26–27.

24. Cyrus Redding, *Memoirs of William Beckford of Fonthill: Author of Vathek* (London, 1859), I, 142.

25. W. Beckford to A. Cozens, November 24, [1777], quoted in Melville, p. 40.

26. W. Beckford to Elizabeth Hervey, undated letter, quoted in Oliver, p. 20.

27. W. Beckford to A. Cozens, October 3, 1777, quoted in Melville, pp. 31–32.

28. W. Beckford to unidentified correspondent, December 4, 1778, quoted in Melville, p. 65.

29. *Ibid.*, p. 66.

30. Chapman, p. 52.

31. Melville, p. 65.

Chapter Three

1. Oliver, pp. 17–18.
2. Melville, p. 40.
3. *Ibid.*, p. 41.
4. "I will seclude myself if possible from the World, in the midst of the Empire, and converse many hours every day with you Mesron [Moisasour] and Nouronihar," W. Beckford to A. Cozens [?], December 4, 1778, quoted in Melville, p. 65; ". . . if you come to see and comfort me, which I trust you will, bring the long story. . . . ," W. Beckford to Samuel Henley, October 13, 1784, in Alfred Morrison, *Collection of Autograph Letters and Historical Documents*, Second Series (Privately printed, 1893), I, 193; "Pray tell me if *Esplendente* is in yr possession? the *long story* I am certain is," W. Beckford to S. Henley, n.d., 1785, in Morrison, I, 195. This collection of letters and documents is hereafter referred to as *Morrison Collection*.
5. "Introduction," *The Vision* [and] *Liber Veritatis* (London, 1930), pp. xi; xiii. All page references to this work hereafter will be based on this edition and appear in parentheses in the text.
6. Parreaux, p. 125.
7. *Ibid.*, pp. 99–100. Parreaux's statement in French from which my translation is made appears as follows:

"1. Cinq pages et demi environ, dont les trois premières et une partie de la quatrième constituent une variante du texte publié par Chapman, à partir de « I was admiring the cheerful air of the cave » (p. 88). Seule la première de ces pages porte un numéro (116); les autres ne sont pas numérotées. La fin de cette première version comporte quelques variantes particulièrement intéressantes.

La suite de ce fragment (deux pages et demie) nous présente Nouronihar lisant des passages tirés des volumes mystérieux; elle converse avec l'auteur et accepte, sur sa demande, de lui narrer l'histoire de sa vie.

2. Dix-huit pages manuscrites, numérotées de 1 à 18, contiennent le début de cette histoire.

3. Quatre pages numérotées de 19 à 22 ne sont qu'une reprise, une amplification, un développement et une mise au net d'une partie du fragment précédent (et notamment des pp. 12–13) — toujours de la main de Beckford.

4. La suite du récit de Nouronihar est représentée par divers fragments, qui forment un total de seize pages:

a) quatre pages non numérotées de la main de Beckford (et dont la première commence par les mots « I looked around »).

b) huit pages numérotées de 1 à s intitulées « For the Keladet where N. remains six months ».

c) une page non numérotée (commençant par les mots « We saw a light at a distance »).

d) deux pages non numérotées dont la première débute ainsi: « a whirlwind of sand clouds the air », et dont la seconde se termine sur une phrase inachevée: « Said had just performed the last sad rites over the body of »."

e) enfin quelques lignes sans lien apparent avec ce qui précède, mais qui se rappor-
tent probablement à la même histoire (« The Deer which bounding across the vast
Forests of Amrin . . . »)."

8. *Ibid.*, pp. 100–01. Parreaux writes:

"On peut en reconstituer les grandes lignes de la façon suivante. *The Long Story* se
composait de deux parties principales:
 1. Un récit initiatique que Chapman a publié intégralement, à l'exception . . . des
cinq pages manuscrites qui se rattachent encore à ce récit. — Cette première partie,
bien qu'elle soit actuellement représentée par un manuscrit plus long, était
vraisemblablement, la plus courte des deux, et ne constituait, en quelque sorte, qu'un
long préambule à l'histoire proprement dite.
 2. La vie de Nouronihar et de ses ancêtres racontée par elle-même. Dans cette
seconde partie, on peut distinguer les divisions suivantes:
 a) Une histoire des ancêtres de Nouronihar qui était, en même temps, un exposé
historico-mythique des origines de l'Inde.
 b) Le récit d'un sacrilège commis par Nouronihar, qui constituait à la fois le point
culminant de *The Long Story* et la péripétie essentielle de l'action.
 c) L'expiation, et les aventures qui adviennent à l'héroïne au cours de cette expiation — cette dernière partie était sans doute la plus considérable par sa longueur."

 9. *Ibid.*, pp. 101–02.
 10. *Ibid.*, p. 103.
 11. *Ibid.*, p. 106.
 12. *Ibid.*, p. 107.
 13. *Ibid.*, pp. 107–08.
 14. Fatma Moussa-Mahmoud, "A Monument to the Author of *Vathek*,"
Etudes Anglaises, XV (1962), 144.
 15. John G. Lockhart, *Quarterly Review*, LI (June, 1834), 427.
 16. The other possible influences identified by Parreaux are Henry Lord's
A Discovery of the Sect of the Banians (London, 1630); Abraham Roger's *La
Porte ouverte, pour parvenir à la connoissance du paganisme caché* (Amsterdam, 1670); Bernard Picart's *Cérémonies et coûtumes religieuses des peuples du monde* (Amsterdam, 1723); J. H. Grose's *A Voyage to the East-
Indies* (London, 1757). See pp. 114–16 of Parreaux's book.

Chapter Four

 1. Cyrus Redding, "Recollections of the Author of *Vathek*," *The New
Monthly Magazine*, LXXI (June, 1844), 151–52.
 2. Henry V. Lansdown, *Recollections of the late William Beckford*
(Bath, 1893), p. 35. Only one hundred copies were printed of this little book.

3. See R. J. Gemmett, "The Composition of William Beckford's *Biographical Memoirs of Extraordinary Painters,*" *Philological Quarterly,* XLVII (January, 1968), 139–41.

4. *Memoirs,* I, 96.

5. "William Beckford, Esq. of Fonthill," *The European Magazine and London Review,* XXXII (September, 1797), 147.

6. *William Beckford of Fonthill . . . A Brief Narrative and Catalogue of an Exhibition to Mark the Two Hundredth Anniversary of Beckford's Birth,* ed. Howard Gotlieb (Yale University Library, 1960), p. 17.

7. Alexander, *England's Wealthiest Son,* p. 273, n. 20.

8. Guy Chapman and John Hodgkin, *A Bibliography of William Beckford of Fonthill* (London, 1930), p. 3.

9. Both letters (J. Lettice to W. Beckford, December 12, 1779 and March 23, 1780) are printed in Melville, pp. 67–70.

10. Melville has the word "illegible" bracketed here, but it is obvious from the preceding sentence that the word should be "Sucrewasser's." See Melville, p. 68.

11. See Melville, p. 69.

12. This date is based upon Lettice's statement in the letter of March 23rd: "The printer promised faithfully to finish by the 10th April, so that I doubt not having the pleasure of meeting you in town on that day or the next." Melville, p. 70.

13. *Biographical Memoirs of Extraordinary Painters,* ed. Robert J. Gemmett (Rutherford, N.J., 1969), pp. 81–82. All page references hereafter will be based on this edition and appear in parentheses in the text.

14. André Parreaux, "Les Peintres Extraordinaires de Beckford Sont-ils Satire des Écoles Flamande et Hollandaise?" *Revue du Nord,* XLIII (January-March, 1961), 16–17.

15. "Biographical Memoirs of Extraordinary Painters," *The Monthly Review,* LXIII (November, 1780), 469.

16. "Biographical Memoirs of Extraordinary Painters," *The Gentleman's Magazine,* L (June, 1780), 290.

17. "Biographical Memoirs of Extraordinary Painters," *The Critical Review,* XLIX (June, 1780), 478–79.

18. "Biographical Memoirs of Extraordinary Painters," *The Monthly Review,* LXIII (November, 1780), 469.

19. *Ibid.*

20. "Biographical Memoirs of Extraordinary Painters," *The Retrospective Review,* X (London, 1824), 173; 179.

21. "Biographical Memoirs of Extraordinary Painters," *The Literary Gazette,* Saturday, August 16, 1834, pp. 558–60. An advertisement for the new edition appeared the previous week in the issue of August 9, 1834, p. 552.

22. Bath, Monday, August 18, 1834. Letters of William Beckford to His Bookseller [George Clarke]. Manuscript copies made in 1894 for Richard

Bentley, III, Letter 347, f. 486. Beinecke Rare Book and Manuscript Library, Yale University.
23. John G. Lockhart, "Italy, with Sketches of Spain and Portugal," *Quarterly Review*, LI (June, 1834), 426.
24. Redding, *The New Monthly Magazine*, LXXX, 151.
25. Parreaux argues, for example, that Beckford attacks an eighteenth-century school of German painters led by Raphael Mengs, a strained mannerist, and Philipp Hackert, a laborious high finisher. *Revue du Nord*, XLIII, 31–36.
26. *Dreams, Waking Thoughts and Incidents*, ed. Robert J. Gemmett (Rutherford, N.J., 1972), pp. 63–64.
27. Redding, *The New Monthly Magazine*, LXXI, 151.
28. Redding, *Memoirs*, I, 97.

Chapter Five

1. W. Beckford to Charlotte Courtenay, February 22, 1781, quoted in Chapman, *Beckford*, p. 82.
2. W. Beckford to Louisa Beckford, January, 1780, quoted in Melville, p. 78.
3. Written by Beckford in 1838. See Chapman, *Beckford*, p. 69.
4. W. Beckford to Count Benincasa, October 21, 1780, quoted in Alexander, *England's Wealthiest Son*, p. 76.
5. Lady Hamilton to W. Beckford, December 11, [1780], quoted in Oliver, p. 52.
6. W. Beckford to Lady Hamilton, December 29, 1780, quoted in Oliver, p. 54.
7. Lady Hamilton to W. Beckford, January 9, 1781, quoted in Oliver, p. 55.
8. W. Beckford to Countess Rosenberg, October 7, 1781, quoted in Alexander, *England's Wealthiest Son*, p. 14.
9. W. Beckford to Lady Hamilton, April 2, 1781, quoted in Melville, p. 105.
10. Only one notebook has been found; it runs from October 26 to 31, 1780. See *Bibliography*, p. 11.
11. Redding, *Memoirs*, II, 310. While in Rome, Beckford did write a few of the letters in full; and he later incorporated them into the book with only slight alterations.
12. Melville, p. 109.
13. W. Beckford to Samuel Henley, January 29, 1782, *Morrison Collection*, I, 183.
14. Oliver, p. 95.
15. W. Beckford to Samuel Henley, January 21, 1782, *Morrison Collection*, I, 183.

16. Oliver, p. 96.
17. W. Beckford to Samuel Henley, January 29, 1782, *Morrison Collection*, I, 183.
18. Oliver, p. 98.
19. W. Beckford to Samuel Henley, April 25, 1782, *Morrison Collection*, I, 183.
20. Melville, p. 48.
21. There is some evidence available which reveals that, while in Padua, Count Benincasa was given access to some unpublished material of Beckford's. Since we know that it was in epistolary form, it is possible that the material was a manuscript version of *Dreams*. What is clear from a letter written by the Reverend Lettice to Benincasa on July 29 and 30 from Naples is that, during the stay in Padua, Beckford, Lettice, and the Count had talked about a plan leading to the publication of a collection of Beckford's "letters." Benincasa's role is not clearly defined in the letter, but it would most probably be as translator. He had done this kind of work for M. de Rosenberg, and it would not make much sense to consult him about an English edition of any of Beckford's works, let alone *Dreams*. This could mean, as Guy Chapman has already suggested, an Italian edition of *Dreams*, or perhaps the publication of a portion of the book in Italian. (No such publication has yet been found.)
The possibility that the "publication in question" refers to another series of Beckford letters cannot be ruled out, however, especially in view of the fact that Lettice's letter describes the work as containing expressions "infinitely beyond the most violent language of ordinary passions," which is not an apt characterization of *Dreams* as we know it today. Another possibility is that the final, published version of *Dreams* was considerably altered from the original manuscript. At any rate, on July 20, Count Benincasa drafted a letter to Lettice in which he proposed "two plans" for the "publication in question." Lettice's reply is printed in Chapman's *Beckford*, pp. 137–38.
22. Melville, p. 153.
23. *Ibid*., p. 157. In his unpublished notes on *Dreams*, now at the Bodleian, John Hodgkin wrote that he believed the "conclusive Epistle" referred to "either Letter VI, dated Rome 30 June 1782, second trip to Italy or Letter VII, dated Naples July 8th, 1782." It seems unlikely, however, that at this stage Beckford had it in mind to include any account of his second tour in *Dreams* and, assuming that he did, that he even knew what the concluding epistle for the second tour would be.
24. W. Beckford to Samuel Henley, August 20, 1782, *Morrison Collection*, I, 186.
25. According to an entry in Thomas Jones's diary, dated September, 1782, Burton died "during the Delirium of a Fever, and execrating in a most shocking manner, the Person who was . . . instrumental . . . in bringing him into this deplorable Situation." See *Memoirs of Thomas Jones*, Walpole

Society, XXXII (London, 1951), 114. Most reference works give 1785 as the year of Burton's death.

26. W. Beckford to Samuel Henley, January 15, 1783, *Morrison Collection,* I, 188.

27. W. Beckford to Samuel Henley, February 13, 1783, *Ibid.,* p. 189.

28. W. Beckford to Samuel Henley, April 15, 1783, *Ibid.*

29. W. Beckford to Samuel Henley, April 30, 1783, *Ibid.*

30. W. Beckford to Samuel Henley, Nov. 18, 1783, *Ibid.*

31. Redding, *Memoirs,* I, 138.

32. Chapman, *Beckford,* p. 153. To substantiate this view, Chapman cites elsewhere the following comment which Beckford wrote on a letter sent to him by his attorney, Thomas Wildman, dated April 14, 1789: "The only method of interfering effectually would be to produce the wretched book in open daylight, and to such an exposition I am certain L. C. (whom I take to be Courtenay, *i.e.,* William, who had recently succeeded to the title) would never consent." See Chapman, *Bibliography,* p. 13.

33. Oliver, p. 129.

34. This theory is supported by a Beckford letter to Lettice, dated March 3, 1787, containing the comment: "I cannot permit the mutilation of the book. . . . Not a word of the first letter can I spare. . . . I cannot agree to expunging the strokes I have launched at the Dutch and Flemings." See Chapman, *Bibliography,* p. 13.

35. Redding, *Memoirs,* I, 138.

36. Louise Necker to W. Beckford, Paris, 1784. My translation of original French text in Oliver, pp. 185–86.

37. *Memoirs, Journal, and Correspondence of Thomas Moore,* ed. Lord John Russell (London, 1853), II, 193.

38. John G. Lockhart, *Quarterly Review,* LI (June, 1834), 428; W. L. N., "Beckford's Letters," *Notes & Queries,* IV, 2nd Series (July 4, 1857), 14–15.

39. A note by Beckford in the flyleaf of a presentation copy of the 1823 edition of *Rogers' Italy* currently among the Beckford papers.

40. Samuel Rogers wrote: "For this thought I am indebted to some unpublished travels by the author of *Vathek.*" See *Italy, A Poem* (London, 1830), p. 252.

41. John G. Lockhart, *Quarterly Review,* LI (June, 1834), 429, 456.

42. The Gemmett edition of *Dreams, Waking Thoughts and Incidents,* pp. 192–93. All page references hereafter will be based on this edition and appear in parentheses in the text.

43. William Gilpin, *An Essay upon Prints* (London, 1768), p. 2.

44. Guy Chapman, (ed.), "Memoirs of William Beckford," *The Travel-Diaries of William Beckford of Fonthill* (Cambridge, England; 1928), I, lvii.

45. Richard Garnett, *Dictionary of National Biography,* II, 84.

46. H. T. Tuckerman, "William Beckford and the Literature of Travel," ' *Southern Literary Messenger,* XVI (January, 1850), 14.

Chapter Six

1. W. Beckford to Elizabeth Hervey, April, 1778, quoted in Oliver, p. 23.
2. *Dreams, Waking Thoughts and Incidents*, p. 119.
3. *Ibid.*, p. 125.
4. Chapman, *Bibliography*, p. 94.
5. *Ibid.*, pp. 93; 100–01.
6. W. Beckford to A. Cozens (?), March, 1780, quoted in Melville, pp. 82–83.
7. W. Beckford to A. Cozens (?), March, 1780, quoted in Melville, p. 80.
8. W. Beckford to Elizabeth Hervey, undated letter, quoted in Melville, pp. 42–43.
9. W. Beckford to A. Cozens (?), December 3, 1779, quoted in Melville, pp. 75–76.
10. Oliver, pp. 89–91. Beckford reconstructed this glowing scene on December 9, 1838, in a note he appended to a letter written in the spring of 1782.
11. Redding, *Memoirs*, I, 243; 245. Oliver, p. 95, cites a similar statement by Beckford: "I composed *Vathek* immediately upon my return to town. It was written, not as Byron says, at 17, but at 22."
12. See Chapters II and III in Parreaux's study for a description of some of the unpublished material that was to be included in the *Suite des Contes Arabes*.
13. W. Beckford to S. Henley, February 9, 1786, *Morrison Collection*, I, 196.
14. *Ibid.*, 197.
15. Letter by S. Henley, February 7, 1787, *The Gentleman's Magazine*, LVIII, pt. I (February, 1787), 120.
16. See Karl F. Thompson, "Henley's Share in Beckford's *Vathek*," *Philological Quarterly*, XXXI (1952), 79–80.
17. S. Henley to Thomas Wildman, October 23, 1786, quoted in Melville, p. 138.
18. Marcel May, *La jeunesse de William Beckford et la genése de son Vathek* (Paris, 1928).
19. John Carter, "The Lausanne Edition of Beckford's *Vathek*," *The Library*, XVII (March, 1937), 386–88.
20. H. B. Grimsditch, "Introduction," *Vathek* (London, 1945), p. xi.
21. Redding, *Memoirs*, I, 246.
22. Melville, p. 128.
23. *Vathek: An Arabian Tale* (London, 1834), p. 4. All page references to this work hereafter are based on this edition and appear in parentheses in the text.
24. Jorge Luis Borges, *Other Inquisitions 1937–1952*, trans. Ruth L. C. Sims, (Austin, 1964), p. 139.
25. Lafcadio Hearn, *Some Strange English Literary Figures of the Eighteenth and Nineteenth Centuries*. (Freeport, N.Y., 1965), p. 49.

Hearn's essay on Beckford was originally a lecture given in 1899 at the Imperial University of Tokyo.

26. "The History of the Caliph Vathek," *The Monthly Review*, LXXVI (May, 1787), 450.

27. Edith Birkhead, *The Tale of Terror: A Study of the Gothic Romance* (New York, 1963), p. 98.

28. "Mr. Beckford's *Vathek*," *The Morning Chronicle*, October 10, 1823, in *The Complete Works of William Hazlitt*, ed. P. P. Howe (London, 1933), XIX, 98; 103.

29. Edmund Wilson, *Shores of Light* (New York, 1952), p. 266.

30. Roger Lonsdale, "Introduction," *Vathek* (London, 1970), p. xxviii.

31. Baker, V, 75.

32. Guy Chapman, *Beckford*, p. 109.

33. Cyrus Redding, "Recollections of the Author of *Vathek*," *The New Monthly Magazine*, LXXI (June, 1844), 150.

34. James H. Rieger, "Au Pied de la Lettre: Stylistic Uncertainty in *Vathek*," *Criticism*, IV (1962), 309–10.

35. Richard Garnett, *Essays of an Ex-Librarian* (London, 1901), p. 189.

36. The full title of the original edition by d'Herbelot provides some idea of the scope of this work: *Bibliothèque Orientale, ou Dictionnaire universel contenant généralement tout ce qui regarde la connoissance des Peuples de l'Orient. Leurs Histoires et Traditions véritables ou fabuleuses. Leurs Religions, Sectes et Politiques, Leurs Gouvernements, Loix, Coûtumes, Moeurs, Guerres, & les Révolutions de leurs Empires. Leurs Sciences, et leurs Arts, Leurs Théologie, Mythologie, Magie, Physique, Morale, Médecine, Mathématiques, Histoire naturelle, Chronologie, Géographie, Observations Astronomiques, Grammaire, & Rhétorique.* Par Monsieur D'Herbelot. A Paris, Par la Compagnie des Librairies. 1697.

37. D'Herbelot, *Bibliothèque Orientale* (La Haye, 1778), III, 574–76. All page references hereafter are based on this edition and appear in parentheses in the text.

38. These and other borrowings from the *Bibliothèque Orientale* are acknowledged in the notes to *Vathek*, pp. 99–118.

39. *Ibid.*, pp. 107; 113. See also Parreaux, pp. 319–20; 341–42.

40. May, pp. 296–309.

41. H. W. Weber, *Tales of the East* (Edinburgh, 1812), III, 58.

42. Anonymous reviews of *Vathek*: *The Critical Review*, LXII (July, 1786), 39; *The Gentleman's Magazine*, LVI, pt. 2 (July, 1786), 594; *The European Magazine and London Review*, X (August, 1786), 104; *The Monthly Review*, LXXVI (May, 1787), 450.

Chapter Seven

1. W. Beckford to S. Henley, January 13, 1783, *Morrison Collection*, I, 187–88.

2. November 18, 1783, *Morrison Collection*, I, 190.

3. *Idem.*

4. "I long to hear if you have finished *Vathek,* & when I may have an opportunity of introducing you to his other relations." January 25, 1784, *Morrison Collection,* I, 191.

5. May 6, 1784, *Idem.*

6. October 13, 1784, *Morrison Collection,* I, 193.

7. March 31, 1785, *Idem.*

8. February 9, 1786, *Morrison Collection,* I, 196.

9. August 1, 1786, *Morrison Collection,* I, 197.

10. *Vathek* (Lausanne, 1787), p. 197.

11. *[Vathek] An Arabian Tale* (London, 1786), p. 204.

12. *Vathek, Conte arabe* (Paris, 1787), p. 160.

13. Redding, *Memoirs,* I, 146. Beckford characterized this episode in the following way: "I think that the *Episode of the Story of Motassem* the Father of Vathek will amuse the Abbé [Macquin]. More than any of my sketches, it has something of the historic, of the paederastic (?), and of the simplicity of Arabian tales; and much of the grandiose, the graceful, the whorish (?) and the holy *(secundum ordinem Melchisedek).* What a strange beast or savage I am!" July 4, 1815, *Life at Fonthill,* p. 182.

14. Lewis Melville, "Introduction," *The Episodes of Vathek,* trans. Frank T. Marzials (London, 1912), pp. xxix–xxx. All page references to this work hereafter are based on this edition and appear in parentheses in the text.

15. Samuel Rogers, *Recollections of the Table-Talk of Samuel Rogers to which is added Porsoniana* (New York, 1856), p. 215.

16. *The Works of Lord Byron. Letters and Journals,* ed. Rowland E. Prothero (London, 1922), IV, 207.

17. March 3, 1818, *Letters and Journals of Lord Byron with Notices of his Life,* ed. Thomas Moore (London, 1830), II, 167–68.

18. S. Rogers to Byron, November 23, 1820, *Works of Byron,* V, 138.

19. Anonymous, "Conversations with the Late W. Beckford, Esq.," *The New Monthly Magazine,* LXXII (October, 1844), 219.

20. G. Townshend Mayer, "The Sultan of Lansdown Tower," *Temple Bar,* CXX (June, 1900), 208.

21. For other editions, see R. J. Gemmett, "An Annotated Checklist of the Works of William Beckford," *Papers of the Bibliographical Society of America,* LXI (Third Quarter, 1967), 253–54.

22. Alexander, *England's Wealthiest Son,* p. 91.

23. See Parreaux, p. 418.

24. Parreaux, p. 426.

25. *Ibid.,* p. 432.

26. Parreaux identified this probable source. See p. 434.

27. "The First Kalandar's Tale," *The Arabian Nights' Entertainments,* trans. Richard F. Burton (New York, 1932), p. 73.

28. Anna Barbauld, *The British Novelists* (London, 1810), XXVI, 1.

29. W. Beckford to S. Henley, 1785, *Morrison Collection*, I, 195.
30. November 23, 1820, *Works of Byron*, V, 138.
31. October 20, 1817, *Life at Fonthill*, p. 227.
32. John Mitford, *The Note-Book of John Mitford (1844–1849)*, British Museum, 32.566, f. 35.
33. Chapman, *Beckford*, p. 145.
34. Alexander, *England's Wealthiest Son*, p. 96.
35. *The Complete Tales and Poems of Edgar Allan Poe*, ed. Hervey Allan (New York, 1938), p. 621.
36. *Baudelaire on Poe*, Trans. and ed. Lois and F. E. Hyslop (State College, Pa., 1952), p. 126.

Chapter Eight

1. *Dreams, Waking Thoughts and Incidents*, p. 224.
2. John C. Loudon, *An Encyclopedia of Gardening* (London, 1824), II, 1083.
3. Chapman, *Bibliography*, pp. 44–47.
4. Gotlieb, p. 64.
5. *Modern Novel Writing, or the Elegant Enthusiast* (London, 1796), I, 41. All page references to this work hereafter are based on this edition and appear in parentheses in the text.
6. *Azemia: A Descriptive and Sentimental Novel* (London, 1797), II, 12, 14. All page references to the work hereafter are based on this edition and appear in parentheses in the text.
7. Chapman, *Beckford*, p. 275.
8. *Lord Granville Leveson Gower. Private Correspondence, 1781–1821*, ed. Countess Granville (London, 1916), II, 544–45.
9. See Robert J. Gemmett, "The Caliph Vathek from England and the Continent to America," *American Book Collector*, XVIII (May, 1968), 12–19.
10. See Alexander, *Life at Fonthill*, pp. 326–28.
11. Hazlitt, "Mr. Beckford's *Vathek*," *The Complete Works of William Hazlitt*, XIX, 98.
12. Oliver, p. 312.
13. W. Beckford to Mr. Scholl, July 8, 1833, quoted in Oliver, p. 313.
14. Lockhart, p. 456.
15. Chapman, *Travel-Diaries*, II, 254.
16. Charles Whibly, *The Pageantry of Life* (New York, 1900), p. 204.
17. Rose Macaulay, *They Went to Portugal* (London, 1946), p. 134.
18. Chapman, *Travel-Diaries*, II, 316.
19. Chapman, "Preface," *Excursion à Alcobaça et Batalha*, ed. André Parreaux (Paris, 1956), p. xiv. An edition of the *Excursion* published in French and English.

20. H. A. N. Brockman, *The Caliph of Fonthill* (London, 1956), pp. 194–95.

21. *The Works of William Hazlitt*, X, 58.

22. Oliver, p. 322.

23. *Ibid.*, p. 325.

24. "Conversations with the Late W. Beckford, Esq., Contributed by Various Friends," *New Monthly Magazine*, LXXII (October, 1844), 217.

25. W. Beckford to Lady Hamilton, April 2, 1781, quoted in Melville, p. 105.

Chapter Nine

1. See John L. Lowes, *The Road to Xanadu: A Study in the Ways of the Imagination* (Boston, 1955), p. 326.

2. Marie E. de Meester, *Oriental Influences in the English Literature of the Nineteenth Century* (Heidelberg, 1915), p. 31.

3. Chapman, *Bibliography*, p. xviii.

4. A. V., "The Palace of Istaker," *The Gentleman's Magazine*, LX, pt. 1 (January–March, 1790), 69–70, 163–65, 258–59. See Appendix.

5. See Fatma Moussa Mahmoud, "Beckford, *Vathek* and the Oriental Tale," *William Beckford of Fonthill, 1760–1844, Bicentenary Essays*, pp. 112–13.

6. de Meester, p. 24.

7. *The Poetical Works of Robert Southey* (London, 1845), pp. 626–27.

8. Garnett, *Essays of an Ex-Librarian*, pp. 190–91.

9. *Medwin's Conversations of Lord Byron*, ed. Ernest J. Lovell, Jr. (Princeton, 1966), p. 258.

10. Henry Lansdown recorded in a letter to his daughter that Byron once called upon the Duchess of Hamilton with a copy of *Vathek* in his pocket, which he identified as "his gospel." See *Recollections of the Late William Beckford of Fonthill, Wilts; and Lansdown, Bath*, ed. Charlotte Lansdown (Privately printed, 1893), p. 32.

11. *Medwin's Conversations*, ed. Lovell, p. 218.

12. *Byron's Letters and Journals*, ed. Prothero, VI, 284.

13. *The Works of Lord Byron. Poetry*, ed. E. H. Coleridge (London, 1899), III, 145.

14. *Byron's Letters and Journals*, ed. Prothero, II, 283.

15. Harold Wiener, "Byron and the East: Literary Sources of the *Turkish Tales*," *Nineteenth-Century Studies*, ed. Herbert Davis *et al.* (New York, 1968), pp. 89–101.

16. *Ibid.*, pp. 102–03.

17. *Works of Byron*, ed. Coleridge, III, 183.

18. André Parreaux, "Beckford et Byron," *Etudes Anglaises*, VIII (January, 1955), 11–26.

19. Now in the library of the late James T. Babb of New Haven, Connecticut. Mrs. Babb has graciously permitted me to examine it and quote from it.

20. In this passage, the phrase "even the most distant" is lined out and the word "any" substituted; the phrase "or point out instances of *petty larceny*" is scratched out.

21. October 18, 1818, *Memoirs, Journal, and Correspondence of Thomas Moore*, ed. Lord John Russell (London, 1853), II, 193.

22. March 23, 1816, *The Letters of Thomas Moore*, ed. W. S. Dowden (Oxford, Eng., 1964), I, 394.

23. *Letters and Journals of Lord Byron*, ed. Moore, II, 167n.

24. *William Beckford of Fonthill, 1760–1844, Bicentenary Essays*, ed. F. M. Mahmoud, p. 115.

25. Robert Birley, *Sunk Without Trace* (New York, 1962), p. 154.

26. Thomas Moore, *Lalla Rookh, An Oriental Romance* (London, 1817), p. 53. See *Vathek*, p. 89.

27. Sidney Colvin, *John Keats, His Life and Poetry, His Friends, Critics and After-Fame* (New York, 1917), p. 184.

28. *The Complete Poetical Works of Keats*, ed. Horace E. Scudder (Boston, 1899), p. 315.

29. See Keith Hollingsworth, "*Vathek* and the *Ode to a Nightingale*," *Times Literary Supplement*, October 27, 1961, p. 771; Robert Gittings, *The Mask of Keats: A Study of Problems* (London, 1956), pp. 101–02.

30. Gittings, p. 107.

31. March 9, 1833, quoted in Melville, p. 337.

32. Quoted by Benjamin Disraeli to his sister, May 26, 1832, in Melville, p. 337.

33. W. Beckford to George Clarke, March, 1833, Melville, p. 338.

34. W. Beckford to George Clarke, [1834?], Melville, p. 339.

35. W. Beckford to George Clarke, [1833], Melville, p. 336.

36. Henry A. Beers, *A History of English Romanticism in the Eighteenth Century* (New York, 1932), p. 43.

Selected Bibliography

PRIMARY SOURCES

1. Important Editions of *Vathek* and the *Episodes*
An Arabian Tale. From an Unpublished Manuscript: with Notes Critical and Explanatory. London: Printed for J. Johnson, in St. Paul's Church-Yard, and Entered at the Stationer's Hall, 1786. First English edition of *Vathek;* Henley's translation.

Vathek. A Lausanne: Isaac Hignou & Compe, 1787. First French edition. The prefatory note makes reference to Henley's indiscretion for having published the English translation of *Vathek* before the original had appeared.

Vathek, Conte Arabe. A Paris, Chez Poinçot, Libraire, rue de la Harpe, près Saint-Côme, No. 135. 1787. Second French edition; text has been refined.

Vathek. A Londres; Chez Clarke, New Bond Street, 1815. Third French edition. Contains some verbal as well as stylistic variations from the Paris edition.

Vathek. Translated from the Original French. From the Third London Edition, Revised and Corrected. Philadelphia: M. Carey, 1816. First American edition from Henley's translation.

Vathek; An Arabian Tale. London: Richard Bentley, 1834. Volume XLI of Bentley's Standard Novels.

Le Vathek de Beckford. Reimprimé sur l'Edition française originale avec Préface par Stéphane Mallarmé. Paris: Adolphe Labitte, libraire de la Bibliothèque Nationale, 1876. An edition of two hundred twenty numbered copies initialed by the editor.

Vathek: An Arabian Tale. Edited by Richard Garnett, Ll.D. With Notes by Samuel Henley, and Etchings by Herbert Nye. London; Lawrence & Bullen, 1893. An edition of six hundred numbered copies; seventy numbered copies were printed on vellum.

The Episodes of Vathek. Translated by Sir Frank T. Marzials. With an Introduction by Lewis Melville. London: W. C. Stephen Swift & Co., Ltd, 1912. Includes both the English translation and the original

French. Two of the three *Episodes* appeared for the first time in French in *The English Review* (December, 1909; August and September, 1910).

Vathek with The Episodes of Vathek. Edited with a Historical Introduction and Notes by Guy Chapman. In Two Volumes with Illustrations. Cambridge; Constable and Company & Houghton Mifflin Company, 1929. The text for *Vathek* is the Paris edition of 1787; that of the *Episodes,* the French version published in 1912.

Vathek. A new translation by Herbert Grimsditch, with ten illustrations by Marion V. Dorn. London: The Nonesuch Press, 1929. This new translation is based on the French version of 1815.

Vathek et les Episodes. Texte établi et introduit par Ernest Giddey. Lausanne: Editions Rencontre, 1962.

Vathek. Edited with an Introduction by Roger Lonsdale. London: Oxford University Press, 1970.

Vathek. The English Translation by Samuel Henley (1786) And the French Editions of Lausanne and Paris (1787). Facsimile Reproduction With an Introduction by Robert J. Gemmett. Delmar, New York: Scholars' Facsimiles & Reprints, 1972.

The Episodes of Vathek. Ed. Robert J. Gemmett. Rutherford: Fairleigh-Dickinson University Press, 1975. Reprints the 1912 translation by Sir Frank Marzials.

2. Other Works by Beckford

Biographical Memoirs of Extraordinary Painters. London: J. Robson, 1780.

Dreams, Waking Thoughts and Incidents. London: J. Johnson, 1783.

Modern Novel Writing, or the Elegant Enthusiast; and Interesting Emotions of Arabella Bloomville. A Rhapsodical Romance; Interspersed with Poetry. By the Right Hon. Lady Harriet Marlow. 2 vols. London: G. G. and J. Robinson, 1796.

Azemia: A Descriptive and Sentimental Novel. Interspersed with Pieces of Poetry. By Jacquetta Agneta Mariana Jenks. 2 vols. London: Sampson Low, 1797.

Epitaphs; some of which have appeared in the *Literary Gazette* of March & April, 1823.

Italy; with Sketches of Spain and Portugal. 2 vols. London: Richard Bentley, 1834.

Recollections of an Excursion to the Monasteries of Alcobaça and Batalha. London: Richard Bentley, 1835.

The Travel-Diaries of William Beckford of Fonthill. Ed. Guy Chapman. 2 vols. Cambridge: Constable and Co., 1928.

The Vision and *Liber Veritatis.* Edited with an Introduction and Notes by Guy Chapman. Cambridge: Constable and Co., 1930.

The Journal of William Beckford in Portugal and Spain 1787–1788. Edited with an Introduction and Notes by Boyd Alexander. London: Rupert Hart-Davis, 1954. Published in New York by John Day in 1955.

Beckford's 1794 Journal. Edited with an introduction by Boyd Alexander in *William Beckford of Fonthill, Writer, Traveller, Collector, Caliph, 1760–1844.* By Howard Gotlieb. New Haven: Yale University Library, 1960.

Biographical Memoirs of Extraordinary Painters. Edited with an Introduction and Notes by Robert J. Gemmett. Rutherford, N.J.: Fairleigh Dickinson University Press [1969].

Dreams, Waking Thoughts and Incidents. Edited with an Introduction and Notes by Robert J. Gemmett. Rutherford, N.J.: Fairleigh Dickinson University Press [1971].

3. Correspondence

Collection of Autograph Letters and Historical Documents. Formed by Alfred Morrison (Second Series, 1882–1893). 3 vols. Printed for private circulation, 1893. Volume I, 182–200, contains the Beckford-Henley correspondence and additional letters.

Collection of Autograph Letters and Historical Documents. Formed by Alfred Morrison (Second Series, 1882–1893) The Hamilton and Nelson Papers. 2 vols. (vol. I, 1765–1797; vol. II, 1798–1815). Printed for private circulation, 1893–1894.

    Letters by Beckford can be found in I, 153; 157; 165; 169–70; 183; 212–13; 215–16; 218–19; 227–28; II, 78; 193–94.

Life at Fonthill: 1807–1822. With Interludes in Paris and London. From the Correspondence of William Beckford. Translated and Edited by Boyd Alexander. London: Rupert Hart-Davis, 1957.

The Life and Letters of William Beckford of Fonthill (Author of *Vathek*). By Lewis Melville. London: William Heinemann, 1910.

SECONDARY SOURCES

1. Bibliography

CHAPMAN, GUY AND JOHN HODGKIN. *A Bibliography of William Beckford of Fonthill.* London: Constable, 1930.

GEMMETT, ROBERT J. "An Annotated Checklist of the Works of William Beckford," *Papers of the Bibliographical Society of America,* LXI (Fall, 1967), 243–58.

———. "William Beckford: Bibliographical Addenda," *Bulletin of Bibliography,* XXV (May-August, 1967), 62–64. Partial listing of secondary sources on Beckford's life and work.

2. Books and Articles

ALEXANDER, BOYD. *England's Wealthiest Son: A Study of William Beckford.* London: Centaur Press, 1962. Indispensable study by the custodian of the Beckford papers; contains a great deal of material drawn from unpublished documents.

ALLEN, WALTER. *The English Novel: A Short Critical History*. New York: E. P. Dutton, 1954. Focuses on Beckford's sense of the grotesque in *Vathek*.

BAKER, ERNEST. "*The Oriental Story from Rasselas to Vathek*." *The History of the English Novel*. New York: Barnes & Noble, 1929. Sees the realistic detail in *Vathek* as an innovation in the development of the Anglo-Oriental fantasy.

BELLOC, HILAIRE. "On *Vathek*." *A Conversation with an Angel*. New York: Harper, 1929. Brief but incisive essay. Belloc believes that *Vathek* is a unique book deserving of a higher place in the history of English letters than it holds.

BIRKHEAD, EDITH. "The Oriental Tale of Terror. Beckford." *The Tale of Terror: A Study of the Gothic Romance*. New York: Russell, 1963. In spite of the misleading title, Birkhead stresses the intellectual and biographical aspects of *Vathek*.

BORGES, JORGE LUIS. "*About William Beckford's Vathek*." *Other Inquisitions 1937–1952*. Trans. Ruth L. C. Sims. Austin: University of Texas, [1964]. Borges discerns in *Vathek* foreshadowings of DeQuincey, Poe, Baudelaire, and Huysmans.

BROCKMAN, H. A. N. *The Caliph of Fonthill*. London: Werner Laurie, 1956. Principally devoted to the subject of Fonthill Abbey; secondly, to Beckford's life.

CARTER, JOHN. "The Lausanne Edition of Beckford's *Vathek*," *The Library*, XVII (March, 1937), 369–94. Extremely valuable discussion of the bibliographical problems involved in the history of the early editions of *Vathek*. Carter has since reported that the retranslation theory set forth here has been effectively demolished by Parreaux's findings.

CHADOURNE, MARC. *Eblis ou L'Enfer de William Beckford*. [Paris]: Jean-Jacques Pauvert, [1967]. Popular account successfully recreates Beckford's life and times.

CHAPMAN, GUY. *Beckford*. 2nd ed. London: Rupert Hart-Davis, 1952. The standard biography — a major contribution to Beckford studies.

———. "Beckford the Caliph, A Traveller of Two Worlds: Passion and Fantasy," (London) *Times Literary Supplement*, May 6, 1944, p. 222. An introductory essay stressing the thesis that Beckford's life and work display the ambivalence of his transitional period.

CHURCH, RICHARD. *The Growth of the English Novel*. New York: Barnes & Noble, 1957. Sees *Vathek* as an exotic dream comparable in poetic grandeur to Coleridge's *Kubla Khan*.

CONANT, MARTHA PIKE. *The Oriental Tale in England in the Eighteenth Century*. New York: Columbia University, 1908. By far the best account of this special literary genre. One of the first critics to recognize that *Vathek* was not an abnormal phenomenon in the eighteenth century, that it was intimately connected with both its predecessors and its successors, and that it deserves a high place among the Anglo-Oriental tales of the period.

"Conversations with the Late W. Beckford," *New Monthly Magazine*, LX-XII (September, October, November, December, 1844), 18–25; 212–21; 418–27; 516–22. Illuminating conversations contributed by various friends.

DE GRAAF, D. A. "Potgieter en Vathek," *Revue des Langues Vivantes*, XXIV (1958), 469–75. Underscores the significance of *Vathek* to the nineteenth-century Flemish writer, Potgieter.

DE MEESTER, MARIE E. "*Vathek* and its Influence." *Oriental Influences in the English Literature of the Nineteenth Century*. Heidelberg: Winters, 1915. Points out that *Vathek* "gave new food to the appetite for eastern literature."

ELTON, OLIVER. *A Survey of English Literature, 1780–1830*. London: Edward Arnold, 1912. Views *Vathek* as representing revival of the real East in the eighteenth century.

FINKELSTEIN, DOROTHEA M. *Melville's Orienda*. New Haven: Yale University, 1961. Finds traces of *Vathek* in Melville's work, particularly *Moby Dick*.

FOLSOM, JAMES K. "*Beckford's Vathek* and the Tradition of Oriental Satire," *Criticism*, VI (1964), 53–69. Provocative article devoted to the argument that *Vathek* satirizes some of the absurdities of the Oriental tradition; "that its extravagances are signs of a literary extravagance within this tradition rather than of psychological infirmities on the part of the author."

GARNETT, RICHARD. "Beckford's *Vathek*," *Essays of an Ex-Librarian*. London: William Heinemann, 1901. This celebrated essay first appeared as the introduction to Garnett's edition of *Vathek* in 1893; helped considerably in the revival of Beckford studies.

GEMMETT, ROBERT. "Beckford in the Saleroom," (London) *Times Literary Supplement*, November 17, 1966, p. 1056. Descriptive summary of the John Hodgkin collection of personal essays, notes, transcripts, etc., relating to bibliographical studies and other work on Beckford, which was bequeathed to the Bodleian Library in 1931.

———. "Beckford's Fonthill: The Landscape as Art," *Gazette des Beaux-Arts*, LXXX (December, 1972), 335–56. Full discussion of Fonthill as a dramatic illustration of a landscape garden in the picturesque style.

———. "The Birth Date of William Beckford," *American Notes & Queries*, VI (June, 1968), 149–50. Provides evidence which establishes the birth date as September 29, 1760.

———. "The Caliph Vathek from England and the Continent to America," *American Book Collector*, XVIII, 9 (May, 1968), 12–19. History of the editions of *Vathek*, including the earliest to appear in America.

———. "The Composition of William Beckford's *Biographical Memoirs of Extraordinary Painters*," *Philological Quarterly*, XLVII (January, 1968), 139–41. Establishes that Beckford did not complete *Extraordinary Painters* until he was nineteen after having begun writing it over two years earlier.

————. "The Critical Reception of William Beckford's Fonthill," *English Miscellany* XIX (1968), 133–51.

————. *Sale Catalogues of Libraries of Eminent Persons, III: William Beckford.* London: Mansell, 1972. Reprints with introductions catalogues of the 1804, 1808, 1817, and 1823 sales.

GIDDEY, ERNEST. "La Vision créatrice de *Vathek* de Beckford." *Mélanges offerts à Monsieur Georges Bonnard.* (Université de Lausanne; Publications de la Faculté des Lettres, XVIII.) Geneva: Droz, 1966.

GOTLIEB, HOWARD B. *William Beckford of Fonthill.* New Haven: Yale University Library, 1960. Includes a brief narrative and catalogue of an exhibition at Yale marking the two hundredth anniversary of Beckford's birth.

GREGORY, WILLIAM. *The Beckford Family: Reminiscences of Fonthill Abbey and Lansdown Tower.* 2nd ed. London: Simpkin, 1898. Useful little book; contains some inaccurate information and relies rather heavily on secondary sources.

HAZLITT, WILLIAM. "Mr. Beckford's *Vathek,*" *Morning Chronicle,* October 10, 1823, in *The Complete Works of William Hazlitt.* Ed. P. D. Howe. 21 vols. London: Dent, 1931–34. XIX, 98–103. Important early appreciation of *Vathek.*

HEARN, LAFCADIO. "*William Beckford.*" *Some Strange Literary Figures of the Eighteenth and Nineteenth Centuries.* Ed. R. Tanabe₂. Freeport, N.Y.: Books for Libraries [1965]. Lecture delivered to the students of English literature, graduate class of 1899, Imperial University of Tokyo.

HEPPENSTALL, RAYNER. "The Palace of Subterranean Fire." *The Fourfold Tradition. Notes on the French and English literatures, with some ethnological and historical asides.* London: Barrie & Rockliff, 1961. A summary introduction to *Vathek* and the *Episodes;* brief account of Beckford's life.

HUNTER, A. O. "Le *Vathek* de William Beckford: historique des éditions françaises," *Revue de Littérature Comparée,* XV (1935), 119–26.

HUSSAIN, IMDAD. "Beckford, Wainewright, DeQuincey, and Oriental Exoticism," *Venture: A Quarterly Review of English Language and Literature* (Karachi University), I (September, 1960), 234–48. Interesting, helpful discussion of Beckford's use of a special cultural atmosphere to articulate his sensuous life.

JANTZEN, HERMANN. "Source of 'The Hall of Eblis' by B. Cornwall," *Archiv für das Studium der neueren Sprachen u. Literaturen,* CVII (1902), 318–23. Devoted to the influence of *Vathek* on the poet Barry Cornwall.

KEEGAN, P. Q. "Gleanings from Anglo-Oriental Literature: *Vathek, Anastasius, Hajji Baba,*" *Colburn's New Monthly Magazine,* XI

(1877), 674–87. Admires Beckford's imaginative power and the portrait of Oriental sensuality in *Vathek*.

KIELY, ROBERT. *"Vathek," The Romantic Novel in England.* Cambridge: Harvard University Press, 1972. Provocative discussion of *Vathek* as an extension of Beckford's character.

LANE-POOLE, STANLEY. "The Author of *Vathek*," *Quarterly Review*, CCXIII (1910). 377–401. Perceptive, sensitively written essay on Beckford's career and works. Concludes that "Beckford was an egoist and a hedonist, like the majority of men; the difference was that he boldly professed his creed and did not pretend to be what he was not."

LANSDOWN, HENRY V. *Recollections of the Late William Beckford of Fonthill, Wilts.; and Lansdown, Bath.* Bath: Privately printed, 1893. Collection of letters about Beckford written between the years 1838 and 1844.

MAHMOUD, FATMA M. "*Rasselas* and *Vathek*" *Bicentenary Essays on Rasselas*. Ed. Magdi Wahba. Cairo: Cairo Studies in English, 1960. Underlines a few similarities between the two works.

——— (Ed.). *William Beckford of Fonthill, 1760–1844: Bicentenary Essays.* Cairo: Cairo Studies in English, 1960. Articles appearing in this collection are as follows: André Parreaux, "The Caliph and the Swinish Multitude"; Boyd Alexander, "The Decay of Beckford's Genius"; Geoffrey Bullough, "Beckford's Early Travels and His Dream of Delusion"; Magdi Wahba, "Beckford, Portugal and Childish Error"; Fatma Mahmoud, "Beckford, *Vathek* and the Oriental Tale"; Mahmoud Manzalaoui, "Pseudo-Orientalism in Transition: The Age of *Vathek*."

MAYER, G. TOWNSHEND. "The Sultan of Lansdown Tower," *Temple Bar*, CXX (June, 1900), 182–212. Prints, selections from an important supply of unpublished letters by Beckford to his bookseller, George Clarke.

MAY, MARCEL. *La Jeunesse de William Beckford et la genèse de son Vathek.* Paris: Les Presses Universitaires France, 1928. Pioneer study on the genesis of *Vathek*. Although a little outdated, a very useful work.

MAYOUX, JEAN-JACQUES. "La Damnation de Beckford," *English Miscellany*, XII (1961), 41–77. Probing discussion of the relationship between Beckford's personality and his imaginative life.

MORE, PAUL E. "William Beckford." *The Drift of Romanticism.* Boston: Houghton Mifflin, 1913. Views *Vathek* as an essential type of Romanticism because of its portrayal of the tortured ego's search for a union with infinity.

OLIVER, J. W. *The Life of William Beckford.* London: Oxford University, 1932. Corrects many of Lewis Melville's hurried transcriptions; includes an important selection of letters by Louisa Beckford. Good biography; a pleasure to read.

OPPÉ, A. P. *Alexander and John Robert Cozens*. Cambridge, Mass.: Harvard University Press, 1954. Discusses relationship between Alexander Cozens and Beckford.

PARREAUX, ANDRÉ. "Beckford et Byron," *Etudes Anglaises*, VIII (1955), 11–31; 113–32. Explores the whole question of Beckford's influence on Byron — an excellent article.

————. *William Beckford, Auteur de Vathek: Etude de la Création Littéraire*. Paris: Nizet, 1960. Solid critical study of *Vathek* and the related Oriental tales which should be read by all serious students of the eighteenth century. Includes an extensive bibliography of Beckford's works together with a checklist of over 175 secondary sources.

RAILO, EINO. *The Haunted Castle: A Study of the Elements of English Romanticism*. London: George Routledge, 1927. Asserts that *Vathek* is a good example of English Romanticism because it contains the elements of terror, sublimity, and suggestivity.

REDDING, CYRUS. *Memoirs of William Beckford of Fonthill*. 2 vols. London: Charles Skeet, 1859. The much-criticized first biography. Redding gathered his material during the course of a nine-year friendship with Beckford. Sometimes carelessly written and badly organized but absolutely essential anyway.

————. "Recollections of the Author of *Vathek*," *New Monthly Magazine*, LXXI (June, July, 1844), 143–58; 302–19. Although allowances must be made for the natural failings of memory, these recollections of conversations with Beckford provide a great deal of information that is indispensable to the serious student.

RIEGER, JAMES H. "Au Pied de la Lettre: Stylistic Uncertainty in *Vathek*," *Criticism*, IV (1962), 302–12. Thought-provoking essay on the incongruous comic element in *Vathek*.

SAINTSBURY, GEORGE. *The Peace of the Augustans*. London: G. Bell & Sons, 1916. Claims that *Vathek* is essentially eighteenth-century in character.

SITWELL, SACHEVERELL. *Beckford and Beckfordism*. London: Duckworth, 1930. An essay composed in 1924 as a preface to a proposed edition of Beckford's works which never appeared.

STEEVES, HARRISON R. "Oriental Romance. Johnson and Beckford." *Before Jane Austen. The Shaping of the Eighteenth Century*. New York: Holt, Rinehart, 1965. Believes that the authentic Oriental tone of *Vathek* brings it closer to the *Arabian Nights* than any other imitative romance of the eighteenth century.

THOMPSON, KARL. "Beckford, Byron, and Henley," *Etudes Anglaises*, XIV (1961), 225–28. Restatement of some of the arguments made in *Philological Quarterly* in Henley's behalf but this time with a rebuttal by André Parreaux appended.

————. "Henley's Share in Beckford's *Vathek*," *Philological Quarterly*, XXXI (1952), 75–80. Attempts to reveal some mitigating circumstances to excuse, in part, Henley's publication of *Vathek* without Beckford's permission.

VARMA, DEVENDRA. *The Gothic Flame*. London: Arthur Barker, 1957. Argues that *Vathek* is intimately associated with Gothic Romance.

WAGENKNECHT, EDWARD. "*Vathek* and the Oriental Tale." *Cavalcade of the English Novel*. New York: Henry Holt, [1943]. Classifies *Vathek* as a minor classic of English literature.

WIENER, HAROLD S. L. "Byron and the East: Literary Sources of the *Turkish Tales*." *Nineteenth-Century Studies*. Ed. Herbert Davis *et al.* New York: Greenwood, 1968. Reviews in detail Byron's use of *Vathek*.

WHIBLY, CHARLES. "The Caliph of Fonthill." *The Pageantry of Life*. New York: Harper & Brothers, 1900. Eminently readable review of Beckford's life and works.

WILSON, EDMUND. *The Shores of Light*. New York: Farrar, Straus, and Young, 1952. Draws a comparison between Ronald Firbank and Beckford.

ZEIDLER, KARL. *Beckford, Hope und Morier als Vertreter des Orientalischen Romans*. Inaugural-Dissertation zur Erlangung der Doktor würde der Hohen philosophischen Fakultät der Universität Leipzig, 1908.

Index

(The works of William Beckford are listed under his name)

Abdalla, Son of Hanif (Bignon), 19
Addison, Joseph, 20, 22, 25, 80
Adventurer, 21
Agamine, 35
Alastor (Shelley), 63
Alexander, Boyd, 30, 46, 55
Alnaschar, 20
Alroy (Disraeli), 144
Amusemens sérieux et comiques (Dufresny), 22
Amusements Serious and Comical Calculated for the Meridian of London (Brown), 22
Arabian Nights, 17–19, 23–24, 26, 33, 46, 86, 99, 105, 110–11
Ariosto, Ludovico, 59
Atterbury, Bishop, 19, 23

Baker, Ernest, 22, 97
Barry, Charles, 140
Baudelaire, 119
Beckford, Louisa, 64, 84, 98
Beckford, Maria, 29–32, 34–35, 73, 98, 103
Beckford, William (Lord Mayor), 29–31, 114
Beckford, William, 27, early years and education, 29–39, emotional crises, 64–67, 103–104, picturesque taste, 76–78, Oriental studies, 35–36, 39, 51–52, 79–81, exoticism, 82–85, landscape activities, 121–22, Fonthill Abbey, 126–29, later years, 129–36

WORKS:
Azemia, 122, 124–26
Biographical Memoirs of Extraordinary Painters, 53–63, 68, 97–98, 122, 129
Dreams, Waking Thoughts and Incidents, 64–79, 98, 103, 131, 166n21
Episodes of Vathek, The, 27, 51–52, 86, 103–21, 135, 141–42, 148
"Excursion to the Grande Chartreuse, An," 69
"Histoire d'Abou Niah," 81
"Histoire d'Aladdin," 81
"Histoire d'Elouard Felkanaman et d'Ansel Hougioud," 81
"Histoire de Darianoc, jeune homme du pays de Gou-Gou," 103
"Histoire de Kebal," 81
"Histoire de la Princesse Fatimah," 81
"Histoire de Mazin," 81
"Histoire du Prince Ahmed," 81
"Histoire du Prince Mahmed," 81
Italy; with Sketches of Spain and Portugal, 61, 74–75, 131–32
"L'Esplendente," 34
Long Story, The, 27, 39–53, 98–99, 135
Modern Novel Writing, 122–26
Recollections of an Excursion to the Monasteries of Alcobaça and Batalha, 131–33
"Story of Motassem, The," 106, 170n13

Vathek, 17, 27–28, 43, 49–53, 58, 60–61, 69, 74, 76, 78–109, 112, 114–15, 117, 119–20, 128, 132, 135–48
Vision, The, See *The Long Story*

Bellini, Giovanni, 133
Benincasa, Count, 65, 70
Bentley, Richard, 61, 108
Bernier, François, 18
Bessborough, Lady, 127
Bibliothèque Orientale, 99–100, 109–11
Bignon, J. P., 19
Birkhead, Edith, 94
Birley, Robert, 143
Blake, William, 83
Boileau, Jorge Luis, 93
Bride of Abydos, The (Byron), 141
Brockman, H. A. N., 133
Brown, Thomas, 22
Burney, Fanny, 122
Burton, John, 70–71, 166n25
Burton, Richard, 20, 26
Byron, Lord, 27–28, 107–108, 112, 114, 117, 128, 137–42, 172n10

Camden, Charles, 32
"Cap and Bells, The," (Keats), 143
"Carazan" (Hawkesworth), 21
Carter, John, 89
Cérémonies et coûtumes religieuses de tous les peuples du monde, 102
Chambers, Sir William, 35–36
Chapman, Guy, 35, 41, 46–47, 49, 76, 80–81, 85, 98, 117, 127, 132, 138
Chardin, Jean, 18, 79, 101
Chatham, Lord, *see* William Pitt (the elder)
Cipriani, 71
Citizen of the World, The (Goldsmith), 22, 24–25
Clarke, George, 61, 73, 108, 144
Clarke, William, 60, 129
Colbert, 18
Coleridge, Samuel T., 82, 137
Colvin, Sidney, 143
Conant, Martha Pike, 18
Conquest of Syria, Persia, and Egypt, The (Ockley), 26

Contarini Fleming (Disraeli), 144
Contes Chinois (Gueullette), 17
Contes Moguls (Gueullette), 17, 19, 101
Contes Tartares (Gueullette), 17, 19
Corsair, The (Byron), 137
Courtenay, William, 64, 73, 84, 88, 98, 104, 113–14, 116
Cozens, Alexander, 35–37, 40, 53, 76, 82, 84, 98
Cozens, John Robert, 70
Curse of Kehama, The (Southey), 137–39

de Bonnet, Charles, 36
de Bremond, G., 19
de Caylus, Comte, 19, 25
de Graffigny, F. Huguet, 19
d'Herbelot, Barthelemi, 79, 99–100, 109–11, 140
de la Croix, Petis, 17, 19–20
de Loutherbourg, Philip, 84–85
de Meester, Marie, 138
DeQuincey, Thomas, 82
de Rosenberg, Madame, 65, 70
de Sassure, Horace B., 36
Descamps, Jean-Baptiste, 62
de Segrais, J. R., 19
Designs for Chinese Buildings (Chambers), 35
Disraeli, Benjamin, 144–45
D'Israeli, Isaac, 138
Dissertation on Oriental Gardening (Chambers), 35–36
Dissertation on the Languages, Literature and Manners of Eastern Nations (Richardson), 26, 102
Dodsley, Robert, 23
"Domain of Arnheim, The" (Poe), 119
Don Juan (Byron), 141
Dou, Gerard, 58, 133
Drahomira, 59
Dryden, John, 58
Drysdale, Robert, 30–31
Düer, Albert, 58
Dufresny, Charles, 22

Effingham, Lord, 30
Ehrhart, Dr., 70
Endymion (Keats), 143

"Fable of the Two Owls, The," 20
"Fall of the House of Usher, The"
  (Poe), 119
Farquhar, John, 129
Fielding, Henry, 126
Firbank, Ronald, 96
"First Kalandar's Tale, The" 111–12

Galland, Antoine, 17–20
Garnett, Richard, 138–39
Gemmett, Robert J., 161n11
Giaour, The (Byron), 137, 140–41
Gibbons, Sir John, 32
Gilpin, William, 76
Gittings, Robert, 143–44
Godwin, William, 125
Goldsmith, Oliver, 22, 24–25
Gordon, Lady Margaret, 103–104
Grimsditch, H. B., 89
Guardian, The, 20
Gueullette, Thomas, 17, 19, 101
Gulliver's Travels (Swift), 22
Gunning, Elizabeth, 123

Hackert, Philip, 165n25
Hai Ebn Yockdhan (Pococke), 18
Hamilton, Antoine, 25
Hamilton, Lady, 65–66, 70–71
Hamilton, Sir William, 65, 70
Hawkesworth, John, 21–22, 25, 80, 146
Hazlitt, William, 95, 129, 133
Hearn, Lafcadio, 93
Henley, Samuel, 68–72, 84–90, 102,
  105, 112, 138, 140
Hervey, Elizabeth, 37, 55, 122
"History of Nouraddin and Amana"
  (Hawkesworth), 21
History of Nourjahad (Sheridan), 25
"History of the Second Old Man and
  Two Black Dogs, The," 110
Hodgkin, John, 166n23
Hope, Thomas, 145
Howell, J. Z., 51
Huber, Jean, 36
Hunter, Mr., 56
"Hyperion" (Keats), 143

Inchbald, Elizabeth, 123
Infernal Marriage (Disraeli), 145
Interesting Historical Events, Relative

to the Provinces of Bengal, and the
  Empire of Indostan* (Howell), 51–52
Ippolito, Cardinal, 59
Irish Melodies (Moore), 74
Italy (Rogers), 74

Jeffrey, Francis, 143
Jerdan, William, 61
John Keats, His Life and Poetry
  (Colvin), 143
Johnson, Joseph, 72, 138
Johnson, Samuel, 21–22, 25, 80, 146
Jones, Sir William, 26, 79

Keats, John, 62, 83, 143
Kinglake, Alexander, 20, 26
Koran, The (Sale), 26, 102
Kubla Khan (Coleridge), 137

Lalla Rookh (Moore), 137, 142–43
Lamb, Lady Caroline, 139
"Landor's Cottage" (Poe), 119
Langhorne, John, 25
Lansdown, Charlotte, 54
Lansdown, Henry V., 53–55
Le Brun, Charles, 79, 101
*Lectures on Science and Revealed
  Religion* (Wiseman), 134
Lee, Sophia, 122
Letters and Journals of Lord Byron
  (Moore), 141
*Letters from a Persian in England to
  his friend at Ispahan* (Lyttelton), 22
Letters from Turkey (Montagu), 102
Lettice, John, 32–33, 36, 53, 55–57,
  65, 67–68, 70–71, 89
Levade, Jean-David, 89
Lippi, Filippino, 133
Lewis, Matthew Gregory, 117
"Ligeia," (Poe), 119
Lockhart, John G., 51, 61–62, 74–75,
  131
Lonsdale, Roger, 97
*Louisa; or the Reward of an Affectionate
  Daughter* (Hervey), 122
Lyttelton, Lord, 22, 32

Macaulay, Rose, 132
Mahmoud, Fatma M., 50, 143
Mallet, Paul Henri, 36

Manfred (Byron), 141
Marana, G. P., 18, 22
Marriage of Figaro, The (Mozart), 30
Marriot, Sir James, 23–24
Marzials, Sir Frank, 108
May, Marcel, 88–89, 101
Medwin, Thomas, 139
Meister, Henri, 136
Mejnoun and Leila (D'Israeli), 138
Melville, Lewis, 33, 108
Memlinc, Hans, 58
Mengs, Raphael, 165n25
Merian, Maria Sibylla, 58
Mierhop, Francis, 58
Mille et un Jours, Contes Persans, Les
   (de la Croix), 17, 19
Mille et une Nuits, Contes Arabes,
   Les (Galland), See *Arabian Nights*
Milton, John, 50
Mitford, John, 74, 116
Monk, The (Lewis), 117
Montagu, Edward Wortley, 81
Montagu, Lady Mary Wortley, 102
Montesquieu, 22
Moore, Thomas, 27–28, 73–74, 122,
   137, 141–43
Morall Philosophie of Doni, The (North),
   18
Morier, J. H., 145
Mozart, 30
Murray, John, 142
Musters, Sophia, 84

Necker, Louise (Madame de Staël), 73
North, Thomas, 18
Northern Antiquities (Mallet), 36

"Obidah and the Hermit" (Johnson), 21
Ockley, Simon, 26
"Ode to a Nightingale," (Keats), 143
Ogilby, John, 58
"Ortogrul of Basra" (Johnson), 21
Ouseley, William, 26

"Palace of Istaker, The," 149–58, 172n4
Paradise Lost (Milton), 50
Parreaux, André, 28, 46–47, 51, 57,
   88–89, 110
Perrault, Charles, 18

Petrarch, 78
Picart, Bernard, 102
Pitt, William (the elder), 24, 30, 32–35
Pitt, William (the younger), 124–25,
   126
Pococke, Edward, 18
Podebrady, George, 59
Poe, Edgar Allan, 116, 119
Polo, Marco, 18
Pope, Alexander, 23, 58, 121
Porta, Joseph, 58
Poussin, Gaspar, 133
Purchas, Samuel, 137

Radcliffe, Ann, 122
Raphael, 133
Rasselas (Johnson), 21–22, 140
Recollections of the late William Beck-
   ford, of Fonthill, Wilts, and Lans-
   down, Bath (Lansdown), 54
Redding, Cyrus, 53, 55–56, 62, 72, 85,
   98, 122
Reiger, James H., 98
Reynolds, J. H., 143
"Rhymes on the Road" (Moore), 74
Richardson, John, 26, 102
Richardson, Samuel, 123, 126
Ridley, James, 25, 110
Robinson, Maria, 123
Rogers, Samuel, 73–74, 107–108,
   114, 117, 122, 127, 141
Romano, Guilio, 58

Saint Anthony, 59
Saint Denis, 59, 61
Sale, George, 26, 102
"Santon Barsisa," 20
Sardanapalus (Byron), 137
Scott, Jonathan, 26, 79
Shelley, Percy B., 63
Shenstone, William, 121
Sheridan, Frances, 25
Siege of Corinth (Byron), 141
Smith, Charlotte, 122
Smollet, Tobias, 126
Solyman and Almena (Langhorne), 25
Southey, Robert, 27–28, 137
Spectator, The, 20
Steele, Richard, 20

Story of Hilpa, Harpath, and Shalum, The (Addison), 20
Swift, Jonathan, 22
Swinburne, 136

Tales of the Genii (Ridley), 25, 110
Tallyrand, 131
Tatler, The, 20
Tavernier, Jean-Baptiste, 18
Thalaba (Southey), 137–38
"Thou Art the Man" (Poe), 119
Thurlow, Lord Chancellor, 103–104
Travels in the Two Sicilies (Swinburne), 68
Turkish Spy (Marana), 18, 22
Turkish Tales (de la Croix), 19–20

van Poelemburg, Cornelius, 58
Vendramin, 65–66
Vie des Peintres Flamands, Allemands et Hollandois (Deschamps), 62
Vision of Mirzah, The (Addison), 20
Voltaire, 25, 36

Voyage dans les Alpes (Sassure), 36
Voyage en Perse et autres lieux de l'Orient (Chardin), 101
Voyage par la Moscovie en Perse, et aux Indes Orientales (Le Brun), 101

Walpole, Horace, 121
Warton, Joseph, 23–24
West, Benjamin, 32, 62
Whibly, Charles, 132
White, Richard Samuel, 73
Whitehead, William, 23–24
Wiener, Harold, 140–41
Wildman, Thomas, 71–72
"William Beckford and the Picturesque" (Gemmett), 161n11
Williams, Helen Maria, 123
Williams, Edmund, 96
Wiseman, Nicholas, 134
World, The, 23, 25
Wyatt, James, 122

Zemir, 80–81

DATE DUE

DEMCO 38-297.